SUFFER AND SURVIVE

Gas Attacks, Miners' Canaries,
Spacesuits and the Bends:
The Extreme Life of Dr J. S. Haldane

MARTIN GOODMAN

SIMON &
SCHUSTER

London · New York · Sydney · Toronto

A CBS COMPANY

First published in Great Britain in 2007
by Simon & Schuster UK Ltd
A CBS COMPANY

1 3 5 7 9 10 8 6 4 2

Simon & Schuster UK Ltd
Africa House
64–78 Kingsway
London WC2B 6AH

www.simonsays.co.uk

Simon & Schuster Australia
Sydney

All pictures courtesy of Richard Haldane except nos 6:
University of St Andrews; 7: Getty Images; 10: Reflective
Images collection; 12: National Coalmining Museum;
20: TopFoto

A CIP catalogue for this book is available
from the British Library.

ISBN: 978-0-7432-8597-1

Typeset in Bembo by M Rules
Printed and bound in Great Britain by
Mackays of Chatham plc

SUFFER AND SURVIVE

Also by Martin Goodman

Fiction
ON BENDED KNEES
SLIPPERY WHEN WET

Non-fiction
I WAS CARLOS CASTANEDA
IN SEARCH OF THE DIVINE MOTHER
ON SACRED MOUNTAINS

For James Thornton

CONTENTS

That man is a success who has lived well, laughed often and loved much; who has gained the respect of intelligent men and the love of children; who has filled his niche and accomplished his task; who leaves the world better than he found it . . . who never lacked appreciation of earth's beauty or failed to express it; who looked for the best in others and gave the best he had.

— ROBERT LOUIS STEVENSON

1

WHY MINERS DIE

Few people found the need to travel to South Wales in mid-winter. Dr John Scott Haldane's own mission, on this late January day in 1896, was one that most sensitive people would dread. The few hours of daylight were never better than grey, and now it was night. The north wind was doing its job, curling the smoke and steam cloud from the engine and down along the carriages. The train was thundering towards the source of its power. As they drew near to Cardiff the stoker shovelled into the furnace the last layers from a pile of coal. The coal was from the mines of South Wales, known to be the finest steam coal in the world.

Such fine coal came at a price. 'The higher the quality of the coal seam,' read a government report of February 1894, 'the more liability there is to explosions of dust.'[1] The source was coal dust, grains of coal that hung in the air and smeared all surfaces. It could snatch the flame from any explosion and send it charging through the dust-strewn workings. On tests of dust from throughout the nation, the dust from Albion Colliery at Cilfynydd, a small South Wales town, 'excelled all others in violence and sensitiveness to explosion'. It stemmed from a high-grade seam of coal that ran through the region. In the last fifty years more than 1,600 men and boys had died in explosions from this seam.

On 23 June 1894 a 2-ounce shot of dynamite was set among this combustible dust in the tunnels below the Albion Colliery, and fired. Two claps of thunder shook the ground and timbers flew from the structures at the pithead. Clouds of dust burst through the tunnels below. The miners' lamps were extinguished while a glare of blue flame streaked above their heads. Survivors told the tale to this point, where they lost consciousness. Such survivors were few: 281 men and boys were killed on that Saturday afternoon.

The weekend passed before news of the disaster touched the world. Five days after the disaster Haldane reached the wreckage of the colliery. Death was an overwhelming fact. One small house alone held the bodies of a father, his four sons, and six lodgers. The underground explosion had killed them. Grieving families wanted to know what caused it, but the explosion itself was sufficient cause of death. Dr Haldane, on the other hand, was far from sure that miners' deaths were inevitable in such circumstances. He picked his way among the underground debris looking for clues. After hacking limbs and drawing organs from the carcasses of pit ponies, he performed more discreet autopsies on some men. And he asked many questions that drew conflicting answers.

What did the rescuers smell? Some smelt nothing although their eyes smarted. Others smelt wool, or burnt matches, or 'something sulphury'.[2] They found many 'asphyxiated' bodies, and some survivors who were enduring what seemed to be epileptic fits, foaming at the mouth or beating their heads against the ground.

Back in his laboratory at Oxford University Dr Haldane studied the blood and organs of the dead. A rash use of dynamite had prompted the explosion, but why did the miners actually die? From fire, from violent blows, from suffocation, from some other cause? Haldane's tests gave some tentative answers which he published in the *Journal of Physiology*, but nothing conclusive. He needed to reach the aftermath of an explosion much faster, to be there when fatal gases still lingered below ground, while survivors still gasped to fill their lungs.

Such disaster fills most men with fear. For Haldane the opposite was true. His pulse quickened when he tore open the Home Office telegram at his Oxford home. It brought news of an underground explosion that very morning, mere miles from the Albion Colliery. If he was quick, if train connections worked, if the aftermath of the disaster was so huge and the weather remained so cold and foul, he had a good chance of wielding his knives and collecting his samples while the pickings were still fresh.

Haldane had a first-class compartment to himself. A small dark leather case borrowed from previous employment worked wonders in maintaining his privacy on such journeys. He held the case so that mothers and nurses could read the words stencilled in red on its lid. *London Fever Hospital*. It glared an initial warning. The man's blue eyes flared another challenge, and his clothes were far from being a gentleman's. His heavy boots and overalls were more like the outfit of a working man, and he had a helmet on his head. A broad moustache quivered like a fat rodent dozing on his upper lip. And what was that smell? Were those really caged mice on the rack above his head? Those wary women peering in at him dragged their infant charges clear of the strange man's

compartment. This was as planned. He was good with children, but their cries and chatter chased out the thoughts that
needed to cohere and settle in his brain.

In Cardiff Haldane located the carriage that would be
hauled up the Rhondda Valley as the first train of the morning, changing at Porth for the mining town of Tylorstown.
After ensuring the safe transfer of his bags and equipment, it
was best if he could close his eyes. Any sleep he collected
through the rest of the night would have to last him for days.

Haldane shared that first night train up through the Rhondda
Valley with a batch of coffins. He would need to work fast
before those coffins were sealed. The faces, the skin, the
blood of the dead, all had a story to tell. He would curl back
their lips, and the dead would talk. They would tell him why
they died. Meanwhile the living were telling their own tales.

Few stories were more compelling than the one told by a
young miner called Jack. Coal was not worked at night, but
about ninety repairmen were below ground, clearing debris,
firming up walls, securing supports, maintaining the underground haulage roads ('roads' were the tunnels leading from
the shaft to the working faces). Jack and his mate, his 'butty',
were working the 12-hour shift, from six in the evening to
six the next morning.

'About twelve o'clock on Sunday evening myself and a
butty sat down to partake a little food,' Jack related just hours
after the incident. 'We noticed there was a great deal of gas
about in that part of the pit, and the dust was fearful. Well,
we had been eating a short time, when I noticed my mate
had dropped off to sleep. I supposed it was under the effects
of the gas. As soon as I'd finished my meal I woke him up.
We resumed work again, but ere long he said to me, "Look

here, Jack, do you know I had a terrible dream, man, in those few minutes of sleep?"

'"Did you?"

'"Ay indeed. I dreamt that the pit was on fire, and that the master haulier was burnt to death."'

The two men gave it a moment's thought and decided, 'Come what may, we would leave the place at an early hour and go up before the hour of "stop cage" would arrive. You see, the men are stopped from going up at 5.30 am, and we have to wait for 6.00 am unless we go up with the last batch. I had a row with the master haulier about my going, but I insisted and defied him. I rushed into the cage. On our way I met an old man we all liked, George Lewis. This old man was about 62 or 64 years of age. I said, "George, come on up, man, we are off. We are not going to stay here in this gas and stuff, I know."

'He only said, "Oh, I think I will clean out this bit of road first and get ready for the six rise." He didn't come. Now he's among the dead as well as the master haulier, who I saw rushing to stop us when the cage had been lifted several yards from the bottom of the shaft. We had only reached the top when we heard the first explosion – for the rumbling noise we heard twice. I was struck on the leg by a piece of timber and thrown prostrate into the yard.'[3]

Three friends had travelled up in that final cage, drawn up the 500 yards from the floor of shaft number 7. Jack's thoughts turned back to a young colleague they left behind.

'Just before the explosion we heard two distant knocks from below. We knew it was poor Johnny Collins knocking to come up. You see, when we four were in, the carriage started up. We saw Collins coming towards us, but we couldn't stop as we had given the signal. So poor Johnny had to wait till his next turn. But, poor chap, he never had the chance, for he must have been killed after he had made the second knock.'[4]

Crockery fell from the dressers in houses 300 yards from the colliery.[5] Dr T. H. Morris, the medical doctor for the whole colliery, snapped out of sleep as his house shook and his windows rattled. He climbed from bed, lit a light, and began to dress. Doors crashed open in the street outside and remained that way, despite the freezing temperature and the slashing rain. The white of a woman's nightgown dashed around her heels as she ran along the street. Her man was down the pit. She feared the worst.

Tylorstown was a well-managed colliery, part of a chain of such businesses that brought up coal from deep beneath the whole stretch of the Rhondda Valley. New safety explosives, bellite and ammonite, had just gone into production. Tylorstown set them to use at once, banning gunpowder from its mines.[6] No major incident had happened in all of its history.

Even so, the mining community lived with fear that was as pressing and constant as the region's grey skies. Pray as they might in their Sunday chapels, it was defying the natural order of things to work tunnels deep inside the Earth. Each miner's return from work was a daily and weary miracle. Miracles were far from guaranteed.

The first shout hit the street. 'An explosion at number 7 shaft!' A man sent from the colliery did not even reach the doctor's door. His bag in hand, Dr Morris was already on his way.

It was black. The air was stuffed with the smell of smoke but he saw no flames. The only lights were the dim ones of miners' lamps. They were dim enough even in the narrows of the mines. Above ground they swung like giddy fireflies, barely visible and lighting nothing.

A crowd pulled at Morris's coat sleeves. They wouldn't normally touch him but he was just pushing through. He was the doctor. He had to help them. They called out the names, names he knew, the names of the husbands and the brothers and the fathers who had gone out into the night. Had he seen them? What could he do?

A policeman pushed through from the rear. He was already shouting for order, calling people back. The crowd eased its swarming, its shifting from foot to foot and place to place to get a better glimpse of nothing. They listened to the policeman's voice. They wanted order. They wanted things restored the way they were.

The roof was blown off the head of the pitshaft. Dawn took an age to struggle into this valley, the winter sun in no hurry to rise above the hills. Training their eyes though, they could see the silhouette of the giant wheel of the winding gear high above them. The tower that held it was still standing. The wheel was not moving. It would have to turn, to wind men down and wind men up, before they knew the full truth of what lay below ground. But at least the tower was standing.

Men spoke of what they had seen and the story passed around. In the way of such stories the details changed. Some heard tell of flames that burst from the ground to lick the sky, but in truth there was no fire. The first force of the blast propelled a black tornado of dust up through the shafts. Clouds of dense smoke chased up behind the initial shot of black dust, but no flames.

David Hannah, the general manager of the Ferndale

Colliery of which Tylorstown was a part, had heard the explosion's rumble though he was sleeping in the town of Ferndale further up the valley. He arrived on the scene at 6.20 am. His first thought was to check the condition of the fan. Though the cover had blown off it, the fan was still working. It was still pulling a vital flow of air up from the tunnels below. The metal of the cages, which could usually lower men down the shaft at 35 feet per second, was bent but not too badly damaged. However the guideropes that steered the cage over the winding mechanism had been displaced. They would need to be freed and reset first.

His next stop was the lamproom. Some men had grabbed their lamps, desperate to descend the mine and help their colleagues below. Hannah called them back. He needed to count. Men returned their lamps to their position on surfacing from the mine. The number of gaps, the number of missing lamps, was the number of workmen caught below. Many were repairmen, maintaining the network of tunnels, roads and seams that spread for miles deep below the valley floor. Firemen were down there, inspecting the distant corners. They had the duty of setting the explosives too. These were not used for releasing the coal. This was too delicate an operation, for lumps of coal had to come out as least as big as a miner's fist. Smaller than that and the miners weren't paid for it. But explosives could shift the rock and help create the haulage roads that led to the 4-foot, 5-foot and 6-foot seams of coal. Ostlers were down there too, caring for the pit ponies whose entire working lives were spent below ground.

Hannah despaired for the pit ponies. They had around 150 of them working out of the stables below. They were one of the colliery's largest investments, not just buying them but training them too. It took a while to accustom a horse to working blind, to hauling trams along the wet and uneven roads, to sweating through the higher temperatures found at that depth.

And the boys, the trappers! He'd forgotten them in his counting. Most trappers did not even have lamps, so the lamps that were missing told him nothing about them. One downshaft carried air down the pits. This would simply rush through the system and out again, pouring out through the two upshafts, never pausing to be still and breathable, were it not for the trapper boys. They crouched beside the brattice doors, thick wooden slabs of doors that closed to seal off the haulage roads. At the sound of approaching men or horses, on hearing the appropriate cry, they would pull the doors open and let the business through. Then close the doors again. The doors and the boys were vital in achieving the right ventilation for the pit. Hannah prayed that doors and boys had been spared the blast. He would ask a man to collect names from outside. The boys could be counted by finding their mothers in the crowd.

Dr Morris was in the lamproom. He was treating the few injuries from above ground. They were the cuts and bruises and shock in those who had been thrown to earth. Hannah paused briefly to interview those who had just come up from below. Above a hundred lamps were missing. He needed to believe that many of those with the lamps could be saved.

They had to fix the guideropes so as to lower a rescue party below. Hannah advised Morris to stay behind and tend to the injured up above. Better a live doctor above ground than a dead one below. At nine o'clock the first rescue party of four was ready to descend. The doctor was with them.[7]

In order to free the ropes and not just hang there when

stuck, they rode on the cover of the cage rather than inside it. Strapping themselves to the metal frame, they held on with one hand and used the other to work the displaced rope back over the guides. The cage now became stuck so firmly that they could not shift the guideropes with their hands. Handhold by handhold they left the cage and edged down the rope, dropping into pitch black till feet touched the first fall of debris.

Air travelled down the shaft above them. That was their one link to sanity, the fact that they could breathe. Their workplace 1,500 feet below ground had been swallowed by shadow. The way shadows distort shapes, the way they melt and merge, the way they bend corners and climb walls, and are formed out of darkness, these were clues from which they could start to relocate themselves in their twisted surroundings. The men took the effects of the blast into their minds to try to make sense of all they saw. So the metal casing that they found slammed and buckled against a wall, one wheel tilted towards a roof, they made out was a tram. From its angle and position, they worked out the direction of the blast. It came from the west.

From above they had heard of old George Lewis. They had no hopes for him. Nothing could have survived the blast at this point, certainly not the bones and flesh of an old man, bent over his broom, standing in the passage of the explosion's full force. They would find his body, some way behind them, but not yet. First they needed to discover any survivors.

Poor George Lewis. He was doing his best. Coal dust lay an inch thick on the floors of the haulage roads, and clung to the walls and roof as well. It was this very dust that picked up explosions and blasted them throughout the workings. Think how easily coal burns, then imagine the incendiary nature of coal dust. Each particle is set to explode in an instant, and charge the particle next to it to do the same. It's a chain reaction of gathering power that can gut a whole mine in one flash. A man with a broom is a despairing creature, asked to create a firebreak to stop such a blast.

Water was piped in to prevent explosions. Wet the coal dust and it won't combust. Those pipes were now fractured and ripped apart. George Lewis's road, the one he was sweeping at 5.30 that morning, was now a river 2 feet deep.

'Get up, man,' a workman insisted. This wasn't a time for niceties. You didn't want your doctor soaked to the skin. Dr Morris gave up his protests and climbed on the workman's back. He was lowered again on to dry ground.

Three men approached from the east side of the pit, stumbling behind the flicker of one lamp. They were dazed. Far from jubilant to escape, they just stopped and stared at where the rescuers were shouting. They had stumbled, felt and crawled their way along the broken roads, but still their surroundings made no sense.

Morris helped the men to the ground and pooled light around them from a cluster of lamps. They had cuts and abrasions but no broken bones. He dressed their wounds with linseed oil. Drops of ether revived them a little.

The rescuers were finding their way now. They brought the doctor to two workmen found injured in the cabin near the base of the shaft. They were alive though sick with fumes. Burns had pitted the skin on their faces and hands. They were bound on to stretchers to be taken up above.

The doctor could do nothing for the engineman. His body was splayed across the top of the engine. Turn your lamp away from such a sight and deal with him later. That was the only thing to do. The roofs of the haulage roads often held for hours after an explosion, and only then would they collapse. This disaster was still unfolding itself.

Over to the west a day-fireman, Roderick Williams, had reached the coalface on his morning tour of inspection just as the explosion happened.

'I heard two reports,' he would later say, 'like great falls, but I thought it was an explosion. I took out my watch and saw it was twenty-three minutes to six.' Roderick Williams was a veteran of two previous mining disasters. He knew from experience the true killer of such explosions. Afterdamp. Many 'damps' plagued the lives of men below ground. As mines grew deeper, these 'damps' grew in number, new gases that leaked into the system. Afterdamp was the poisonous residue of explosions underground, a gas born of the fusion of coal dust and fire.

He smelt it now. He tasted it, and backed away. Finding a rise in the ground that led him away from the haulage road along which the afterdamp flowed, he followed it away from the passage of the gas. This gas streamed towards its exit through the upshaft, and with the doors blown away it did not need to turn from its route to seek him out. He waited four hours for it to depart.

Dr Morris was working his way west towards the scene of the blast. This meant passing the stables, individual stalls that housed the pit ponies. He was no veterinary surgeon, but reaching a hand up the flank of one of the felled beasts and round to its head the body felt in good condition. The animal had not died from burns or injury.

He clambered over the next fall in the tunnel to move further. He was moving towards Roderick Williams. But the way ahead was blocked. David Hannah, the general manager, had disappeared, along with the fireman Evan Evans. They had located more than thirty survivors by now. It was time to follow them up to the surface, and see what help he could give there.

Back above ground and across at shaft number 8, Dr Morris found himself surrounded by a whole team of professionals and experts in various fields including medicine, all of them waiting to give help. None of them was eager to go down the pit to where help was most sorely needed. Morris descended shaft number 7 one more time.

The lodge room near the base of the shaft became his centre of operations for an hour, as he tended the injured men who were brought to him. Over to the west the afterdamp had passed. Roderick Williams felt free to move back on to the main road and work his way across the debris towards freedom. On his way out, from about a mile and a quarter away in the west part of the workings, he discovered a man. Apparently dead, on bending closer he detected a slight movement in the man's chest. Through the hours after the explosion when the pit had been sealed to rescuers; while survivors had reached the surface, thanked their God, and returned into the hellhole of the pit in search of their unlucky colleagues; while hopes had gone of finding anyone alive; for fifteen hours this young man had lain there, unconscious but still breathing.

Roderick Williams found Dr Morris in the lodge room. The doctor picked up his bag and followed. The fallen man, 24-year-old Griffith Phillips from Brynamam in Carmarthenshire, was 800 yards away from the shaft in the main level. This was 800 yards of crawling through the smallest of openings, and wriggling under fallen timber.

Griffith Phillips had not been alone when he fell. Five bodies of his colleagues lay around him, and four lamps that were still burning.[8] If there was oxygen enough for the lamps to burn, why could the men not breathe? This young man, still breathing, must survive and tell them.

Hannah, the manager, who was relentless in leading search parties through the shattered roads of the pit, knelt by the unconscious man's side. He pressed his mouth to the young collier's mouth, and thumped his pressed hands down on to the man's chest, attempting artificial respiration. Dr Morris eased him to one side and took over. Drops of ether brought a slight shift in the young man's consciousness. Griffith showed enough signs of life to be carried back to the shaft. Dr Morris followed. At eight in the evening, with a full ten hours underground behind him, he emerged from the mine himself.

The doctor worked on, and came to see how a man could do without daylight, just as miners could get by without a glimpse of it all winter.

By midnight twelve bodies had been recovered. It was hard to tell how many more would be found. Men had been paid that Saturday, so some who were missing might just have left the district. The number of dead was becoming clear though. Fifty-seven. They should all be examined before burial. Morris thought it best to start at once. Work, even the examination of corpses, could distract him from the horrors of all he had seen.

It was not simply a matter of issuing death certificates. The Home Secretary had commissioned an additional inspector to help determine the causes of death. He was a lecturer in Physiology, on his way from Oxford University.

Dr John Haldane was known to Morris by name and reputation. Morris would meet him off his train with as salient
a series of observations as he could muster.

'Dr Haldane?'

Haldane paused a moment. His hands were full. In one
was the London Fever Hospital case. In the other his
Gladstone bag. This concertina-style bag, with its metal clasp
and faded leather, was more suited to a nanny than a scientist.
At least that was the opinion of Mrs Haldane. So much did
she dislike it, that keeping the bag with him had become an
act of amused rebellion. Haldane put down the bag and
reached out his hand.

'Dr Morris.'

Haldane had little time for the doctors of Edinburgh, but
such doctors would be held laughable in a Welsh mining
town. Collieries employed more practical men as their medical practitioners. Dr Morris was clearly of this latter breed.
Their handshake was warm.

Though they had never met, Morris recognized Haldane
on the instant. Two years before, in the aftermath of the devastating explosion at the Albion Colliery further up the valley,
Haldane had made a distinct impression. For other doctors it
was sufficient to attribute a miner's death to an underground
explosion, even when no obvious burns or injury were
apparent. Tales spread of this new doctor who questioned
every conjecture, and who took away the blood of dead men
and the organs of horses. It seemed as eccentric and backward
as sifting through the entrails of sacrificed beasts in order to
predict the future. Haldane drew men towards him, however,
with his clear description of scientific measures. His explana-
tions were so practical as to make sense. As the doctor

returned to his Oxford laboratory, the spell of his intense focus was broken. People remembered him with some fondness, but their memories began to fail them about the exact nature of his investigations.

That intensity of focus was part of Haldane's physical effect. Though only thirty-five, his hair had receded from an overarching brow that hooded his eyes. His eyebrows were bushy, a thick moustache lined his upper lip, and the whole assembly of the man's head craned towards you. Still more distinctive were his travelling clothes. He had apparently travelled from London in the garb of a miner, in belted overall and boots, a miner's helmet in place of a hat. Haldane clearly had no wish to refresh himself, nor any expectation of changing his attire. He asked Morris to lead him directly to the pithead.

Their feet crunched against the hard frost on the road. Haldane listened as the colliery's medical officer gave his account of the previous day. Though Morris spoke of his time underground as being 'indescribable', in flash after flash he revealed images that helped Haldane piece together the aftermath of the disaster.

Strands of wire cordoned off the pit mouth. Haldane announced himself to the attendant police officer before walking through. In the first hours of the tragedy crowds had swarmed the area. At midday panic had set in, people falling to the ground and crying, as a further explosion was heard below ground. It seemed that all rescuers must have perished alongside those they had gone to save. In fact the noise was just the crash of one pit cage hitting another, the sound reverberating up the shaft to jangle people's nerves. Since that moment order had set in. Though men still waited at the pithead there were seldom more than twenty women among them. It was understood that the women were better deployed in the homes of the town, where they could care for the wounded, the bereaved and each other.[9]

The sounds of saws, of hammers on nails, came from the colliery sheds. Carpenters were hammering rough-hewn wood into biers so the corpses could be carried to their homes. A rescue party led by Griffiths, the under-manager of shaft number 8, was currently underground.[10] Some hours before rescuers had reached the epicentre of the explosion. The blast had been triggered by a shot of dynamite. The body of Richard Evans, the fireman who had set the shot, was recovered and brought to the surface. An hour afterwards the bodies of two brothers-in-law, Jacob Jones and Thomas Scourfield, had come up in the cage.

A group of townsfolk were swirling behind the wire as Haldane arrived. A number of women stood amongst them, wringing their hands or clutching a child to their sides. As the winding gear turned and the cage rose to the surface, news spread. More bodies had been found. Friends, colleagues and family waited, tense in the cold air, clinging to their last moments of hope.

One young woman, the newly married Mrs Jones, had spent the previous hours in the home of her mother-in-law. The body of her brother-in-law Jacob, still single though courting, had been among the first to be recovered the previous day. Now the young Mrs Jones was back at the pit. From the distance she watched as the body of her husband Gwilym was carried from the cage. The two brothers would lie side by side for a while, before being carried to their separate homes.

The body of a second man, William Jenkins, was brought up at the same time.

And then a third.

A woman cried out at the sight of it, and let go of the child by her side to bring her hands up to her face as though she would pull off its skin. She was Mrs Barrett. The third body was that of her eldest boy, George. She had last seen him on the Saturday night, when she made up his sandwich pack and walked by his side to the pithead. It was his very first day at work, his very first trip down the mine. His voice had not yet broken – he tried to keep it low but she heard the quaver in it as he said goodbye. George's job would be to sit in the dark beside the large air doors on the haulage road. He was to pull these doors open at the sound of an approaching truck, man or pony, then close them again. If these 'trappers' were lucky they would have a lamp to cast some shadows in the black that surrounded them. George was not so lucky as yet. He simply had to be glad of a job, and the extra pennies it would bring in to the family.

He had almost survived his first night in the dark. In just another hour he would have been back on the surface. He could have run home to tell his tales. Instead his body was returned to his mother.

Some bodies had come to the surface with apple cheeks, a fresh pink flush, and every sign of apparent health once you washed off the grime and ignored their lack of breathing. Not George. He must have been the wrong side of the door as it was blown away. His body was burnt. The force of the blast had torn off his clothes. The body was so small that it was folded into the arms of just one workman.[11]

Haldane stood back some way from the proceedings. He wished for a close and early inspection of the bodies, but it was better for now that Dr Morris took control. The familiar doctor could administer some degree of calm as the bodies were removed to the quiet of the lamproom.

Haldane prepared his equipment as men gathered around. First he uncoiled the tubes of his breathing apparatus, explaining the principles of its design to the men as he did so. Then he took out a metal cage. The sight of its occupant was enough to make the workmen snort in disgust. A white mouse. Rats were one thing. Rats knew a little respect, a little fear. They kept their distance when a man came near. Lousy mice would stream all over a man, swarming through his clothes in search of a crumb. Strings hung from the roofs of mines for men to attach their sandwiches to. It was the only way to keep the creatures from nabbing them. Mice were no friends of miners. No miner in his right mind would take a pet mouse down below.

Haldane had an explanation. This was another life-saver. Just as no man should attempt a mine rescue after an explosion without a supply of oxygen, no rescue team should go in without such a small creature to hand. Carry it in a cage like this, or in the chimney of a lamp perhaps, suitably closed off with mesh. White ones were clear to see. These mice detect gases that won't trouble the flames in lamps. Before a man ever sniffs at danger, a mouse will have lost control of its limbs and be panting on the floor. Watch their mouse and the men would know when to turn back.

Birds would do just as well. Birds had a similar metabolism and body surface to mice. They were less easy to handle, less easy to revive, but the effects of gas on a small bird can be even more conspicuous. A mouse collapses. A bird falls off its perch. When the small bird topples, the miner must retreat at once. A dark bird might be hard to see in the dim light of a mine. But a caged canary maybe? Miners could be more comfortable with that.

Another man had neared the outskirts of the group. He now stepped forward and introduced himself as David Hannah, the general manager of the Ferndale Colliery. Haldane wouldn't be needing any mouse, it seemed. Hannah informed him that the workings were all clear of afterdamp.

Except in the case of firedamp, little had been done to analyse the irrespirable gases in mines. Haldane had surprised a gathering of top scientists in the field some time before, stating that most books of chemistry on the subject were 'slovenly'.[12] The professional field was strewn with popular error. The very names, 'chokedamp', 'firedamp', 'whitedamp', 'blackdamp' and the like, were balefully simple. Afterdamp was simply the term for a gas produced by the effects of explosion, the 'damp' that came 'after' an explosion, 'damp' drawn from the German word for steam, 'Dampf'. Did Hannah have the expertise to pass judgement on whether or not the afterdamp had cleared?

As the scientist and the manager spoke, it became clear that Hannah's verdict rested on the back of considerable experience.

At noon on the previous day a rumour had spread around the pithead that Hannah had been overcome by afterdamp. The news was only partly true. Hannah told Haldane how, moving deep into the mine with fireman Evan Evans as his companion, he began to feel weak and was unable to walk steadily. He felt drowsy, needed to keep stopping and sitting down, and found great difficulty clambering over the falls. His lamp remained burning.

Appreciating the acuteness of Haldane's interest in his tale, Hannah brought in others with their own stories of afterdamp. A man with the surname of Thomas was the manager of shafts numbers 1 and 5 in the same network as the explosion.

'We went into number 6 through the separation doors,' Thomas told Haldane. 'Feeling affected, we went back into the fresh air behind the closed doors, and after a short time we made another attempt to penetrate along a road leading towards the shaft. My lamp burned perfectly, even when the afterdamp was at its worst. I felt smarting of the eyes, but the first definite symptom was loss of power in my legs. We began to feel weak after walking a little way, and turned to make our way back to the doors. Just as I sensed I was reaching fresher air, I fell.'

Both he and his companion were unconscious. The precaution of leaving several men in the fresh air saved them. These men reacted at once, and with real difficulty dragged their companions out of the toxic gas. Still unconscious and lying on top of coal trucks, they were brought back to the shaft.

Haldane could guess at the symptoms that accompanied the men's subsequent recovery: severe headache, nausea or vomiting, and great fits of shivering. His guesses were confirmed.

Just beyond where the manager and his companion fell was a group of four miners. They were sitting corpses, their bodies leaning against the walls, yet their Cambrian safety lamps still burnt at their sides.

'You smelt sulphur?'

Sulphur was the name given in Wales to afterdamp, and though Haldane had smelt the gas so described he did not believe sulphur was the main constituent. Thomas confirmed the smell.

'That smell was probably due to a very small amount of sulphurous acid. But these other symptoms? The only gas which could cause them, under the circumstances, is carbonic oxide [now known as carbon monoxide]. Lack of oxygen could have a similar effect, but your lamp still burned perfectly you say?'

'Perfectly. As those lamps were still burning beside the dead.'

'For lamps to burn, there must have been at least 18 per cent of oxygen in the air.'

Haldane spoke as though his statement were a question posed for himself to answer, the words drifting into a period of thought. He had come to Tylorstown hoping to prove a theory. This theory in itself had startled the scientific community. Common assumption held that 70 per cent of the deaths in such disasters were due to the effects of injuries from the blast. On the contrary, Haldane was sure that the cause of death in around 75 per cent of the cases was suffocation. His analysis of blackdamp, otherwise known as chokedamp, had shown that only 10 per cent of it was carbonic acid and the rest nitrogen. People died not from an excess of carbonic acid, but from lack of oxygen which was displaced by nitrogen in the damp.

Yet here Haldane faced an anomaly. In instance after instance, he was discovering that afterdamp and oxygen coexisted. Men died even while their lamps burned. There was therefore sufficient oxygen to have kept them alive. Why had these men died?

Haldane disliked having his theories challenged. It angered him. Such theories were the fruits of a continual flow of thoughts and calculations in his mind. They were expressed when irrefutable, their logic so clear as to seem obvious, but only because he had wrestled with near-infinite permutations before delivering them to the world.

The burning lamps beside the dead men now contradicted him. They told him that his theory of miners' death by suffocation was wrong.

It amazed Haldane to have the facts of a case disprove his theory in such a way.

It also intrigued and excited him. Among scientists he was well aware of his own supremacy. In the realm of pure science he delivered unassailable conclusions. Applied research, in which he observed the working environment and sought to address its needs, was a more bracing form of science altogether. It corresponded with his take on philosophy, which was his abiding passion. Life contained an intelligence. Life, not the scientist, was the master. The very best scientific career would weave its way through all the intricacies of life, always seeking control but always prepared to be astonished. Constituent parts of an organism might be appreciated in detail, but a scientist must also come to know the organism as a whole. Beyond that, he must remember that an organism does not exist outside of its environment.[13]

Taking his laboratory into the field was vital to Haldane's sense of himself as a scientist. It shifted his science from the realm of theory and into practice. In his laboratory he had studied the effects of different gases, and understood at first hand the effects of breathing the different 'damps' that arise in mines. He knew that afterdamp contained no oxygen, so that a man would suffocate in an atmosphere consisting of the gas. Yet in this mine, far removed from his laboratory, men had clearly encountered afterdamp yet suffocation was not the cause of their deaths.

Haldane had to discover what made the conditions in mines so dangerously unique. He was already working on new suppositions. The burning lamps were a clue. More evidence, more clues, were down there. He must find them.

The rescue party below was now resigned to being a recovery party, bringing back the bodies of dead colleagues. Initial efforts were also under way to clear the carcasses of the horses. Repair gangs were focusing on replacing air doors, to restore the proper circulation of air. Haldane set aside his own eagerness to continue his researches underground and switched to investigating the pithead. He needed to be sure of the state of the fan, both now and in the immediate hours after the explosion. He had to know where the bodies were found, and to be sure that their location was recorded. It would help if he could be directed through a detailed plan of the workings. He had much to do.

The manager accepted Haldane's request that he be his guide.

'I am sure you took note of where the bodies were recovered,' Haldane stated. 'Were many of them found along the haulage roads?'

It was so. The elements of a new theory were slotting into place.

Three biers emerged from the colliery sheds and bodies were laid across them. The dead men would be carried to their homes. Haldane took a chance to survey the others while they still lay in ranks. Many showed some sign of burns. In occasional cases these were considerable, but the flesh of other men was unblemished.

Morris stood to one side, his eyes blank. He had busied himself as a doctor. Now he took time to be weary of death. Haldane approached him.

'You told me of the man found unconscious beside others that were dead, and lamps that were still burning.'

Morris nodded. 'Griffith Phillips.'

'Could you take me to him?'

Morris nodded again.

'At once? I see little opportunity of examining the lungs of the dead. If we can examine this Phillips while he lives, we will have much to learn.'

Haldane drew out his watch to keep note of the times of various investigations. The watch lacked a minute hand, but judging time by the fractions to which the hour hand had passed seemed accurate enough. When he placed the stethoscope to Griffith Phillips it was near enough 11.30 am, less than thirty hours after the explosion. The man was barely conscious, though Haldane was confident he would survive. Morris helped the miner sit up, holding him in place while Haldane ran the stethoscope across his back.

The breathing was shallow, but clear. The young man's lack of consciousness showed that he had clearly been exposed to the afterdamp for a long time. Yet he showed no sign of bronchitis or pneumonia. It seemed increasingly unlikely that the men found beside him had died of suffocation.

Darkness closed in before four o'clock. Haldane had used the hours of daylight to investigate damage at the pithead. He had examined and interviewed the survivors, and studied plans to gain some picture of how the blast shot through the network of haulage roads and seams below ground. It was time to start investigating the bodies of the dead.

Terraced houses, each built of the same thick blocks of grey stone, were strung along each side of the road by the hills that formed the sides of the valley. The streets of Tylorstown were entirely unfamiliar to him, yet Haldane could have found his direction around this next task by smell alone. He walked past several houses, tracing the current of noxious fumes to their source. Though the weather was damp and chilly the single downstairs window of one of the houses was open on to the street.

'Putrefaction has set in early,' Haldane observed. 'It must be the effect of lying so long in the heat of the mine before recovery.' These mines of the Rhondda were particularly deep, heat rising considerably at their 500-yard depths.

The household was awake. A young wife opened the door. With her black clothes, her hollowed eyes, she was a wife no more but a widow. Offering his condolences, Dr Morris announced the purpose of their visit.

The dead husband was laid out on a table. He had been washed but not scrubbed.

'He looks so peaceful,' the widow observed. 'So fresh. So well, but for the blackening. And his moustache. You see how his moustache is singed?'

She bent close. Her face, always pale and now bleached of hope, had the pallor of death while the man's had the bloom of life to it. The hairs of his moustache nearly touched her. Her lips were cracked with the cold. His lips where not blackened were pink and seemed ripe for a kiss.

The woman shivered. She was cold, the body was colder. The stench of death oozed from it. She twisted her nose away and stood up.

'It's a blessing he didn't suffer,' the widow concluded. 'A blessing he died so quickly.'

Haldane chose not to challenge her assumptions. It would do her no good, and besides in many ways the man's death had been peaceful. Haldane received her permission to draw blood from the body. She left them alone for a while.

'See this coal dust,' Haldane announced, as his examination began. He was generous with his students, leading them step-by-step towards discovery. Now he was not only leading Dr Morris through the process of analysis, he was rehearsing the findings of his eventual report. 'It covers one half of the face and not the other. It's adhered to the skin through the force of the blast. This part of the face must have been the exposed side. We'll scrape off a sample and analyse it microscopically later. I expect we'll find both angular and rounded particles.'

An initial explosion in a mine often ignites the coal dust that mats the walls, roofs and floors. This combustion carries the initial blast as a charge throughout the workings, along the roads and to the coalface. Such an explosion should burn up all oxygen and extinguish all lamps. Miners would suffocate in such an atmosphere. Yet though miners died the lamps continued to burn. One rescue crew had even reported seeing a small fire. It seemed the coal dust was far from pure, that it was mixed with the likes of shale dust, so that the oxygen levels of the afterdamp were higher than expected. If so, men would take longer to die. Improve the flow of air back into the pits, bring in an oxygen supply, and they might well recover and survive.

As Haldane collected his sample of dust engrained in the man's face, he instanced the possible nature of the blast.

The sample of dust collected from the face was evidence in Haldane's developing theory. For the lamps to burn beside dead bodies, the coal dust could not have been pure. Oxygen could not have been burnt up in the blast. The coal dust that carried the explosion must have had a high degree of shale dust within it. Analysis of the dust engrained in the young man's skin offered possible proof of this.

The skin on the back of the man's hands was completely loosened, and peeled off in the same way as when a poultice has been applied for some time. The colours were clear even in the lamplight of the room.

'The nails are pink, the fingers quite white,' Haldane observed, and then turned the hand over. 'Only towards the palmar surface, where the blood supply is normally more abundant, is the red colour to be seen. This, as you very well know doctor, would be leaden-blue or pale in death from any other cause.'

Such remarkably lifelike appearance of pink and red on the skin of the deceased had one likely cause. Death from carbon monoxide poisoning.

Cutting into the man's external jugular vein caused blood of a dark carmine-red to spurt into the collecting tube. The colouring announced the presence of carbon monoxide. To make certain, Haldane deployed his spectroscope there and then. He diluted a drop of the blood in a test tube of water. Two absorption bands became sharp and distinct to the eye. Adding an ammonium sulphide solution to absorb any oxygen that was present, he then warmed the test tube over a small spirit flame. The bands remained almost as sharp as before. Carbon monoxide was not only present. The haemoglobin was nearly saturated with it.

House to house, home to home, Morris and Haldane conducted forty-five examinations together. Carts with coffins moved around them. The coffins were of fine quality. Ferndale Colliery provided them, as was traditional in such disasters. The colliery added the gift of £1 to each bereaved family, to help with funeral expenses. No colliery had ever extended itself in such a way. Some miners' families accepted this, while others preferred to bear the costs themselves.

Widows sat by the embers of fires. Laundry hung on a wooden rack connected by pulley to the ceiling. In the darkness the cotton shirts seemed blazingly white. These women would no longer have to combat the coal dust brought home on their husbands' and sons' clothes. They would not have to check the folds of clothes for the mine beetles or the lice caught from mice. They would not have to haul water from the well to the fire, and scrub and pound and boil the miners' clothes clean for the next working shift. It was a tough and cruel domestic life but it had satisfied them. Now they had nothing.

The post-mortems took the two doctors through the night, through the following day, and on into the next run of darkness. Everything confirmed the supposition that the men had died not from suffocation or the direct effects of the explosion, but from carbon monoxide poisoning.

Bloodletting of humans was only just this side of ghoulish given the current social setting. When asked, the bereaved families had readily granted permission for Haldane to take blood samples, putting aside their own disquiet in tribute to the doctors' expertise. A fuller autopsy, allowing for dissection and the removal of organs, was clearly out of the question. It was time for Haldane to switch partners. Back at the colliery brattice doors were being lowered down the shaft for the repairing gangs to install. The doors went down, and into the cages for the upward journey came the bodies of the first two ponies.

The colliery's veterinary surgeon, David Rees, had assembled a fine team of 150 pit ponies. Eighty of these had died, along with five of the ostlers who had been caring for them in their stables. Four of these men had been overcome by carbon monoxide. The fifth ostler was found near living ponies and a companion who escaped. His head had been crushed by fallen timber and split open by a panicked horse's hoof.

The veterinary surgeon joined Haldane in an examination of the animals. Thirty were studied in total, fifteen of these very completely. Some they examined in the colliery yard, before the animals were skinned and taken to be buried in the tips; others were examined below ground.

Haldane saw no need to bring down his white mice to test for gas. Brown and black mice darted between the horseflesh, running off with samples. Remaining horses kicked and whinnied, recovering their strength as oxygen re-entered their bloodstreams. Ostlers, and other men new to the task, calmed the beasts and led them away to drag clear fallen timber.

Haldane focused his work on a stable in which twenty horses had died. In the stable opposite, just across the haulage road, thirteen horses had survived.[14] The stench of rotting horseflesh was almost overpowering, the light from the Cambrian safety lamps falling dim pools over scenes of horror. Notes Haldane made on one horse might have served for all of them, since the death of each horse resembled others so closely:

From stable on west side of No. 8 pit. No burns. Several slight bruises. Tail slightly singed. Muscles and subcutaneous tissue bright carmine-red. Stomach and intestines pink or

carmine-red in parts where blood was visible. Liver light
pink. Spleen very dark. Lungs mottled black and bright
carmine-red, not abnormally congested; and on section no
liquid exuded. Windpipe carmine-red on internal surface,
and containing a few grains of coal dust, but quite clear.
Blood of heart dark cherry-red. Samples taken from right and
left ventricles, and from spleen.[15]

The process meant wielding hacksaws as well as scalpels
and needles. These hours of butchery in the stink and swel-
ter of the mine developed their own rhythm to see Haldane
through, as severed limbs and organs soaked in the crimson
pools of their own poisoned blood.

Haldane and Rees passed a rescue party pulling debris
from a 4-foot seam as they walked back to the shaft. The cage
closed them inside itself and they were hauled back up to the
last of the daylight. A deputation met Rees, the veterinary
surgeon, as they stepped out of the cage. They were horse
traders, seeking to sell the colliery fresh beasts to consign to
a life underground.

This was Thursday afternoon. The last train that could
carry Haldane home left at 3.30 pm. He had done enough.
He was determined to be on it. He would not need his
London Fever Hospital case to keep children from his
carriage for this journey. His slaughterhouse smell, his blood-
stained attire, would guarantee a carriage to himself.

The streets of the town were filled by men dressed in their
Sunday best. Though only thirteen funerals were held that
day, bodies carried in their coffins to the cemetery on the
summit of a hill, word had gone around that this would be
the day of most funerals. Miners throughout the valley left
the coalfaces unworked for the day. They would do without

their pay, and pay their respects to fallen colleagues. The windows of the houses were draped in the traditional white of mourning.[16]

At four o'clock, as Haldane's train pulled him south, the body of fireman John Bowen was discovered beneath debris in the 4-foot seam of shaft number 7. He was the last to be retrieved of the fifty-seven men who had died.

Haldane was already working out the calculations that would go into his official report. Of those bodies he had examined, 32 per cent were not burnt. Of those burnt or injured, he reckoned nearly half would have ultimately died apart from the effects of afterdamp. So but for the afterdamp, 66 per cent might have been saved.

His mind seldom discovered one figure without running it past a whole set of related calculations. About one-fifth of the male population of Britain between the ages of twenty-five and sixty-five were miners. Over the last forty years the number of men employed in the mines had trebled, though the number of deaths had stayed fairly constant. That average was 1,061 per year, the highest of any industry save perhaps the railways. He would need to be alert to future mine disasters, and check his new findings against those, but if the Tylorstown average applied nationally then 700 miners a year would be saved.

Haldane's report was published throughout the English-speaking world and immediately translated into several languages. The message had to be passed among all miners. 'Listen and learn. Don't trust your brains when they are addled by gas. Have this knowledge in place any time you go underground. You're already alert when you are down there. Even when everything is well, you are tense for the sound of an explosion. Any workman who hears the blast approaching should never attempt to run. Instead he should instantly fall flat, if possible in a sheltered position, and out of the way of any wagons which might be blown over him. Gas is lighter than air, so crouch below it. Seal yourself away from the main roads and wait.'

Effective rescue apparatus had to be provided, and men trained in how to use it. Rescue parties must be taught the use of mice and canaries. The exquisite care of Haldane's mind would soon be seen in a future invention, the 'Haldane box'. This held a canary, but as soon as the creature fell from its perch, the sides of the cage were sealed. The carrying handle was also a miniature oxygen cylinder. Turn a valve and oxygen was released into the box. As miners retreated to safety, each fallen canary was already on the way to recovery.

Mines should be safe places for any creature. Haldane should be happy to send his own son down there. Come to think of it, why not hurtle young Jack into the peculiar abysses of his father's working life as soon as possible?

Sit Haldane on one scale, place around 3,000 mice on the other scale, and the scale would balance. Skin Haldane, however, lay his skin on the ground, and it would only take the skins of 150 mice to cover it. Creatures produce carbon dioxide and absorb oxygen at a rate that accords with their surface area, not with their mass. A mouse's lungs are hectic little things. In an hour, a mouse produces about 10 grams of carbonic acid per kilo of its body weight. A man, on the other hand, breathes much more leisurely and produces only about half a gram per kilo in the same period. Relate man to mouse and you find that the exchange between air and blood is about twenty times as rapid in a mouse's lungs as in a man's.

Require your mouse to breathe poisonous gases, and it will be affected twenty times as fast as a man would be. Conversely, remove that mouse to a safe atmosphere and it will recover twenty times faster than would a man.

Priestley placed a mouse under glass, Lavoisier used a sparrow, both discovering how these creatures used up the various constituents of air. It is handy to use such small warm-blooded creatures for experiments, due to the sheer speed of their responses to the surrounding atmosphere. Haldane had already taken the ponderous step of replacing such animals with himself, so spending 7½ hours in his wooden chamber for effects he could have achieved in 22 minutes with a mouse under glass.

Now he devised an apparatus to take those tests several stages further. Oddly this apparatus was simpler than the wooden chamber, and involved reintroducing a bottled mouse. Water was set to drip through a tap at a regulated rate. These drops fell into a cylinder filled with pure carbonic oxide, displacing the gas into a tube through which a constant flow of air was streaming. This tube dipped down into a sealed bottle containing a mouse.

Normally an experiment might stop at this point. Take the data received from the mouse and extrapolate it to estimate the relative effect on humans. However these individual mice had a colleague. The mixture of air and gas that they breathed, now mixed with a modicum of mouse breath, passed out of their bottle through a second tube which ended in a valve made of glycerine-soaked intestine. This was Haldane's mouthpiece. As the mouse breathed the poisonous vapours, so did Haldane. A further intestine valve, and a bag made of bladder, prevented any of Haldane's breath flowing back to disturb the regular current of air.

The apparatus was set to deliver 0.39 per cent of carbon monoxide into the airstream passing above the mouse and into Haldane. After 1½ minutes the mouse was panting. On 3 minutes it was sprawling on its belly and failed to move again. After 13 minutes its role was over. It was removed and placed on its side, pending recovery.

The advantage of the mouse's quicker reaction time in such a situation is that the scientist has fair warning of what will happen to him if he persists. It is a sensible time to stop. In the twentieth century, drivers would close garage doors and run tubes from their car exhausts to die of carbon monoxide poisoning. For Haldane, the gas was an unknown poison. No person had, as yet, troubled to breathe in the gas for measured durations and in measured quantities, so as to measure its physiological effects and its rate of absorption into the bloodstream.

When the mouse fell senseless it was no sign for Haldane to stop. Rather it was encouragement to persist. The mouse's collapse was a sure indicator that 0.39 per cent of carbon monoxide in his atmosphere was set to have a dramatically toxic effect.

Haldane took a sample of his own blood, and compared its dilution to one taken before the experiment. This new one was distinctly pinker, even though he felt no symptoms as yet. The evidence of his own poisoning shone before him. His blood was saturated with 23 per cent of carbonic oxide. After 29 minutes he was panting fast, 18 times a minute. His limbs were shaking, his pulse ran at 120, and he felt 'distinctly abnormal'. The mouse had shown such signs of trouble at 1½ minutes. In man it had taken half an hour. The expectation that gases affected small warm-blooded animals 20 times faster than humans was borne out.

At 30½ minutes a fresh blood sample was bright pink in dilution, his blood saturated with 39 per cent of the gas. Haldane pulled himself away from the gas and ran up a flight of twenty-four steps. 'A little later became giddy,' run his lab notes at this point, 'much out of breath, had palpitations and could not see as well as usual. On standing for two or three minutes felt all right again. Vision cleared, and hyperpnoea [panting] disappeared. Afterwards singing in ears. Ran upstairs again.'[17]

Each time he ran up the stairs the symptoms returned, but a little less severely. A few hours after the experiment he was able to run up and down the stairs in his Oxford home at Crick Road without any ill effect. Those journeys between laboratory and home were not without their own dangers. Police stopped him on one such fuddled walk, suspecting drunkenness. For her part his housekeeper kept her distance when she saw Haldane weaving his way along the pavement, but offered her sympathies to Kathleen later. 'I knows how you feel, ma'am,' she said. 'My husband's just the same on a Friday night.'[18]

Haldane was modelling the affects of gas on miners in the wake of an underground explosion. In introducing mice into these experiments a motive beyond normal experimentation on animals was in play. He 'had partly a directly practical object in view. The presence of carbonic oxide in the air is in certain cases a source of great danger in coal-mines and other places . . . A miner usually trusts his lamp to give him indications of the presence of dangerous gases in a mine. A lamp is, however, of no service in detecting small quantities of carbonic oxide in the air.' Haldane was examining the use of small animals as a detector of such gases. How much time would a miner have after a small creature shows signs of distress? And how much would physical exertion exacerbate the effects of poison on man? A miner would expect to flee a situation underground once it was proved to be dangerous. This was likely to mean rapid exertion up a gradient. As Haldane ran up his flights of stairs, an imaginative scenario saw his actions reflected in tunnels below ground.

Time and again Haldane reset the apparatus, set the air flowing, and stationed himself at the far end to breathe in the poison. The percentage of carbonic oxide in the mixture ranged from 0.021 up to 0.5. The length of time to which Haldane would stand breathing it in varied from 11 minutes to 4½ hours.

He took notes every few minutes of each experiment. A scientist might measure an animal's convulsions or note the moment at which its legs start to tremble, but the mouse is never going to give voice to a headache or report the first onset of nausea. Haldane added his own quality feedback.

'John's end of the enquiry in which he is now engaged,' John Burdon Sanderson wrote to his sister Mary at the end of 1895, 'the one which relates to the causes of death in consequence of black damp – is excellent.'[19] The following month this work was brought to its climax in the wake of the colliery disaster at Tylorstown. At the beginning of March 1896, Haldane travelled to Wales to hear the coroner's verdict on those Tylorstown deaths. He was writing the official report. Its results could not come soon enough. Already on 18 February that year, forty-nine bodies had been brought out of the Vulcan Mine in Garfield, Colorado, following an explosion.

The Welsh coroner's verdict 'seemed a very fair one, and did not throw blame on anyone,' Haldane wrote. 'The owners of the pit had done all they could to water the dust and avoid any source of danger. The watering was not effectual, however, and no doubt these explosions will go on until someone finds out by experiment what will stop them.'

On 20 April twenty men were killed in Brancepeth Colliery, near Durham. On post-mortem examination, Haldane determined that nineteen of these had died of carbon monoxide poisoning. On 30 April an explosion rocked Micklefield Colliery near Leeds. Rescuers and victims all showed signs of poisoning by the afterdamp containing about 3 per cent of carbon monoxide, a seemingly small yet near-lethal amount, carbon monoxide binding so readily with haemoglobin that the life-giving oxygen is displaced. Thirty-six hours after the explosion a pony was found alive and well. A little further on rescuers discovered a man alive but unconscious, lying beside dead colleagues.

'I was in the pit at the time when the living man was found,' Haldane observed in an addendum to the official report, 'and proceeded to the place with a cylinder of oxygen.' Oxygen was administered to clear the carbon monoxide from the bloodstream, the man stretchered to the surface and placed to warm beside a fire, though he died in Leeds Infirmary the following day.

Mining authorities throughout the world recognized the importance of Haldane's report on the Tylorstown disaster. Years later he would hear from the Department of Mines in Canada that 'this country, and the mining world in general, owe a great deal to the careful, painstaking, and valuable investigations made by yourself and your colleagues'.[20] Haldane delivered, for the first time, an accurate diagnosis of the greatest cause of death among miners. He gave clear recommendations about how the miners could protect themselves, and invented breathing equipment that would allow rescue teams to operate. His introduction into mines of the canary, as an early warning indicator of dangerous gases, would become so universally adopted that everyone knows the significance of 'the canary in the mine'. Haldane was himself such a canary, putting his own health and life on the line to protect others.

Investigating the cause of disasters, delivering the science, alerting the world to proper safety measures, were steps in an almighty and everlasting battle. A twenty-first-century Haldane would be disgusted but not altogether surprised to find safety measures still being sidelined for the sake of profit and convenience.

In February 2007 the *Globe and Mail* reported from the town of Linfen in China. Just as industrial expansion in the Western world led a drive for coal from the deepest seams, and resultant encounters with hitherto unknown gases, coal is the driving force behind China's twenty-first-century industrial expansion. A Canadian reporter found a scene in the China of 2007 that was Dickensian in feel, 'an apocalyptic vision of clanking factories, spewing smokestacks, burning flames, suffocating fumes, slag heaps, constant haze and relentless dust'.[21] Estimates for miners' deaths in China in 2006 range from 4,700 to more than 7,000. The exact numbers will never be known, for it can be convenient to bury statistics of miners' deaths along with the miners themselves. In February 2007 the director of the Coal Mine Safety Bureau in Henan province admitted 'the deaths of seventeen miners were deliberately concealed' in reports of a recent underground fire.[22] In the same month *China Daily* reported: 'Many Chinese coal mines ordered shut by the government for safety reasons are still operating – some seven years after being told to close – and accidents are still happening there.

The government has taken aim at small coal mines in the last few years as many have few or no safety measures in place, to try to cut the death toll in the world's deadliest mining industry.'[23]

In February 2006, sixty-five miners died in an underground mine in Mexico. Ricardo Ramirez, a 25-year-old miner who survived the blast, stated, 'That mine has no remedy because they never took precautions, and I doubt they will start now.'[24] One year later the bodies of the dead miners had still not been recovered, their colleagues walking out on strike in support of stricter safety measures.

Inside a Colombian mine a spark ignited gases, and thirty-two men died in the blast. Mines in the Andean region have few or makeshift safety features or rescue apparatus.[25] Earlier that day, 3 February 2007, mine authorities had been pleading over the radio for a gas extractor to remove methane from the underground tunnels. Trapped methane gas made it unsafe for rescuers to retrieve the bodies.

It is unwise for the developed world to grow complacent. In America *The Nation* reported in 2006: 'Mine workers have faced increasingly unsafe conditions because of rollbacks of health and safety regulations, the appointment of former mining industry executives to federal mine safety agencies, and the slashing of the budget and staff for safety inspection.'[26]

The percentage increase in US coal-mining deaths in 2006 was the largest in 107 years. Forty-seven miners died, sixteen of them in Kentucky. Melissa Lee was the widow of one of those sixteen, her husband Jimmy killed in a methane explosion in Harlan in May 2006. She stood up in Kentucky's General Assembly to plead for a mine safety bill that was being allowed to fade away through lack of attention. 'If sixteen of you all were killed last year, do you think there would be no change?' she asked the legislators. 'Do miners not mean anything? Are they not important? Please don't turn your backs on us just because you don't know what mining is like.'[27]

Haldane knew what mining was more precisely than any man who had gone before him. He would explore all forms of mining in the most extreme conditions. He would come to know what it was like for sailors trapped in submarines too. What it was like to be a soldier in the trenches, a diver on the seabed, a stoker in front of the hottest of ovens, or a mountaineer on the highest points of the Earth. And he was wise and sane enough to know that you never presume you have resolved a matter and hand it over to the authorities to take care of. Human ignorance feeds on itself, its bloated form always eager to assume control to its own advantage. From the outset, Haldane pitched his career as a battle to keep the Earth progressing along as sane a track as possible. Such a battle is not a matter of winning. It's about never giving up.

SON OF SCOTLAND

What could John Scott Haldane tell his children about his childhood and family background? Son Jack would gain his own fame as a scientist. Daughter Naomi would be acclaimed as the novelist Naomi Mitchison. Their father's tales of his early life could set a model for their own growth into adulthood.

On Haldane's death, his books and papers were sent into the care of Jack. Haldane's library included a first edition of Darwin's *Origin of Species*, signed and presented to him by Darwin, among its many treasures. By then Jack was known to the world as J. B. S. Haldane, geneticist and popular science writer. He was a Marxist with individual ideas about ownership. If a book strolled from a library never to return, then someone who cared enough for it to steal it now owned it.

Haldane's own papers sat in Jack's house in India to be chewed by termites. Jack's widow called in a friend to witness their burning. These papers were her 'dowry'. Should her in-laws ever complain that she had burnt what was precious, her friend must corroborate the fact that insects got there first.

Haldane's private and handwritten papers were tipped from a suitcase on to a bonfire and consumed by flames.

His daughter Naomi had the only copy of her father's memoir. It has vanished. Had it survived, it is unlikely that it would have whispered a word about his upbringing. Haldane lived a sensational life, but he was not a sensationalist. He cared enormously for science, for public welfare, and for achieving a unifying philosophy of life, but did not give a damn for personal glory. He went to tremendous efforts to promote the scientific career of others, but his own scientific papers were shepherded into publication by those who loved him. This biography is an attempt to nudge him out of the shadows and into world renown, just as Brunel's first biography reclaimed a genius from obscurity. Haldane's son and daughter, his sister, his brother, his mother and daughter-in-law, his uncle, all have their biographies and autobiographies. Had Haldane felt any need for world acclaim, he could have achieved it. He could have trumpeted his scientific breakthroughs, and championed the mode of personal suffering that brought them into being. This he never did.

His early life is drawn from scraps dropped by those whose lives were tangential to his own. Since he was a Haldane through and through, it pays to pause a little and draw those scraps together into as clear a picture as we can manage. What was a Haldane? What made this remarkable man?

Wind sliced through the grid system of Edinburgh's New Town and hurled itself across the expanse of Charlotte Square. The skies roared breath against the glass as windows rattled. The servant bent down in her morning print dress and used tongs to place fresh nuggets of coal upon the fire.

The mistress usually graced these rooms in moiré silk.

Now her limbs kicked against her white cotton gown as gusts of pain gasped from her mouth. Her firstborn, a boy called Elijah, had died in the aftershock of his birth. He was three days old. Two more sons since then had survived, first Richard then George. The mother was prone to sickness but also strong. Pile fresh linen by the side of the bed, fetch the hot water, say your prayers, and stoke the fire.

Her waters broke. Her body spasmed. In a flush of blood a head emerged. The midwife's hands reached for the baby's shoulders and eased him loose. Scissors snipped his umbilical cord. A clock in another room struck midday on 2 May 1860. A hand beat a rhythm against the baby's back, kick-starting his tiny lungs. They jolted, contracted, and sucked in their first independent breath. The baby took a taste of air, thickened with carbon dioxide and sulphur dioxide pumped from the smouldering coal. Oxygen diffused from the lungs and into his bloodstream.

In a thin and juddering cry that brought happiness to the household, John Scott Haldane forced the vitiated air from his system.

The heart was beating, the blood was coursing through the veins, and the brain was transmitting neural impulses to the limbs. The greatest sustained physiological experiment in the history of the human lung was under way.

His cot was in the nursery on the top floor of the house. It was a long haul up four flights for the men who carried in the weekly sacks of coal, bought in at ten shillings a ton. They spilt it into the bunker on the landing. At the crash of each sack of coal, the baby jolted.

As Mary Haldane's first baby, Elijah, died, a white turtledove appeared at the front door of 17 Charlotte Square. No one ever found out where the bird had come from. The grieving mother took it as a sign of grace. The white bird stayed with the family for ten years when, no longer a 'living organism', it was stuffed and mounted. The indoor flight of the bird, its death, its subsequent return in its still, taxidermized form, was one of the infant Johnnie's first memories.

Infant Johnnie Haldane looked down to see his face reflected in patent leather shoes. He stared at his image in a mirror and saw a young girl staring back, her fair hair in curls, her dress flounced out by petticoats. His older brothers wore similar girls' attire when infants, beribboned and smothered in velvet. Babies looked beautiful in frocks.

Baby Johnnie looked up into his nurse Betsey Ferguson's eyes, magnified by her spectacles. A black velvet and lace cap crowned her head. The nurse distrusted perambulators so carried her babies through Edinburgh, taking the air around the perimeter of Charlotte Square.

Number 17 was on the west side of the square, just an alley separate from St George's Church. Its façade was a palace front, built to Robert Adam's design. High ground-floor windows opened on to a dining room. The drawing room spanned the entire front of the first floor. Replete with marble mantelpieces, its furniture made of rosewood and Utrecht velvet, glass-drop chandeliers dropped light on to what was in truth a grand ballroom. The servants' bedrooms, the closets and stores, the wine cellar, the scullery and the kitchen were all found in the basement. The children's realm was at the top of the stairs.

The house was grand for socializing, but cramped for living. An earlier Mrs Haldane died in childbirth. Her five children were now growing up to leave and form families of their own. John was the third surviving son of his father's second family. A daughter and a further son squeezed beside him into that upstairs nursery world. His siblings and nurse shaped young John's life.

'The influence of a good man or woman has a profound effect on a child when their principles are carried out in practice,' Mary Haldane wrote. 'I have watched this in many cases and have endeavoured to follow it as far as possible with our own. A parent can only guide at a distance by supplying other channels of good influence so as to reach her children.'[1]

John's father Robert Haldane was a Writer to the Signet, with special expertise in conveyancing. The Signet was the private seal of the early Scottish kings, and 'Writers to the Signet' were those officials allowed to supervise its use. The first recorded use of the Signet was in 1369, its membership of 'Writers' formalized into a legal society in the sixteenth century. Such lawyers were confidential advisers to Scottish landowners, dealing with their financial affairs. Many of these landowners were Robert Haldane's relatives. John met with them many times, and through them came to know a wide network of other influential people.

The Haldanes worked on the principle that social strata had to be maintained, yet all women and men were equal in the eyes of God. In terms of the house's geography, some people would come through the front door of the house, while others would come to the back. For the children, whose lives on the bare top floor were balanced by access to the servants' quarters of the basement, the back-door patrons were as significant in their lives as any others. With no pensions or state benefits to rely on, several women turned up for their weekly allowance from the Haldanes. 'The tree-legged man', named for his wooden leg, came on a more occasional scrounge. The children made deals with packmen, the travellers who lived by barter. They swapped skins peeled off rabbits by the cooks for small china ornaments. A popping beer-bottle cork meant it was midday, and 'Jimmie the Post' was in the kitchen.

Down in that empty basement kitchen early one morning, young John and his small brother William placed a poker in the fire. This fire was kept burning, turning the smoke-jack of roast meat. The poker glowed red. A movement at the window made the boys glance left. A white figure peered in at them. Maids' stories of the time buzzed with fears of Spring-Heeled Jack. This demonic figure first terrorized London in 1837. Now he had leapt out of urban myth to bedevil the young girls of Edinburgh. He was a rapist and a kidnapper, jumping clear of all crimes on his fabled heels.

Young Johnnie guessed at once that Spring-Heeled Jack was in his back yard. Snatching the poker from the fire, he led Willie on a charge out through the back door. Terrified, the figure ran to the high wall and jumped to clear it.

Rumour spread among adults that the figure, in truth, was a wayward medical student on a maid-startling spree. Demon or student, it was Johnnie Haldane and a red-hot poker who put an end to his career.

A naked gas light hung over the table in the middle of the nursery. Another, lit on darker days, was by the fireplace. Betsey Ferguson, known to the children as 'Baba', sat in the nursing chair by the fire, a silk apron protecting her full dress, reading out snippets from the newspaper on her lap. Her father had died in an accident, the mother scrimping to save for her children's education. Baba was schooled till the age of ten. She prized education very highly. How lucky they were, she told the children, that their father worked to give them food, clothes and schooling. They must understand they were privileged, and give their lives to helping other people.

Their nursery window looked out to the tree-lined banks of the Firth of Forth, and beyond them to the hills. Charlotte Square contained the family through the winter. The summer saw them escape to those hills.

The estate of Cloan was built on a flank of the Ochils in Perthshire. It centred on a fine square farmhouse, a new rocket-shaped turret switching it to a more Scottish baronial style. As in Edinburgh, the nursery was on the top floor, with views across to the Grampian mountains. 'Clean chintzes covered the chairs', and the children had 'home-made scones instead of baker's bread and plenty of milk in old-fashioned white jugs adorned with ferns'.[2] Robert Haldane bought the house in 1851 and worked hard to fence, plant and drain the land, becoming landowner as well as lawyer.

These were ancestral lands. The principal family home of the Haldanes of Gleneagles stretches across the glen below. The name Gleneagles in fact stems from the Haldane family chapel, a thirteenth-century stone building standing at an ancient crossroads. It was prominent as the church, or in French *église*, of the Glen – 'Glen église' eliding into Glen-eagles. The ruins of the Haldane castle crown a small hill nearby.*

A large black Newfoundland dog led the children out into the gardens, around the estate, and over the land beyond. A pool near the house was so deep it was black. The dog dis-

---

* Much to the objection of the Haldanes, a railway company would later rename the station of Crieff Junction near Cloan. They called it Gleneagles, and built a vast hotel with its internationally renowned golf course nearby. The 2005 G8 summit conference added to the worldwide fame of the Gleneagles name.

liked the children swimming there. It jumped in to claw at their backs, urging them back to land. Safest was to herd the children into its kennel, and guard the entrance.

The boys built a loghouse out of wood, tarpaulin and moss. Inside the children built fires and roasted potato dinners, singing their secret 'Song of the House' and speaking their secret 'Language of the House'. Outside they played cricket, climbed trees, and fished for trout in the burns. The new sport of lawn tennis was easygoing. Croquet was fiercely competitive. Young Johnnie lay on the grass to line up his shots, and jumped up, crying with frustration, whenever he missed. Croquet stirred him to the same excitement throughout his adult years.

From the age of twelve boys were encouraged to shoot. John found no pleasure in killing. Instead he and his sister Elizabeth headed for remote glens in search of rare ferns.

The whole family loved walking. Her layers of skirts sweeping the earth, Mary Haldane led family parties up the glens. John and his older brothers once started at two o'clock in the morning and headed down in the dark through Auchterarder. The sun rose on their distant goal: the 4,000-foot summit of Ben Lawers. At the base of the mountain they met a party of climbers just emerged from the local inn. Those climbers planned to climb up and down the peak in record time. The boys had momentum on their side. They left their rivals far behind, reached the top, descended, and walked home, the teenagers covering a distance of seventy-three miles all within twenty-three hours.

Sunday walks kept to the garden. Each day began and ended with chapters read from the Bible, though Sundays also meant a 4-mile trip to church by barouche. Built on C springs for a comfortable ride, the children rode on its front seat. In rain the back of the front seat was pulled forward, the hood was pulled across, the curtains drawn, covers pulled up to protect the legs, and the children squatted among the feet of the adults.

Robert Haldane was a man 'to whom all animals were intimate friends. The pigeons lit on his shoulders when he went out to feed them after breakfast, and the horses and ponies nosed his pockets for the bread which he carried there for them.'[3]

Robert's own father James, once a swashbuckling captain on the lucrative East India Company trading route, sold land in order to fund a preaching mission around Scotland. Robert Haldane had that same missionary fire in his belly. 'He was a man of an old-fashioned type and he loved a simple country life. He was very devout, and he had a barn fitted up where he used once a week to preach to a considerable audience of old-fashioned Scottish country folk who came to hear the Word of God in all its strictness. On alternate Sundays he used to ride miles to various villages and preach there.'

'Religion permeated our lives,' John's sister Elizabeth recalled, 'and the sense of sin and its consequences seemed to dog our footsteps when we remembered what it meant. But strangely enough the churches did not influence us as did the influence of home. Church in the country had a pleasant aroma of outside life and outside people, and the oppressive theology that was apt to overshadow our lives was blown aside by the fresh country breezes.'

With the looks of an Old Testament prophet, their 88-year-old minister read the text 'Into Thy Hands I commit my spirit', left the pulpit, and died. John visited the corpse, with sods of earth placed on its eyes. Death rooms were training grounds for children. Death was part of life and held nothing to fear.

Murder was part of life too. Robert Haldane led his children on tours through the closes and tight alleys of Edinburgh's Old Town. In the shadows and damp of old, dark stone he told them tales of robberies and murders. He stood them outside the debtors' refuge near Holyrood. How did lives of such misery come to lurk among the streets? The father had his answer. These sinners had never heard the good news of the Gospel. Calvinists like him visited the sick to throw a religious text at their heads. The children rode in carriages and helped throw tracts, many of them terrifying, at the cottages along the road.

The doctrines of the father felt hollow to the children, but the sights of so many forms of suffering triggered what in different ways would be lives of social activism. Their mother Mary Haldane was active in her own way.

'My weans, my weans, what will they do?' a condemned woman cried from the dock. She had killed her husband's lover and now would hang. What would happen to her children?

Let her hang, was the opinion of a visiting Haldane aunt. It was only proper to care for the good people. Others must be left to the fruits of their sinning.

Mary Haldane came from different stock, and thought differently. All people were the same and needed equal help. Pregnant herself, knowing what it meant to be a mother, she wrote a letter of support to the condemned woman. Her letter reached the press. Relatives found it shaming. Mary Haldane's own sense of mission continued. She would go among women who were deemed to have 'fallen' and point out that men must have 'fallen' with them.

Tutors delivered John's early education, and continued to do so through the autumn terms when the family stayed at Cloan. A tutor in Edinburgh, Hugh Wilson, primed Johnnie with the necessary Latin and Greek. At Cloan, Duncan MacDonald was more amiable than brilliant. He taught the basics, but made the greatest impression as a companion out in the wilds, where he would swing up through the highest branches of trees. He left Johnnie with a skill that would be vital should he ever, who knows, need to hurry through a network of underground tunnels in the wake of mass explosions. He taught the boy to jump over crevasses without fear.

Novels were discouraged, though Johnnie could read Charles Dickens and Charlotte Brontë, because their books had done so much to help children and the poor.

Mary Haldane's own education had been vile. She was determined to spare her own children anything as severe. Her governesses were supplied by Mrs Stevens, whose niece Mrs Carus Wilson ran the school that became the model for the cruel schooling of Charlotte Brontë's *Jane Eyre*. The typical governess was 'a perfect hypocrite, and neglected her charges while she amused herself. She was in the habit of singing hymns and putting on a sanctimonious face before her employers.'[4]

One such governess shut young Mary up for a day at a time and fed her only on bread and water. 'Sometimes it was an empty room, and once in a room never opened in a so-called haunted house which my father had taken for the shooting season. I remember to this hour the sound of the closing heavy door . . . While with Miss Taylor our feet were placed in stocks during lesson time, and we held a black board behind our backs, being seated on narrow seats that only just held us. The day commenced by us being waken by our nurses, taken by the two, and plunged over head in a deep bath of cold water.'

The Haldanes are said to be one of only fifteen families in Britain who can trace their ancestors in the male line back to 1250.[5] Two of those ancestors died across the Border, resisting an English invasion. They kept their battling skills primed by defending the plainsmen's cattle against raids by hill tribes. Stories from the Haldanes on his father's side, and the Burdon and Sanderson families on his mother's side, were ancestors' tales from which the boy should learn. One spoke of his mother's great-grandfather: 'When eighty years old he used to insist on my father following him out on a mule, and he was in the habit of riding over hedge and ditch, never allowing the child to think or say he was afraid. The result was that his namesake and grandson never knew what fear was.'

Another tale spoke of how her father learnt to swim. The little boys were all called out in the morning by Mr Birkett, the headmaster of Ovingham preparatory school, with the words, 'All out to bathe, boys.' Each was taken hold of by one foot and plunged into the Tyne. 'They became excellent swimmers in consequence.'

These lessons tied in with the single-word Haldane family motto: 'Suffer.' Suffering was not a good in itself. Putting your own life and comfort on the line in order to relieve the suffering of others? That was an ultimate good. It was a lesson the children must learn.

The food in Edinburgh was steady and simple, carried up the four flights of stairs by the under-nurse. Breakfast was porridge with bread and butter. 'Dinner', served at lunchtime, was mutton and plain puddings. The children stood and looked down through the stair rails as couples emerged from the drawing room and descended to the dining room for their feasts. The younger ones made an appearance at dessert. Given a slice of apple or orange, they were dispatched to the drawing room to admire some paintings before heading up to bed. Children were to be seen, just occasionally, and not heard. They kept back from the glittering, chattering adults, longing to scamper back to their 'real lives' upstairs.

Ten-year-old Johnnie Haldane walked down the steps from his front door into Charlotte Square. D'Arcy Wentworth Thompson, exactly his age, came along the side alley to meet him. D'Arcy hoped no one saw him emerge from his downstairs quarters in Alva Street, where servants should normally be housed. His mother had died as he was born. His father had moved from a teaching post at Edinburgh Academy to become a Professor of Greek in Galway. D'Arcy lived with his grandfather Joseph Gamgee, a noted veterinary surgeon specializing in horses.

Johnnie and D'Arcy headed down Church Lane and on through the village of Stockridge, where barefoot 'keelies' (as city boys termed kids of a lower class than themselves) were waiting for them. In their knickerbocker suits and balmoral bonnets, with books in a strap over their shoulder, Johnnie and D'Arcy were clearly heading for the Edinburgh Academy. This made them 'cads'. 'Cads' and 'keelies' were destined to fight.

Sir Walter Scott was one among illustrious men who set up the Academy in 1824. Sixty-five boys in total entered the class of Dr James Clyde, at a fee of £4.15s per term. They kept the same teacher for five years, who taught them all subjects before passing them on to the Rector for 'finishing'.

Clyde drew his charges into the imaginative realm of the Mediterranean plus a good smattering of the Bible. 'We knew extraordinarily little about Clive* or George Washington or even Buonaparte,' D'Arcy later reflected, 'but we knew a good deal about Greek and Roman and Israelite.'[6] Some mathematics and languages were added, which still left a narrow curriculum.

> It was all very wrong, no doubt, and very medieval and absurdly antiquated; we ought to have been learning chemistry and physics and physiology, to get us ready to make our living, and to grow rich, in a scientific and technical world. But that was not our way. In all our seven years we never had a single lesson in science of any kind, physical or biological; we were never 'shown any experiment', never taught a single lesson in mis-called 'Nature-study.' But one after another we became 'scientific men'.

D'Arcy was known as Daftie or 'Daft Thompson', his head always in hot pursuit of some fresh idea. Later to become Sir D'Arcy Wentworth Thompson he would hold a professorial Chair, largely of Natural History, for a world-record sixty-four years. His classic book of 1917, *On Growth and Form*, brought years of experience to the same thrill of the natural world he experienced in boyhood. Daftie and Johnnie joined up with some other boys to pursue their own interests. They formed the Eureka Club together. Come Saturdays they would head out into the country on botanizing expeditions, 'howking fossils in quarry and railway-cutting, grubbing in

---

* Robert Clive 'of India', 1725–74, the soldier and statesman who helped establish British supremacy in the area covered by the East India Company.

the rock-pools at Wardie, or searching the jetsam of Newhaven fishing boats'.[7]

In the Pentlands they climbed to the roosting sites of wild birds, and cycled over the border with England to the coast around Berwick-on-Tweed. As teenagers they donned knapsacks and strode off on 40- or 50-mile hikes.

The Royal Society had two more future members in the Eureka Club, besides Daftie and Johnnie. William Herdman's passion for marine zoology took him to a Professorship by the sea, first the Chair of Natural History at Liverpool and later that of Oceanography. Diarmid Noel Paton became Professor of Physiology at Glasgow, flashing out quick blackboard sketches to support magnificent lectures, dying on the day of his retirement in 1928.

Aged eleven, the boys went on a school outing to Mander's Menagerie in the Vegetable Market. Lions, tigers, bears, elephants, wolves and zebras added breadth to young Haldane's known world. Out of school he rode up and down on the new open-topped trams, pulled by horses along iron tracks.

D'Arcy reckoned Johnnie was 'an unathletic and rather clumsy lad', yet forgot about his 'great reserves of power'. The 14-year-old D'Arcy challenged Johnnie to a race up Church Lane. 'Puffing and blowing, using his arms almost as much as his legs, John won by a neck.'

Johnnie's teacher Dr Clyde 'was in his outlook an old Roman, and he was also in classical learning a fine scholar, though he did not inspire us with much of the higher meaning of classical literature. But he taught us always to seek for truth in the first place. It was his duty to read the Old Testament with us. While setting himself to avoid disturbing our faith in the Old Testament narratives, he could not help letting us feel that he himself did not accept what was recorded.'[8]

Richard Haldane, the oldest son, studied under Clyde in an earlier class. 'One result was that I soon became detached in my attitude towards the earlier Bible teachings.' As heaviness of religious doubt settled on Richard, John's brother George brought lightness to the balance.

Known as Geordie and two years older than John, he was 'a beautiful child, very fair and with large expressive dark blue eyes. He had great physical energy and an extraordinary musical gift from little more than a year old.'[9] The boy beat out time on his knees, and hummed tunes so loudly that passers-by stopped to listen. 'Green Grow the Rushes Oh' was a favourite, his singing or whistling filling the house, and he could turn to the piano and play any song from memory. His mother's father was a close friend and supporter of the great Robert Stephenson. George likewise was fascinated with developments in railway engines. New building methods excited him. Richard fostered the philosopher in John, but George brokered the engineer and field scientist.

Later kids found jazz or rap. The Haldanes found 'The Music of the Future'. To the parents it was just noise. For the young Haldanes, this music meant Wagner. He was their star. The thrill of his music was frightening. Music was pleasure, which under the Puritan ethic of their upbringing was sinful. They had to find ways to turn pleasure to the service of God and their fellow men.

For George, music held the same place as faith. Both were natural wonders that gave strength to life and need not be questioned. 'He could not bear to see the weak oppressed by poverty or bodily infirmity of any kind, and did all in his power to help them.'[10]

Richard, in the meantime, was posing profound religious questions to himself, and doubtless to John. 'The divines to whom I turned for personal guidance in those days could not help me much, for they had not themselves gone deeply enough down. I was driven to look to the philosophers, and I then began the study of metaphysics.'[11] He couldn't find the answers he needed, and in April 1874 his mother and nurse waved him off from Leith harbour. His ship was bound for Hamburg, from where he continued by train to the university of Göttingen.

The town of Göttingen dismayed him at first. The people and their customs were so unfamiliar they upset him. Looking out on to the street in the grey of his first dawn there, he watched a woman and a dog pulling along a cart which contained a man and a calf. Blood spurted an inch high from veins sliced open in duels between his fellow students. The streets held that odious reek of tanning, the town known for manufacture of a rough kind of leather. Effluents from the tanning works polluted the river Leine, yet even so this was the only place Richard could rely on for bathing. Washing facilities were scanty, and the student rooms were filthy. Yet the professors 'were a very brilliant set'.

Chief among these was the Professor of Philosophy, Rudolph Hermann Lotze. A leading philosopher of his age, he sought to establish the role metaphysical speculation could play in science. 'A quiet, reserved old man,' Richard remembered how 'he saw the nature of the crisis my mind was passing through, and set me to read Fichte's popular works, and particularly *The Vocation of Man*. With the aid of these and of Berkeley I began to work myself out of my mood and, under the stimulus of Lotze's teachings, to acquire a wider point of view.'[12]

When Richard returned to Cloan in the August of 1874, John scarcely recognized the brother who got out of the train at Crieff Junction. His hair was long, he had become very thin, and he had grown a moustache. The greater change in him was more subtle. At Easter he had been depressed and confused. Now he was electric with intellectual excitement picked up from his encounters with the idealist philosophy of the great Germans and of the eighteenth-century Irishman George Berkeley. John learnt the names as his brother talked, and moved into the realm of all these new ideas.

In February 1875 Geordie went to one of the series of Edinburgh concerts given by Charles Halle, whose Halle Orchestra would delight audiences through the years to come. He raced back to Charlotte Square to play the music through for his aunt, his mother's sister. The following Sunday he felt unwell so did not go with the rest of the family to church. On the Monday he felt no better, but nobody worried. It was seen as some passing ailment. Friends gathered in the drawing room on the Wednesday to hear an appeal by Miss Leigh for a mission in the north of the country. Life was going on. Geordie remained in bed. On the Thursday he turned the colour of copper. His uncle Dr Rutherford Haldane was called in from his home at 20 Charlotte Square. He examined the boy and turned to the mother.

'He is thoroughly and completely possessed,' he told her.

The boy had diphtheria. 'Baba' Ferguson and Mary Haldane fell to nursing him. His fever intensified. A membrane-like obstruction developed in his air passages to block his breathing. Back from his day at school John was kept away from the room. He only heard the panic of short and forced breathing, and the final silence that followed.

From Italy, Mary Haldane's brother John Burdon Sanderson wrote to her: 'We shall always, to the end of our lives, think what he would have been to us had he lived, and we cannot wish it otherwise. Would that it were possible to bring him back again! But it is not possible. May God help you to bear it, and give you so much joy in those that still remain and surround you that in time you may be able to think of the dear life that has passed away without pain.'[13]

It is hard to know when a boy might decide to become a doctor, to give his life to investigating the passage of air through human lungs, to understanding the workings of oxygen on the human body and finding ways to administer it. John watched and heard his brother dying of diphtheria. Mary Haldane contracted diphtheria as a result of her nursing. John studied the process of her illness from a safe distance, wondering if she too would die. His life had changed.

Richard summoned his father to the sickroom when it was known that George was dying. 'He received the summons with profound sorrow but without moving a muscle, and then, in a tone of deep solemnity, said, "Before the foundations of the world were laid it was so ordained."'[14]

The family retreated to Lowwood on the banks of Windermere, for anywhere new and in the countryside would do, free from the memories of Geordie running as a free spirit through the summer grounds of Cloan. Mary Haldane slowly recovered her health. The family returned to Edinburgh, then dared to go to Cloan again for the autumn of 1875.

On 22 January 1876 the Scotch Express was barrelling down the west-coast line in a snowstorm. By the hamlet of Abbots

Ripton in Huntingdonshire, a couple of hours north of King's Cross and its destination, the express crashed into a coal train which was in the process of shunting itself out of the way. On board the express was Mary Haldane's older brother Richard Burdon Sanderson. He was travelling with his wife Isabella, the sister of Robert Haldane. The marriage of these siblings, Robert's sister to Mary's brother, had brought the two families especially close. Richard and Isabella had two daughters, Elizabeth and Margaret, and an only son who was a law student in the Temple in London. All were travelling with them from Newcastle down to London.

Elizabeth, twenty-seven years old, was not too badly hurt, just locked into position by a twisted part of the carriage she was in. Her brother was trying to release her when the northbound train to Leeds ploughed directly through the already wrecked carriage, killing her instantly. Her sister Margaret, aged twenty-four, had also survived fairly well. After the second collision, the Leeds-bound train smashing through the Scotch Express, her brother found Margaret's body entangled among the iron framework of one of the carriages. She complained that she had lost all feeling below the waist, and died a few moments later.

Dr John Burdon Sanderson, brother to Mary and Richard, received news relayed from the George Hotel in Huntingdon, which had been requisitioned as a home for the dead and injured. His nieces were dead, his brother and sister-in-law both badly injured. The following morning he was able to travel up to the town and take care of some of the sick. Isabella eventually recovered. Richard Burdon Sanderson had a broken leg, fractured right arm and collarbone, and was suffering from extreme shock. He remained in intensive care for three months, after which he died.[15]

The mourning period for the loss of a close relative lasted two years. Mary wore full black, and a 'weeping veil' of black 'crape' made from silk threads to mark the deaths of her son, her brother and her nieces. Robert Haldane wore his hatband to the regulation height, a bow of crape, and on Sundays 9-inch-long cuffs made of plain-weave cotton known as 'weepers' because they could be used to wipe away tears. Soon Mary's period of grieving was extended yet again, this time to mark the loss of her husband Robert. He suffered from diabetes, and died in 1877 aged seventy-two.

'He passed away as he had lived,' his son Richard Haldane remembered, 'full of faith in what for him were eternal verities. He had been throughout too far away from the subjects that were interesting us who were his younger children ever to enter much into our inner lives. But he was full of affection, and when we succeeded in anything he took pride in our success.'[16]

A letter of that year from John to his mother is bound by the requisite thick black border of mourning. The year before he had transferred from Edinburgh Academy to Edinburgh University, studying for an Arts degree with Philosophy as a principal component. He told of his safe arrival back in Edinburgh following a 'comfortable' journey in a third-class carriage with wooden seats and sawdust on the floor. Previously even the servants had travelled second class. The ladies of the family would continue to travel first, but the death of the father brought what was to be the first round of financial restrictions.

'In my classes at College I fear I have got too far behind to make up this session, so I think I will not go in for the remaining examination rather than go in and make a bad paper, especially . . .' he notes, for a Haldane must never languish in the role of victim, 'as neither of the classes is of any importance.'[17]

His main inspiration in philosophy was Alexander Campbell Fraser, who encouraged the free play of thought and inquiry in his students. In 1871 Fraser had brought out the standard edition of Berkeley's *Works*, and he shared Berkeley's sense of the self as conscious activity. No existence beyond the self could be established by sheer reasoning. 'My old philosophical teacher, Professor Campbell Fraser of Edinburgh,' Haldane recalled in later years, 'used frequently to speak of "our mysterious universe." The advance of scientific knowledge does not seem to make either our universe or our life in it any less mysterious.'[18] In 1879 John bagged his First Class Merit in Arts, with high distinction in the class of Moral Philosophy. The mourning period for his father was coming to an end. Set to enrol as a student of Edinburgh's Medical Faculty in the autumn, it was time to assign himself some light relief. Light relief for a Haldane meant signing up for some additional classes. Richard had been revitalized by his stay in Germany. Now it was John's turn.

3

IN THE FOOTSTEPS OF GOETHE

'You may have some estimate of the beer-drinking power of the students,' Haldane wrote from the university of Jena in 1879, 'from the fact that 5,400 seidels of pretty heavy beer were drunk at the Commers the other night by about 400 students. A seidel is about 1½ pints.'* The drinking led to fights, and the fights to seventy duels. 'They look rather dangerous, as the two students who are fighting slash at one another as hard as they can. Their skulls must be very thick. Some of the swordcuts came with apparently tremendous force fair on the side of their heads. The wounds looked ghastly enough, though they never seemed to get seriously hurt.'

Beer drinking and fresh-cut wounds – all grand preparation for a medical student. Jena offered still more besides. Situated in Thuringia, known as 'the green heart of Germany', lime-

* The arithmetic has this work out at around 20 pints per student. One could doubt the figure, but for Haldane's future reputation for meticulous experimentation.

stone slopes rising from both banks of the river Saale give the area a mild enough climate for vineyards. Schiller had lectured there in History, Johann Gottlieb Fichte and Georg Hegel taught and devised the most compelling Philosophy of the age, while Goethe became Jena's 'Superintendent of Direct Measures in Science and Art', living in an official residence in the town's botanical garden. He took those twin responsibilities of art and science very seriously, attracting leading thinkers of the day through his organization of the garden, the libraries, a natural history archive and science laboratories.

A century had passed, but Haldane now found himself in both the intellectual and physical space of Goethe. Haldane would proceed to disprove scientific dogmas of his time. One dogma of Goethe's time was that man and animal were distinguished by the absence of the intermaxillary bone in the head of a man. In what could be seen as a model of targeted medical science for young Haldane, Goethe worked alongside the chemist Johann Wolfgang Döbereiner and the anatomist Justus Loder, and located that human intermaxillary bone for the first time.

Haldane visited 'the church where Schiller went for cheapness sake to get married. It is a queer little church something like a hayloft. We also saw the place where Goethe wrote his "Erlkönig". The alder trees along the banks of the Saale are certainly very ghostly looking, especially at night. No wonder there are all sorts of traditions about them.' A botanical excursion to Dormburg achieved very little botany, but allowed for a fine sequence of sausage meals, beers, song and dance and a visit to another of Goethe's houses, 'one of those castles of Dormburg, and there is a splendid view from the windows'.[1]

A daily hour-long German lesson helped the lectures

which Haldane attended to rise from the fog of incomprehensibility. The lessons also paved the way for his further studies, since many of the most significant papers in his field were written in German. Each week Haldane met with two theology students from Glasgow, John Herkless (later principal of St Andrew's University) and Lewis Muirhead, plus his philosopher friend Andrew Seth, to discuss Hegel's *Rechtsphilosophie* (Philosophy of Right). Another vigorous workout came from the series of lectures given by the Professor of Comparative Anatomy, Ernst Haeckel.

'He is a capital lecturer, and full of enthusiasm for "Monism",' Haldane told his brother. He was so taken with Haeckel that he ordered a photograph of the man, full-bearded and then aged forty-nine, for himself. 'He has a very pleasant face, and wonderful eyes, and is said to be a very pleasant man.'

Besides championing 'monism' Haeckel coined such words as ecology, phylogeny and phylum to help his ideas permeate the culture. Trained as a doctor, he gave up medical practice in 1859 on reading Darwin's *Origin of Species.* 'Monism', with its principle that all aspects of existence adhere into a unified form, can be seen as a basis for Haldane's philosophy, as can Haeckel's stance as a post-Darwinian evolutionist who did not accept the notion that biodiversity was a result of natural selection. Haeckel's own position was that environment had the most significant part to play in evolution, environmental impact on organisms producing different races, natural selection coming into play through the necessity of each organism's interacting with its environment. His magnificent paintings of animals and sea-creatures illustrated his masterwork of 1904, *Kunstformen der Natur* or *Art Forms in Nature.*

Two others of the highest scientific rank became Haldane's

teachers through these months in Jena. They formed essential models for his whole working life. Professor William Thierry Preyer, a friend of Haldane's uncle John Burdon Sanderson, helped direct the young man around the town and found him his German tutor. Preyer was in fact half-English, born in Rusholme near Manchester in 1841. His meticulous observation of children saw him become a leader in the developing movement of child psychology. Similarly influential in his field was Eduard Strasburger, the Professor of Botany who lectured Haldane and oversaw his botanical research. Then aged thirty-five, Strasburger was playing his own role in the evolutionary debate, preparing the third and final volume of his studies which clarified the phenomena of cell division, and the roles played in heredity by the nucleus and chromosomes. 'These German Universities are infinitely ahead of us,' Haldane would write after his time at Edinburgh University. 'A student there has, as a rule, the chance, if he likes to use it, of coming into real contact with men who are making the scientific history of their time.'[2]

Haldane lodged at Fürstengraben 675. At a rent of just £3 18s for the whole summer he had a bedroom with a sitting room attached. As the late spring moved into summer he took his books out to four summer houses in the front garden. His daily Bible excerpts came from Hebrews, to coordinate with his mother's Bible study back home.

'One really very seldom feels at all dull or lonely,' he wrote. He was surrounded by mechanical clocks, for which Jena was famous, and a watchman blowing a horn from a tower every quarter of an hour. 'My rooms here are quiet, but somehow very lively. I think the old clock and the watchman on the tower make a great difference. There are two other clocks quite close, which strike the hours also.'[3]

Lunch every day was at the Bär inn, shared with the budding philosopher Andrew Seth.[4] A friend of his brother Richard, Haldane found Seth shy at first, and then warmed to him enormously. Germany was cheap but for the outlay on books and one essential, a microscope from the local manufacturer Carl Zeiss. Zeiss, now a leading brand name, was 'about the best maker of microscopes anywhere'.

Haldane came to see that German universities, by focusing much of their research on industrial potential, were leaving the universities of Britain in the shade. Zeiss was a prime example of the trend. Carl Zeiss started as a university mechanic developing optical instruments in his own private workshop. He commissioned Ernst Abbe, then an Associate Professor at Jena, to develop his theory of microscope image formation. Otto Schott, who obtained his doctorate from Jena in 1875, was in turn prompted by Abbe to set up his 'Laboratory for Glass Technology', which would produce lenses to Zeiss's exemplary standards. The glass and chemical works Schott & Gen. and the Carl Zeiss corporation went on to prompt a 150 per cent increase in Jena's population by the end of the century.

In afternoon walks around the Thüringen hills Haldane picked flowers to send home to his mother; a large white anemone one day, a scented violet the next, blooms from seeds from as far away as Japan which were once strewn in the hills by a roaming professor. A 15-mile walk, once through a storm of hail and fierce rain that flattened grasses and flooded the roads, led Haldane and his friends to Weimar. Wagner's *Das Rheingold* was the big Saturday event at the Weimar Court Theatre. 'The scenes all melted into one another, in a mist, so there was no pause at all . . . The Grand Duke was there, and the theatre was quite crowded with the aristocracy of Weimar, which is an immense improvement on that of Jena. Liszt, who loves Weimar in Summer, was probably in the theatre, but we did not see him. He is said to conduct occasionally and we hoped he might have done so last night.'[5]

On 1 August 1879 Professor Strasburger signed the record of John Haldane's attendance, praising his exceptional engagement with his course in Botany and his great success on the microscopic course. His summer months in Jena had helped Haldane see the path for his new career. 'I had become interested in questions, the answer to which can only be obtained from the study of the processes of life. And it seemed to me that I could wish for nothing more than a profession which would imply the constant observation of these processes, and which, moreover, would assuredly bring me into close and living contact with my fellow-man.'[6]

Haldane had Jena to lift his spirits out of mourning. Mary Haldane chose Paris. She had been there on honeymoon, modelling her clothing and hairstyle on the young Empress Eugénie. Now as a widow she decamped there again, spending the winter of 1879–80 with her daughter Elizabeth and the nurse Betsey Ferguson. The stay liberated the whole family 'from the shackles of Scottish Victorian and Puritan authority,' Elizabeth remembered. The Seine froze, snow piled in the streets, but the shops and galleries were warm and delightful. Mary copied paintings in the Louvre, later exhibiting her work in the Scottish Academy. Mother and daughter could not quite bring themselves to see Sarah Bernhardt in the theatre – that would be unbecoming for true ladies – but they collected her photographs and snatched the chance to see her in the flesh at a charity reading. On their Christmas visit the boys waltzed Elizabeth off to the Grand Opera de Paris and a performance of Gounod's *Faust*.

Mary Haldane had never written a cheque before the death of her husband. Accounting never became her strong suit. Poor weather of the late 1870s meant little income from farming, and Robert's income as a lawyer was now gone. She packed her wardrobe with Parisian fashions, and quite out-stripped her resources. Reality struck on their return to Britain. Mother and daughter would have to quit Edinburgh, and make do with what society could offer on their estate at Cloan.

Charles Darwin, an earlier alumnus of the Edinburgh Medical School, was bored by its lectures. He preferred find-ing things out for himself. 'I think I am superior to the common run of men in noticing things which easily escape attention, and in observing them carefully.'[7] He went on to Cambridge to study for the clergy, but preferred collecting beetles to attending lectures, and left with his pass degree to take an unpaid post as a naturalist aboard HMS *Beagle*.

Haldane was similarly exasperated by the Edinburgh Medical School and 'the common run of men'. He failed to find there 'any intellectual life other than of a very superficial kind'. His teachers were mostly kind, but 'between them and myself an impassable gulf seemed to be fixed. They influ-enced me little more than the reading of a dictionary might have done.'[8]

Some of his fellow students he found to be 'intellectually dead. The rest were in the same plight as myself. We were all hurrying on from one examination to the next; we had to take as it came all that was taught us, without stopping to inquire as to its significance, and far less as to its truth.' The university's examination system put a block on students questioning those facts that were deemed 'favourable' or correct. This was fine for what he termed 'well-trained prize-takers' but wrong for any truly questing student.

In fact as Britain's first civic university Edinburgh stood against elitism. The medical school's Dean and Professor of Anatomy, William Turner, told how 'we draw . . . a considerable proportion of our students from a class of the community that one cannot exactly call poor, but still people of limited means'.[9]

Haldane's uncle Burdon Sanderson, a Professor at Oxford, disagreed with his nephew on Edinburgh's professorial methods of teaching:

> In Edinburgh and the other schools, most often students are incapable of reading by themselves and have no-one to help them. Consequently the lecturer *must* grind them up on all the parts of his subject . . . The great evil is not the system, but simply that the men who teach the most important subjects are not strong in the subjects which they teach and do not devote themselves with anything like sufficient competence to their professional work. How *that* is to be remedied I do not know.[10]

For Burdon Sanderson, Haldane's studies at Edinburgh under Professor William Rutherford made him hugely attractive to the laboratory at Oxford. Rutherford was a captivating teacher, his squat body topped with a powerful chest. The opening statements of his lectures boomed into the classroom before he got there himself. Arthur Conan Doyle, Haldane's fellow as a medical student, used Rutherford as a model for

Professor Challenger in his novel *The Lost World*. Rutherford set up a practical laboratory and trained his students in histological and microscopic techniques and the analytical methods of physiological chemistry, sometimes using experiments on live animals as demonstration.

Haldane was quick to decide what teaching was acceptable, and what was not. In addition to Rutherford, the School Dean William Turner's course in Human Anatomy involved 'good and for the most part necessary work . . . The methods of teaching were on the whole admirably suited to their purpose.' Haldane's ground rule for a good lecture was that he and other students 'had the opportunity of verifying for ourselves the facts and theories we were learning, and of understanding their real bearing'.[11]

His lecturers failed his test. 'I purposely paid little attention to any of the lectures of my examiners, as I consider that the present system of working for examinations by students is one which is doing a great deal of harm in every way.'[12]

He skipped classes and spent time doing clinical work at the Infirmary instead, observing the practical application of medicine to the sick. For three months in 1881 he dispensed medicine at Fountainbridge. That same year he was elected president of the Edinburgh Philosophical Society, votes coming in from two new friends. Both children of Scottish Free Church parents, James Lorrain Smith and James Wilson would share medical and philosophical enthusiasms with Haldane through the rest of their lives.

Haldane's first paper, co-authored with his brother Richard, was on the relation of Philosophy to Science. It was published in 1883 in *Essays in Philosophical Criticism*, edited by Richard and Andrew Seth. 'The book was devoured by young philosophers when it appeared,' the *Scotsman* recalled in 1933. It marked 'the climax of T. H. Green's influence in British philosophy'.[13]

Green and his contemporary at Oxford, Arnold Toynbee, 'made for an outlook on the universe which was not only satisfying to reason but also encouraging to those who wished somehow to work for their fellows,' Elizabeth Haldane wrote. 'This movement, which was founded on the idealistic philosophy dominated by Hegel, influenced us all greatly.'[14] The Haldane siblings read T. H. Green's *Lay Sermons* and his *Prolegomena to Ethics* alongside Bradley's *Ethics*.

To follow Green, Haldane had to take the three steps which he advocated. Step one: answer the question 'What is man?' Step two: discover man's relation to his environment. Step three: knowing man's relationship with his environment, determine his function, what he is best suited to do in the world. One sentence from the brothers' early essay sums up a related philosophical standpoint which would see them through their lives: 'The fact is that every part of the organism must be conceived as actually or potentially acting on and being acted on by the other parts of the environment, so as to form with them a self-conserving system.'[15]

The Haldane children were moved by the novels of Hale White, who wrote as Mark Rutherford. His early books told of a dissenting minister's suffering when he had to leave the Church. The year 1883 saw Haldane resolving his own situation with his Dublin Street Baptist Church. He wrote to inform them that he and his brother William should no longer be considered part of their congregation.

I joined the Church at a very early age – an age at which it was not to be expected that I could have found anything like mature opinions as to religious matters. On those who persuaded me to take this step rests the responsibility of the consequences for my having taken it . . . Perhaps there are few professions in which one is brought in more close and living contact with sin and imperfection than in medicine – or in which the contradiction between what ought to be and what is seems so terribly real. It is not, therefore, the fact that I am unaware of the meaning of sin that prevents me from accepting literally the reconciliation proposed by the teaching of the Church. But it is because that reconciliation in its literal form does not and cannot satisfy me . . . To make religion depend on historical facts is, to my mind, though I know not to yours, to make the existence of God have no deeper significance than a mere physical fact. Both the world and the self are thus left outside of God in their own innate imperfection and sin, & the spiritual unity of all things in God becomes only a name. All this at any rate appears to me, after a long and careful consideration of both sides of the question, to follow from the doctrine that a man's religion depends on his belief in matters of history. This you will see is no mere scientific difficulty. It is a difficulty which I know is not present to many men, but it is vividly so to me, and I cannot shut my eyes to it without being dishonest to myself. It is quite impossible that I should ever return to the doctrine of the Church on this matter.[16]

He remained steady in his views. In 1924 he told an audience in Oxford: 'I simply cannot believe some of the dogmas and teachings of the churches. That is why I do not belong to an English Church. If I did belong to a church I believe it would be my own Scottish Church, for one advantage it possesses is that it has no prayer book.'[17]

That these decisions were resolute did not make them easy

ones to reach. He closes his letter with an acknowledgement that it was painful to write, as it will be painful to receive. 'Respect has prevented me from writing in a less direct manner,' he tells his Dublin Street minister. 'In lives that are real there must always be pain as well as happiness.'

The showpiece of the new Medical School buildings was the Anatomy Lecture Theatre, a circular building with seating raked high so students could look down on surgical demonstrations. Its main star was Professor Joseph Bell, a tall man with a beaked nose, grey eyes and a curious juddering manner of walking about the stage.

'In teaching the treatment of disease and accident,' Bell said,

> all careful teachers have to show the student how to recognize accurately the case. The recognition depends in great measure on the accurate and rapid appreciation of *small* points in which the diseased differs from the healthy state. In fact, the student must be taught to observe . . . Nearly every handicraft writes its sign manual on the hands. The scars of the miner differ from those of the quarryman. The carpenter's callosities are not those of the mason. The shoemaker and the tailor are quite different.[18]

Conan Doyle turned Bell into his Sherlock Holmes. For Haldane, whom *The Times* would later term 'a medical detective', Bell was the model of how to tune the powers of observation on man and environment.

Bell would become a frequent guest at 17 Charlotte Square, though a twist in this tale must happen first. Mary Haldane was set to return to Cloan. Miss Kathleen Trotter had scouted out possible rentals for the family's winter in Edinburgh. She brought her mother for an afternoon viewing. Led into the downstairs dining room by the letting agent, they found a young man on the hearthrug surrounded by open books. He jumped up, claiming he was 'just working'.

'No, you were fast asleep,' Kathleen retorted.

'He followed us when we went round the house with his mother,' she later wrote. 'Not a tactful young man, as we had to enquire about sanitary arrangements and service bedrooms. This was my first sight of John Haldane, my future husband.'[19]

Their marriage was eight years in the future. The Trotters did take over Charlotte Square, gradually moving in their own belongings. Professor Bell 'knew all the family and could sum up their characteristics in a couple of scathing sentences, which were usually excruciatingly funny. He used to say that they only consulted him professionally when they were bored by their own doctors and that he usually began his treatment by making them exceedingly angry, which was at any rate stimulating!'[20]

Faced with final exams Haldane wrote to his mother: 'This year the examiners are apparently trying to raise their standards in view of the commission.'

This commission was chaired by a Haldane relation, Robert Haldane, Earl of Camperdown. Raising standards was an ongoing process of the universities, faced with a great increase in student numbers. They decided a medical licence must show full competence in all areas: surgery, medicine and midwifery.

In 1870, the ten-year-old Haldane had seen 2,000 people line the streets for the funeral of Sir James Young Simpson. It was a day of public mourning. Queen Victoria's use of chloroform for the birth of Leopold prompted a wholesale switch to this anaesthetic introduced by Simpson, who became one of the most famous men of his time. His fame helped him choose his own replacement as Professor of Midwifery. His nephew Alexander Simpson was duly installed in the post. That Simpson now failed Haldane in midwifery.

'It seems scarcely worthwhile to waste another of the best years of my life because a man of the intellectual capacity of Professor Simpson is not of opinion that I am sufficiently qualified as regards his department of medicine,' Haldane wrote to his mother. 'Of my ultimate success at medicine I feel little doubt, however unsuccessful I may be in exams.'[21]

His treatment by the examiners was a 'very gross impertinence,' he told Richard. 'The intellectual degradation involved in cramming up notes on, say, Prof Simpson's lectures is at any rate a good deal more than I could stand.'[22]

On advice, he appealed Simpson's decision to fail him, 'largely so that if the decision is confirmed the responsibility may rest as far as possible on the whole of the professors'.[23]

The decision to fail him was upheld. Friends sympathized. His uncle sought to arrange a meeting between Haldane and the venerable Joseph Lister. Haldane's refusal of the offer showed a man in resolute control of his own mind. 'As to consulting Lister, or any other person,' he told Richard, 'I am willing to take this advice only on matters on which I am convinced that I cannot form a correct opinion myself. The general question as to what I ought to do is not one of those matters. Outsiders may be perfectly impartial, but they have not sufficient data in a matter of this kind.'[24]

Haldane believed the qualification of MD was not, in any

case, vital to his proposed career in medical research. However he did bow to his uncle's advice and proceed to gain his medical qualifications. Haldane was registered with the General Medical Council in 1884. In the following year Dr Haldane, MD, had his full set of qualifications ratified by Edinburgh.

He could no longer be accused of fighting the faculty in order to gain some extra qualification. This meant he was free to fight on behalf of others. 'I am not sorry that circumstances have made it incumbent on me to bring up the matter here in Edinburgh. Intellectual freedom used to prevail in the Edinburgh School of Medicine, and I hope that before long it may do so again. I have both the money, and I think, the ability to stand against any number of professors on this matter, and probably my reputation, such as it is, in philosophy will be of use to me.'[25]

'Intellectual freedom' was a worthy cause. 'Any number of professors' were a suitable adversary. Like a knight of old, Haldane had a public mission. He could now ride into battle and keep the first of many jousts going for all the years to come.

4

BAD AIR

Take the process of putrefaction, study it as close as you dare, and the oddest things can emerge. Burdon Sanderson brought Haldane down from Edinburgh to work in his physiology lab on just such a study. In the gathering decomposition of foul waste, Haldane looked for the production of antiseptic substances.

Such an investigation is fine for the working day, but it leaves free time to fill. On 11 May 1884 Haldane tried 'some experiments, mostly on myself, with sulpho-carbolate of soda. It is practically not an antiseptic at all when tested on cultivations, and seems to pass through the body almost unaltered in the normal condition.'[1]

This was his first recorded scientific self-experiment. Short of having a laboratory under his command, the dark and sublime organism of his own insides offered a fine alternative arena. What a body it was. Its entire volume of blood, later increased perhaps through altitude experiments to a recorded eight litres, pumped through its heart every thirty-five seconds.[2] Put something in one end of that body, collect it out of the other, and you could see how it was treated by its environment as it travelled in between.

All life is a physiological self-experiment. Sit still, eat loads, we get fat. Lie on our backs, we snore. For some the process is more self-conscious and extreme than for others. Haldane wished to work in medical science. That meant laboratory work. However, simply observing the effects of a changing environment on organisms and chemical compounds was too detached a procedure ever to engross him. He was an organism as much as any bacterium or cat was an organism. 'We of the medical profession are not mere chemists and mechanicians,' he would come to say. 'Our business is to understand organic regulation, and where necessary to assist it.'[3]

One way to understand organic regulation was to experience it in your own body. A subtle but significant element of Haldane's career in self-experimentation involved the vast variety of conditions in which he set his body to work. Haldane's laboratory work was extraordinarily mobile. After mere months in his uncle's laboratory he was relocating himself.

Studying 'the elimination of phenol and indoxyl in disease', he left the laboratory to set up shop in Radcliffe Infirmary. 'I am setting to work in the little clinical laboratory at the Infirmary to do six phenol estimations of different cases daily,' he wrote to his friend James Wilson in 1884. 'You may imagine the smell caused by twelve distillations & evaporations of a day's urine going on simultaneously!'

Oxford had too few fever patients for his needs. First stop in his search for more took him to the Smallpox Hospital in London. Work in such locations, when the causes of disease were not yet known, involved real risk in itself. Experimenting on the inoculation of smallpox virus to cattle in 1866, Burdon Sanderson infected his wife Ghetal from a small vial of the virus that he brought home. Haldane spent July and early August of 1884 living at 24 Richmond Crescent, Islington, near the London Fever Hospital, where he set up a small laboratory to investigate the excretion of phenol in scarlet fever.

Since he was measuring the excreta of smallpox victims, why not measure his own? 'Oddly enough,' he wrote to Wilson, 'I have found that I excrete quite a large quantity of phenol and cresol myself.' While some excretion of phenol is standard, a later letter explained: 'I had an unusually liberal supply at Oxford for some reason or other – possibly from constipation . . . In working at the phenol excretion in scarlet it will of course be necessary to exclude increase due to decomposition in the alimentary canal. This of course can only be done indirectly, and by comparison with other fever cases on the same diet.'

In typical Haldane fashion, he found experimental data to disprove a commonly accepted hypothesis. Phenol production during scarlet fever, to everyone's surprise, actually decreased rather than increased. His first independent scientific paper concluded that there was 'no ground for regarding scarlet fever as analogous to a putrefaction process'.

Hospitals were tough environments for doctors and nurses as well as patients. Much was still to be learnt about the spread of disease and how to contain it. Haldane carried an acute sore throat away with him from his spell at the Fever Hospital, so severe that he put it down to an attack of diphtheria. For six months in 1884 he worked as House Physician at the Edinburgh Royal Infirmary, where he not only supervised patients, but also took up the gauntlet of teaching medical students. Could he do better than those Edinburgh teachers he criticized so severely?

His consulting physician at that time recalled the 'quiet persuasiveness about his enthusiastic scientific aspirations, and his attractive personality, that is intensely stimulating and encouraging to those working under or along with him'. Through his work he sought answers to 'obscure questions . . . connected with the causation, meaning and cure of disease. Even at that early period his fellow-workers recognised the presence among them of a man of masterly mind.' He took breaks from the Infirmary to turn his investigative powers to 'the health and well-being of communities rather than of individuals. In that respect what may be expected of his work in the future is of immense importance.'[4]

Due east of Cloan, 40 miles north of Edinburgh, the seaport of Dundee had experienced a rapid, fierce yet brief industrial boom. Big on fishing and textile manufacture, a new use for jute fibre was discovered in 1822. Mix it with whale oil, and you could weave it into materials for making sacks and the backs of carpets. Dundee pulled in workers from Irish and Highland rural communities, crammed them into cheap housing stock, and set about meeting world demand for the new material. The town prospered.

The University College of Dundee was set up in 1882. In 1884 Dundee acquired city status. So far, so impressive. Step into the working-class areas of the place, however, and its cries and smells set you thinking. Something had gone badly wrong.

Jute was shipped in from Bengal. Within Bengal, Calcutta had its own mass supply of ready workers. They could undercut any Scottish wages. Calcutta's first jute-processing plant opened in 1855 and others soon followed. A process of closures affected Dundee's mills as a result.

Dundee's new Professor of Biology was D'Arcy Wentworth Thompson. He knew how much his Academy companion, Haldane, yearned to bring scientific breakthroughs to the cause of public health. Haldane walked the slums with Wentworth Thompson and the new Professor of Chemistry, Thomas Carnelley. It was easy to feel pity and disgust for the living conditions of the slums. This new breed of scientists looked around and saw beyond that. These slums were a laboratory in which to investigate the human condition and instigate improvements in public health.

On a Tuesday night a covered cart set out from University College and rattled over the cobbles of Dundee. With a guard of two policemen, the team of Haldane, Carnelley and Dr Anderson, the Medical Officer of Health, prepared their first raids. Fists raised, watches ticking at half past midnight, they knocked on the first door.

They had three questions for which they sought answers. What is bad air? What makes air dangerous to breathe? How can its bad effects be prevented?

Boards creaked, the door opened, and the first of many men and women stared out at the scientific investigators. Men in frock coats did not come calling in these parts. No one came calling in the early hours of the morning. Yet here they were, these representatives of a high social order. Their requests were unnatural, their need apparently urgent. You didn't stand in the way of such men.

The investigators did their best not to tread on any family members. It was a job to find somewhere to stand, with so many bodies lying around. All the homes they chose were poor, the poorest being houses of just the one room. Inside this room seven or eight people shared the one bed, when there was a bed. The scientists reached tubes and bottles

above the startled faces, and sucked in the air. Samples collected, they measured the room. It was an important survey,
for sure. Who knew what the men were truly doing, but they
were gentle and courteous enough. This couldn't be an evic-
tion. The room-dwellers did their best to cooperate. Breathe
and make room somehow, that was the best they could do.

The trips had to be stealthy. Give advance warning and the
investigators would be presented with the best that could be
offered for show. Open the window, open the door, let a little
fresh air into the place. The investigators did not want that.
They wanted to capture stale air from above sleeping bodies.

The covered wagon formed a laboratory for the first stages
of work. Samples of air bottled from inside and outside each
home were stacked on a rack for later analysis, and the troop
rattled on. Knock knock, one more house, one more astonished set of inhabitants, one more sample for the rack. The raids
continued till 4.30 in the morning, the horses carrying the
bottled air back to the space Wentworth Thompson had set
aside in his own laboratory. On Friday at midnight the men
set out again. Then on the Tuesday, and on the next Friday.
The investigation was comprehensive, the results startling.

The air from those Dundee homes was analysed for bacteria, moulds, carbon dioxide and 'organic matter'. People in
rooms that gave them 180 cubic feet of space each, compared
to those with more than 1,000, were breathing air containing
62 per cent more carbon dioxide; twice as many moulds; 254
per cent more 'organic matter' which included the highly
poisonous hydrogen sulphide known as stinkdamp; and 1,080
per cent more bacteria.

The investigators used the daytime of each week to collect
air from the city schools. Pupils had as little as 56 cubic feet
to study in, with even higher carbon dioxide and bacteria

rates than in the one-roomed houses. The children looked sick. The reasons were obvious. 'We need not be surprised at the unhealthy appearance of many of these children,' the scientists' final report read.

The authorities in Dundee were shaken by the report. Wentworth Thompson was asked to join the Board of the Dundee Royal Infirmary. They wanted a pathological laboratory such as that designed around Haldane, to do similar work. As for Haldane: 'His experience of the Dundee slums may not have made him a radical,' his son later reflected, 'but it kept him one. He was a strong supporter of National Insurance, Old Age Pensions, and the like, and had little patience with statements by the rich that the poor were really well off, or could be if they tried.'[5]

'Bad air' was a hot topic at the time. If air smelt bad, it was dangerous. As jail fever struck down hundreds of prisoners in Victorian prisons, it was presumed that the fever was carried by 'bad air'. Bowls of flowers were set in courtrooms, so that their scents could act against the smell of prisoners and protect the judges from this jail fever. In fact the jail fever was typhus fever carried by lice.

Among the likely vectors of disease, scientists held faith in 'miasma', the thought that foul-smelling air itself was infectious, until the end of the nineteenth century. By the early 1870s some debate flourished around 'germ theory', but the thought that the spread of disease might derive from germs was still outrageous to many.

When Joseph Lister was appointed Professor of Surgery at Edinburgh in 1861 it was hoped that he would reduce the post-operative mortality rate. He failed. By 1865, more than half his amputees had died of sepsis (infection of the blood

by disease-carrying micro-organisms). Working from a
theory that disease was spread by a pollen-like dust, he
applied carbolic acid (an effective antiseptic) as a seal
between the operative wound and the air, which also happened to prevent infection from the surgeon's hands and
instruments. By 1869 the mortality rate in the male accident
wards under his care had fallen to 15 per cent. Lister now
placed his own theories of antiseptic surgery alongside Louis
Pasteur's findings of the ways micro-organisms caused fermentation and disease.

Lister was celebrated in Germany, where surgeons had had
great success applying his techniques on the battlefields of the
Franco-Prussian War. The scientists of England and the
United States were much more hesitant. They could accept
the usage of carbolic acid, but suspicions that Lister was advo-
cating the controversial 'germ theory' meant he was largely
ignored. He left Edinburgh to take up a post in London so as
to win mainstream recognition for his efforts.

Haldane now took the same route down to London.
People must learn that the increased illness and mortality rates
in the slums of Dundee, the sickness among poor school-
children, were the effects of overcrowding and poor
ventilation. It had nothing to do with 'bad smells'. What
better way to prove this than to delve inside the lower depths
of government and analyse the stink that flowed beneath? A
Select Committee of the Houses of Parliament was appointed
in the spring of 1886 to investigate complaints about the
smells that rose from its sewers. In the wake of the scientists'
report on conditions in Dundee, Haldane and Carnelley were
called in to investigate.

The current belief in the evils of 'bad air' was especially
heightened when it came to what was termed 'sewer gas'.

Descent into the sewage tunnels was simultaneously a self-experiment, since a fair consensus of scientific opinion believed such air was dangerous to health.

The Houses of Parliament were built alongside London's primary sewage outlet – the River Thames. Londoners knew the river as 'the Great Stink', its rising tides flushing the untreated contents of nearly four hundred sewers into its flow. Tons of lime were tipped into the waters by the Palace of Westminster in a bid to counteract the stench. It failed to work for police constable 36 AR, positioned near the Old Palace Yard gates, who reported being 'quite ill' from sewer gas. 'He believed thousands of feet of coal gas mingled with sewer gas escaped weekly,' making the atmosphere 'positively poisonous'.[6]

Haldane and Carnelley's initial observations were made in the main sewer of Westminster Palace, running beneath the open courts in the centre of the building from Victoria Tower to the Clock Tower that housed the great bell Big Ben, beyond which it joined the low-level metropolitan sewer. The height of the sewer kept dipping and rising between 4½ and 10½ feet, the researchers taking care to stand to leeward of the rapid flow of sewage so as to breathe no additions of their own to the atmosphere they were collecting.

A furnace under the Clock Tower sucked air through the sewers as ventilation, this being where almost all the grates to the open air were situated. The police constable had been right to suspect coal gas in the mix of air around him. A leak from a fractured coal-gas pipe was once found to be streaming its gas directly into the sewer. Only a trapdoor stopped its reaching the furnace and causing an explosion that would have sent Big Ben crashing into rubble.

Further down the tunnels where there were no open gratings the air current was feeble. Opening up a manhole cover by the Victoria Tower brought a rush of air and condensed vapour into the investigators' faces. Between a first and second set of experiments the investigators made sure that extra ventilation was added, a new shaft opening on to the furnace, and grates set in appropriate positions to bring a draught running through the entire system.

The aims and methods of their collection of sewage air from under Parliament were the same as in the schools and homes of Dundee. For comparison they spent some of the summer of 1886 examining the sewers of Bristol, near where they opened out into Clifton Gorge beneath Brunel's suspension bridge. These sewers were not ventilated at all. To round off their research they returned to investigate Dundee's sewers.

Thirty-five years later, revisiting Dundee for a British Association meeting, Haldane navigated his way around the streets of Dundee from his memory of the sewers that coursed beneath them. His memories brought back vivid images of the scenes below his feet. The sewer beneath Overgate was egg-shaped in cross-section and 3½ feet high. Below Murraygate was a circular sewer 5 feet high. The flat-bottomed sewer under Dock Street had been altered to reflect the egg-shaped sewers, all of it alternately filled and emptied by the tide.

'It is very interesting work,' Haldane wrote to his mother, from his base at 20 Airlie Place,

and one learns a great deal by it. The sewers here are much smaller than the one at Westminster, but more interesting. One is getting very expert in disappearing down man holes in the street, though I find the Dundee man holes a very tight fit sometimes, and had to be pulled up one in which I had got stuck. One sewer in which we were on Tuesday smelt quite like an orange grove. It received all the insides of the bitter oranges used at Keiller's marmalade works. The sewer men seem sometimes to have very exciting adventures, but do not appear ever to come to any harm. The sewer from Hilltown, which comes down a very steep hill into the main sewer, seems to be difficult to manage. Even today, when there was no rain, the roar of the water coming down sounded very impressive and one could hear it a long way off along the sewer, like the sound of a very large waterfall. We have got to manage very well with our apparatus, which are let down with ropes; but it is very difficult to manage matters when a sewer is less than 4 feet high, as is often the case.[7]

Parliamentarians might fear whiffs of sewer gas from the tunnels that ran beneath them, but the bacteria in the sewer air were actually fewer than in the open air, while in Dundee's schools children had to breathe in vastly increased amounts of both bacteria and carbonic acid. Comparisons between the air of the parliamentary sewers and that of the schools, sewers and homes of Dundee were tabulated in the resulting paper, making a forcible case for government action.

Haldane took his conclusions to the Sanitary Institute of Great Britain in 1887, and posed the question: 'What is the supposed evidence for the causation of typhoid fever and other diseases by the inhalation of sewer air?'

A doctor stood up to declare that he 'had met many cases of fever himself where there was absolutely no other cause except sewage emanations to which the results could be attributed'. Another declared, 'If they were to accept all the teachings of Mr Haldane's paper they would have to put aside all the teachings of sanitary science and all past experience as to the spread of disease and fevers.'[8]

This was a tall order, but it was exactly what Haldane's data gathered from samples of the supposedly fatal 'sewer gas' demanded. His findings required sanitary science to reconsider the bases on which all their knowledge was based. It would take some years to complete. The last occasion on which experts were prepared to attribute an outbreak of disease to miasma was just ten years away, with the typhoid epidemic of 1897.

Once embarked upon a cause, Haldane tended to stay with it. The year 1902 would see him back in the sewers beneath the Houses of Parliament, roping in members to help with experiments, while above him the House was sitting in debate over the Boer War. The data he and Carnelley collected from sewers proved the fallacy of miasma, the notion that 'sewer gas' was infectious, by showing it had a lower bacteriological content than outside air. However the air of sewers still clearly brought dangers other than infection. Haldane's most dramatic encounter with sewers happened in the hot summer of 1895.

'I was busy at the time with the air of wells,' he told a meeting of Edinburgh's Natural History Society the following year, 'and from the newspaper accounts I thought that this was no ordinary well accident such as those referred to. I accordingly went off at once to the scene of the accident to make investigations.'

The main sewer in the sewage works in East Ham, in London's East End, was 680 feet long, 4½ feet high and 3 feet wide. This being the lowest sewer in the complex it ran fast, full to within inches of its ceiling. A grate near the end of its run stopped large objects passing through that might clog the pumps which sucked the mixture up into the pump house. A manhole opened on to a 27-foot shaft so that workers could climb down and clear the grate of large objects pressed against it. This operation had been performed twice daily for three and a half years without anyone ever sensing any danger.

On 1 July 1895 Walter Digby descended the shaft to clear the grating as usual. Before reaching the bottom he called up to say he was ill and began to climb up again. Just short of the top he let go of the ladder and plunged into the 4 feet of sewage below.

His companion at the top called out for help and three colleagues came running: Arthur Butter, Robert Turrant and Frederick David Jones. One after the other each climbed down the ladder, blacked out, lost his holding, and fell. The absence of the four men was noted and Fred Mills, the chief engineer in charge of the pumping station, was called to the scene. Peering down he saw that Frederick Jones had been caught by the top of the screen and was clear of the water. The chief engineer jumped to the ladder and hurried to his assistance. Those above watched as he let loose his hold, fell past Jones, landed in the sewage, and drowned.

A bucketful of live coals was brought from the engine house and lowered down the shaft, to burn off any gases that might be there. With a rope tied around his chest another man climbed below. Hoarse and retching when Haldane interviewed him the following day, he felt the gas was still inside him. He recalled that 'the gas affected him at once, before he got to the bottom. It "caught him in the throat" and made him stupid, so that he would have fallen had he not had a rope round him.' His colleagues pulled him up.

Yet one more man descended, again tied with a rope. This time he managed to keep his footing. Frederick Jones, caught on the top of the screen, was still breathing but was otherwise insensible. With a rope looped around him, he was pulled to the surface and hurried to West Ham Hospital.

The breathing of Jones, aged twenty-eight, was slow and rasping. His temperature soon rose to 102 degrees. There was no corneal reflex to his eyes, which kept staring to one side and giving off some discharge. His body went into spasms every thirty seconds, which made it almost impossible to administer artificial respiration. He kept passing urine in spurts. After fifteen hours in hospital the spasms ceased. Three hours later he was dead.

On 4 July, three days after the accident, Haldane lowered a caged mouse down the well, then pulled it up again. The mouse showed no ill effects. With men holding the far end of a rope tied around his chest, it was now Haldane's turn. Carrying the mouse he climbed down to the stream of sewage at the bottom. The mouse remained fine, and Haldane's lighted candle remained alight. Filter paper moistened with lead acetate solution failed to blacken after three minutes. Haldane took a sample of the air, then skimmed the surface for a sample of the sewage that pushed slowly past his feet. Fragments of kitchen refuse, lots of unused food, vegetables and lumps of meat rode the surface. It all looked relatively fresh, though the smell was very offensive. Before reaching the sewer, kitchen water had passed over grease boxes, metal containers patented in 1884 to hold grease back from clogging waste pipes. The material in these grease boxes was already putrefied before it was thrown away, hence the stench.

The summer was unusually hot. The body of Frederick

Jones was already in an advanced stage of decomposition when Haldane joined the team conducting his autopsy. Analysis of the young man's blood showed Haldane that no carbonic oxide was present. Four men had drowned after passing out from some gas, while Jones had been killed by a gas. What was the gas?

The local police provided Haldane with one clue. Silver coins and a watch chain taken from the recovered bodies had all turned black. Haldane had a clear suspicion as to the identity of the fatal gas. Back in his laboratory he extracted some of his sewage sample so as to half-fill a jar, and shook it.

Recent experiments by Lehmann in Germany concluded that 0.07 per cent of sulphuretted hydrogen (now called hydrogen sulphide) in the air would be fatal. Normal kitchen waste would have had no time to reach levels of putrefaction to discharge such gas in the relatively short distance it would travel along the East Ham sewer, but the material contained in the traps and grease boxes had been subjected to unusual summer heat. Drought conditions applied and water supply was diminished. Normally 30 gallons per day passed into the sewers for each head of population. With the drought this amount was down to 18 gallons. Hydrogen sulphide is highly soluble, about 170 times as soluble in water as air is. With less water in the sewers the solution was far less dilute than usual, but it would stay in solution unless it was disturbed. Haldane noticed the constant slow movement of the body of sewage. He saw that the partial blockage of the screen caused the sewage to eddy as it surged around it. This shaft had been safe from gas for three and a half years, but such a combination of factors was unlikely to have occurred before.

Having shaken up his bottled sewage, Haldane lowered a mouse into the upper part of the bottle. The creature showed signs of unease at once. Its respiration dropped from 140 to 30 breaths per minute. After two minutes it was lying on its side. Twenty minutes later it could still not be roused, but was no worse. When taken out it made a gradual and complete recovery. Moist lead paper lowered into the bottle became discoloured in a few seconds. Haldane could smell the sulphuretted hydrogen. The addition of a little caustic soda saw the gas absorbed. Adding sulphuric acid and shaking the bottle saw the same effects created for the mouse and the paper. Lead acetate removed the gas once again. The fatal gas was definitely sulphuretted hydrogen. Haldane had found the culprit for the five men's deaths.

What could be done in the future? Flushing toilets would stop the putrefaction of the materials in grease boxes and traps, but till then it was hard to avoid the conditions that would spring sulphuretted hydrogen into the air currents above sewage flows. 'Catching of the breath and smarting of the eyes are signs of imminent danger,' Haldane warned, though trusting to smell was unreliable. Not only might the stench of the sewer obscure other smells, truly strong-smelling substances tended to paralyse a sense of smell. 'I have myself met with gas (coming from a heated coal-heap) which at once blackened lead paper, but in which I was quite unable to smell the sulphuretted hydrogen. The smell was quite perceptible, however, when I opened in the fresh air a bottle containing a sample of the same gas.'[9]

At the inquest into the death of Frederick Jones, W. H. Savage, a surveyor for East Ham District Council, stated that the man's death had already prompted the introduction of a new safety measure. Since then, 'acting on the advice of Dr Haldane, a mouse or a bird had been lowered each time a man went down, and no foul gas had been discovered'. Use of Haldane's canaries thus sneaked into public record for the first time. Years of patient and dangerous research away from the public eye were bearing fruit. Lives were already being saved. A mark of how far Haldane's work had to move on before full acceptance may be noted from the jury's verdict on the death of Frederick Jones. The young man had been poisoned by sulphuretted hydrogen. In the official record, however, old fears and ignorance were retained. Death was still accounted as being 'due to suffocation by sewer gas'.[10]

MAN AS BIRD OR MOUSE

The American steel magnate Andrew Carnegie bought himself a country house near Cloan. He had travelled far since his beginning as the son of a Dunfermline handloom weaver. Remembering those Scottish origins and early days of poverty in America, he used his vast wealth to bring education to the masses.

His friend J. S. Haldane offered up early proof of success at such a venture, delivering a series of St John's Brigade Ambulance Lectures in Auchterarder in 1885. Lectures before him had been hit-or-miss affairs, the hall cold and either the lecturer or the operator of the magic lantern frequently failing to deliver. A large mixed crowd drawn from all classes of society turned up for the Haldane lectures, so many that he roped in former student colleagues to help in such areas as bandaging. Prominent alongside him on the platform was a skeleton. The lectures included such practical demonstrations as the workings of a stomach pump, producing the contents of his own stomach for mass delectation. The findings of Louis Pasteur were demonstrated by the

process of developing bacteria on a jelly. Surgeons would perform operations clad in bloody gowns through to the 1890s,
while Haldane was giving Auchterarder's townsfolk proof of
the need to keep wounds clean a decade earlier. 'I never
attended more original lectures,' his sister Elizabeth remembered, 'for he had no idea of following the beaten track or
the syllabus laid down.'[1]

Cloan now housed Haldane's first private laboratory,
rigged up in the attic. His sister Elizabeth was his assistant in
a series of experiments over the next ten years, measuring the
amounts of carbonic acid in the outside air. Standing among
evergreen shrubberies they drew air through an aspirator into
a tube, taking samples into the laboratory for weighing.
Haldane reckoned this system of air analysis was 'a new and
thoroughly accurate method'. Their observations 'showed
that even in summer, when the absorption of carbonic acid
by plants in the day time was at its maximum, the percentage
of carbonic acid did not fall in the day below .025% or rise at
night above .035%. Now if the percentage of carbonic acid in
free air is constant to .01%, it is at least exceedingly probable
that the percentage of Oxygen is equally constant.'[2] This
investigation was one step in Haldane's continuing quest for
proof of self-regulation of organisms.

Elizabeth was so inspired by these experiments with John
that she carried out her own. On holiday in Italy with her
mother in 1898, she dashed in and out of the Grotto del
Cane near Naples. Tourists had been brought there for years,
to be amused as a dog led on a rope into the cave passed out
due to the carbonic acid gas near the surface. The dogs either
died or were brought out to the open air for fresh amuse-
ment, tourists watching to see if they revived. Elizabeth's own
mission was to collect a sample of the gas so fatal to dogs and

bring it home for John. The souvenir was a reward for the time they had spent working together. 'John was infinitely patient,' she recalled, 'and as he explained everything carefully he was delightful to work with.'[3]

Before he took up his Oxford appointment as a physiological demonstrator, Haldane spent the autumn of 1886 in Professor Salkowski's laboratory in the Pathological Institute at the University of Berlin. He found rooms with Frau Höhne, a 'very pleasant, homely sort of person', in Dorotheen Strasse 70.

Ernst Salkowski was the Professor of Medical Chemistry. He was immensely impressed by the young Haldane's 'diligence, perseverance, powers of observation, and his dexterity in his work', most evident in the manner of his experimental research, which was conducted in ways that amounted to 'the height of science'.[4] Berlin also brought Haldane into contact with Emil du Bois-Reymond, Professor of Physiology at Berlin, who was a pioneer in experimental electrophysiology.

The street outside du Bois-Reymond's house was half taken up with stacks of spruce trees on sale for Christmas when Haldane paid his visit. The Professor, with his head of white hair and patrician beard, gave Haldane the full attention of soft eyes beneath a forehead that crinkled curiosity. Haldane wrote to his mother:

He impresses me more than any of the other professors I have come across as yet, even than Virchow, who is on the whole better known. He looks as if he might have been even greater as a statesman or as a soldier than he is as a physiologist. One of the lectures in the first volume of his addresses is on the

German War, & we discussed the advisability of translating it. I think it should be translated, although it is plain spoken with a vengeance. At present it would have additional interest, in view of what the French have lately been doing and saying.[5] The Germans are thoroughly exasperated at the necessity for constantly increasing their army, but they can hardly do anything else. They all seem to expect an attack from France soon, & are evidently thoroughly prepared.[6]

On 10 December he wrote of the professor's lectures:

Among other things he did a very curious experiment with a frog, which if the antivivisectionists heard of it they would probably make a great fuss about. He dipped the frog into boiling lead. However it was none the worse, & one can do the same with one's hand if it is wet, only that the lead scorches one's nails. The experiment sounds a very horrible one when one doesn't know what its nature exactly is – just like the experiment of 'baking' a live rabbit. Du Bois Reymond impresses one as a very able man, but he gets into curious attitudes in lecturing. Today he lectured for a good while with his elbow resting on the desk & leaning the side of his head on his hand. However he didn't continue with his eyes shut & his back to the class like Uncle John.[7]

The antivivisection movement, whose aims found sympathy with Queen Victoria, had now risen to full force and focused its energy on 'Uncle John's' Oxford Physiology Lab. Haldane returned there to develop a series of drastic experiments that did indeed involve animals. The animal that most frequently bore the brunt of these experiments, however, was himself.

★

Haldane's Edinburgh professors may have felt their one-time student Haldane had faded into history. He was in fact maintaining discretion for a while. An anonymous article attacking practices in the medical faculty appeared in the *Scotsman* in 1886, and conjured a satisfying stream of correspondence. 'Please do not say anything to anyone about who the authors of the Scotsman article were,' Haldane wrote home. 'As yet no one knows except those who were concerned in writing it, and yourselves, and it might cause unnecessary trouble were the authors known . . . So far as I can make out it has served its purpose effectively.'

'Medicine is truly a God-like profession,' John Burdon Sanderson proclaimed to the new intake of students at Middlesex Medical School in 1868, but 'how few there are who, even while pursuing a divine art, are animated by divine motives.'[8]

Where J. S. Haldane turned to Germany for his models of how to do medical research, the young Burdon Sanderson had turned to France. He arrived in Paris in 1851, in time to view the massacres that accompanied the *coup d'état* of 2 December that brought Louis Napoleon to power (later he would perform the autopsy on Napoleon III, who died in Chislehurst, Kent, in 1873). The importance of Burdon Sanderson's Parisian year was affirmed by the bust that presided over his study. It was of Claude Bernard, his physiological lecturer at the Collège de France. Haldane's colleague Francis Gotch would recall Burdon Sanderson declaring, 'Bernard was the most inspiring teacher, the most profound science thinker, and the most remarkable experimental physiologist that he had ever known.'[9]

Bernard's work on the pancreas and the liver revealed

much about the internal environment of the organism. From that stems much of our understanding of homeostasis, the self-regulation of vital processes in an organism, a basis for much of Haldane's own pioneering work on respiration. Bernard also demonstrated the rapacity with which carbon monoxide substitutes for oxygen in combining with haemoglobin, a fundamental discovery for Haldane's future research. Perhaps beyond all that in terms of Haldane's own career, and his place in a lineage that reaches back to Bernard through his uncle, was Bernard's powerful advocacy of experimental physiology as being vital to the progress of medicine. He would propound this in his masterwork of 1865, *An Introduction to the Study of Experimental Medicine*.

'Why think when you can experiment?' Bernard was reported to have told one of his students. 'Exhaust experiment and then think.'[10] Besides attending Bernard's lectures, Burdon Sanderson was part of a small group that performed experiments under his direction. Several rabbits and dogs perished in the young man's early attempts to extract pancreatic juices from them. He brought with him to Oxford not only Bernard's belief in the necessity of vivisection, but his zealous regard for experimental exactitude.

In terms of experimental exactitude, on the eve of one trip from Cloan down to Oxford a remarkable physiological experiment took place. The participants were John Scott Haldane and his brothers, Richard and William. For some brothers this outing might have been simply labelled 'a walk'. Indeed Haldane wrote to his friend Wilson that 'One gets a wonderful idea of a country by a long walk through it, and we thoroughly enjoyed our journey.' Haldane's input as a physiological experimenter is clear, however, in the exactness and methods of this journey's planning, the notes taken, and the sheer extremity of the outing.

At 'half a minute past 7 am' the trio set off from Ballater, a nineteenth-century town in Royal Deeside whose train station served royal parties visiting Queen Victoria's Scottish home of Balmoral. The young men were running to an exact schedule, for by the Bridge of Dee at Invercauld they had walked almost 14 miles, it was 12.25, and they reckoned they were ten minutes late. The planning took a further knock at 1.30 with 'first refreshment milk, oatcake, sausage, water & butter (collapse in practice of theory that no-one should drink)'. Pausing by a spring for ten minutes to take in 2½ grains of caffeine produced no perceptible effect. They continued along ancient drove roads, where Haldane's ancestors had likely driven cattle. A telegraph was sent to Cloan, announcing their 6.30 arrival at Blair Atholl. Dinner at the Atholl Arms consisted of soup, steak, pudding and tea, John and Willie drinking two glasses of claret while Richard contented himself with champagne. Eleven and three-quarters of a mile further on Richard is stiffening, helped over a fence by his brothers, helped still more by the application of brandy. He soon 'shewed signs of distress for want of food. A tendon of his right leg was painful and his right stocking burst at the heel.' At ten minutes to one, '55 minutes late' and 66¼ miles into their journey, they took off their boots at a house near Aberfeldy, soaked their feet in water and supped some beef tea. Richard lay down on a bed beside John and 'displayed stertorous breathing'. Sooner than mention the snoring, Haldane wrote to Wilson, 'Richard stopped here, as his feet were blistered and he found a bed a very comfortable thing!'

John and Richard continued at 2.30, the moon setting two hours later. For the 10 miles before dawn John walked on tiptoe, due to burst heels of his stockings. John's stockings mended, Willie's feet soaped, breakfast of ham, eggs, jam, tea and milk delaying them a touch, they walked on till lunch of sandwiches, brandy and water. Cloan was reached at 1.57. 'Total distance 102¾ miles, J.S.H. no blisters', all in less than 31 hours. When Richard arrived by train at 2.27 he was met at the station by Willie, who was weighed and found to have lost 7 pounds.

'We found that the great thing was to eat plenty and have a meal every four hours or so,' Haldane told Wilson. 'By doing this we got on splendidly, and might have gone another 50 miles I believe, and still easily kept up four miles an hour. Of course we might have done the distance a good deal faster had we been on roads the whole way, and not had to wait for meals.'[11]

Haldane chose the Oxford appointment for its teaching commitment. This would enhance any future job prospects. 'I am enjoying work there very much,' he wrote in 1887 to his friend Wilson, who was now in Australia, 'and have no mind for any other appointment anywhere else. The want of a decent scientific library is fatal to good work in Scotland just now.'[12]

Library provision at Oxford he deemed so 'splendid' it helped anchor him to the city for the rest of his life. 'A good library is really the most important thing in many respects. When one has time to read the most original papers or really original books in any subject it certainly makes an enormous difference.'[13]

Haldane now had the opportunity to put into practice the teaching methods he felt to be lacking at Edinburgh. His pupils later recalled how 'his teaching was characterised by his efforts to make the students observe and think for themselves'. For them, Haldane was 'personally gifted with a unique power of encouraging the faculty for research in those who are beginning to work in Physiology'.[14] His friend Samuel Alexander noted of Haldane: 'To his great ability he adds both force and charm of character, the effects of which in securing the attachment of his pupils I have often observed.'[15]

Haldane was doing fundamental research on new calorimetric methods, fine-tuning apparatus that saw a rabbit enclosed in a metal jacket as its weight loss was measured. The true excitement of the year remained the pursuit of the air studies he shared with Carnelley. Papers were now being read at the Royal Society, those further experiments were conducted in the sewers of Bristol and Dundee, and even a lecture given by Burdon Sanderson on 'The Germ Theory of Disease' 'was taken up with my experiments at Dundee'.[16] His laboratory work centred on microbial experiments, but as he told Wilson:

There is a tremendous lot of work to be done in Public Health, and it is a very interesting subject. I wish I could go on with it. You will see from the two papers what a lot of interesting things there are to be worked out in connection with air alone. The way in which we are beginning to fall behind the Germans in the science, though not perhaps in the practice, of Public Health is a disgrace to this country. There is five times as much being done there, I should think, as at home.

He switched from lodging with his uncle to his own rooms at 59 St Giles, given a touch of style by his sister's addition of William Morris wallpaper. However by January 1888 the teaching commitment was already becoming onerous. 'Mr Gotch [his fellow demonstrator] has no teaching, so I shall have almost the whole practical teaching to do, both for the men going in for honours in physiology and the ordinary pass students.'[17]

The honours students were up to a total of eleven from the previous year's six, the chemistry lab always filled. A new plan of closing the lab from two till four, so that students could get to the river or play football, allowed Haldane some freedom. He took his tricycle out for long rides in a bid to keep rheumatism at bay, or took walks with his friends. Chief among these were Samuel Alexander, an Australian, and in Haldane's mind the best philosopher at Oxford after Herbert Bradley; and the idealist philosopher D. G. Ritchie. Ritchie gained Haldane membership in the Common Room of Jesus College, such membership vital in Oxford's exclusively collegiate world.

'It is mostly a Welsh College,' he explained to his mother. 'The Welsh Fellows are very hospitable. They are mostly Home Rulers, and I suppose the College is the only distinctly Liberal one in Oxford. For the present I shall have to dine without a gown, and it was a difficulty to find a precedent for admitting a non-member of the University. However Ritchie found a precedent somewhere in the Middle Ages, which seemed to satisfy everyone.'

April 1888 found Haldane sailing to Germany once again. 'If there had been even moderately respectable science teaching at Edinburgh I should not have needed to go to Germany now,' he wrote to his mother in February, 'but there wasn't, and as I don't wish to become a second edition of one of the present Scotch professors, I almost must spend more time in

Germany. I might do some of the work I wish to do in Oxford, but I'm sure it will be best to go to Germany.'[18]

Haldane's main aim was to develop his microscope skills at the university of Freiburg. He also attended lectures from Professor August Weismann, the era's key figure in the philosophical project to reduce the organic world, including life and God, to a mechanical sphere. In 1890 Weismann would be a focus of Haldane's return visit to Freiburg with his brother Richard, in which Richard was chasing down his old German philosophical influences.

Haldane took German classes from his landlady and a fellow student. 'I have breakfast at 7.30, have my German lesson at 8, and go to the laboratory about 9. Dinner is at one, & takes a good while, as there is no hurrying the waiters at the restaurant, or indeed anyone else here. The clocks on the churches have only one hand, so you may imagine how easily people take things here. Afterwards I work at the laboratory till seven, & then have supper at home, & usually go out for a turn on the hill afterward.'[19]

Haldane's visit coincided with the death of the Emperor. 'He had just reigned long enough to show what he might have done,' he wrote to his mother. 'He seemed to be personally liked everywhere, but it is curious to hear people say that his son will probably be a better Emperor for Germany. Bismarckism is certainly in the ascendant just now and the great majority of people seem to believe in brute force in dealing with the French, the Alsatians, Jews, socialists and other people. One wonders how long it will last, and what will happen when Bismarck is gone.' Freiburg was close to Alsace-Lorraine, the largely German-speaking area of France that had been annexed by Germany in 1871. The loss would rankle with the French and Alsatians until the region's restitution to France after the First World War. Haldane showed a talent for openness as well as prophecy in his conclusions from what he saw. 'I must say that I have now much more sympathy with the French than when I came here. As long as things in Alsace Lorraine are as they are just now there must always be the greatest risk of war.'[20]

Despite the poisonous social climate in Germany, Haldane observed to his mother in the same letter, 'One sees what an enormous advantage the German Universities and higher schools are to the country, and there is no reason why we shouldn't have the same advantages at home. The contrast between a German and Scotch University as regards the quality of the teachers is very great, although the two systems are much more alike than those of Scotland and England. One gets more and more indignant that matters should be as they are at home. It is a disgrace to the whole country.'

Haldane had completed his pamphlet *A Letter to Edinburgh Professors* in 1887, and released it to a few friends, including a friend of his brother Richard, John Kemp. Kemp responded with his sympathies and support, saying of the professors at Edinburgh:

I can only say that Simpson and his colleagues have materially increased their chance of immortality. Their names will be handed down to posterity – which would certainly not otherwise have been the case – as the narrow and ignorant pedants who refused the degree of the University, in which a perverse fate had made them Professors, to a man who was already their master in true scientific knowledge, and was soon to be recognized as incomparably superior by a tribunal that pays no heed to the paltry authority they delight to magnify. Your action will no doubt be condemned by the dull mediocrity of Edinburgh opinion, but no one who knows you can for a moment doubt that you view the whole matter from a standpoint that is far above all merely personal aims.[21]

Interest had waned in the debate about Scottish University reform as the Home Rule issue took precedence. The pamphlet, which though anonymous was Haldane's first published book, came out priced sixpence in 1890. The anonymity was a transparent device. Few but Haldane had cause to compare Edinburgh, unfavourably, with Jena: 'In spite of the enormous size of the Edinburgh Medical School, it may safely be said that no Medical School, in Germany, not even in a little out-of-the-way country town like Jena, is one half so barren in scientific work possessing any significance. There is intellectual life in all these little German Universities. Some, at least, of the teachers *think* and make their pupils think. There are always some teachers whose work and the work of their laboratories or hospitals represent a real scientific movement.'[22] As the pamphlet was handed around the faculty, as lecturers recognized the identity of the ex-student who was hurling such calumnies their way, it is doubtful that any decided to accept the criticism as just and true and therefore to mend their ways. A much more likely response was that, in retaliation, they should seek to block Haldane's academic career. However Haldane was too wise a student of German culture ever to have accepted a Faustian pact. He was never the type to stay silent in order to ensure his own advancement.

In a fine and playful fictional device Haldane had *A Letter to Edinburgh Professors* be the work of a dying medical student, delivered into the hands of his friend.

He sat up (for he was now confined to his couch), his eyes glistening with that peculiar mania which is apt to afflict consumptives. 'The "facts" which we were taught at the College,' said he, 'were to us students little else than rubbish, formed from the skeletons of dead theories. Do you suppose that "facts" are even one-tenth as real as the false theories that Black and Priestley helped to overthrow? And can you not also see that all scientific "facts" are altering every year with the advancement of knowledge, just as the "facts" about phlogiston were then doing, and that "facts" depend for their very existence on a relation to other facts which is for us constantly changing?' And with that he fell to lecturing me about the true methods of Natural Philosophy, and I know not what beside.

The 'letter' proposed two scientists as models of how professors should behave. One was Joseph Black (1728–99), 'who not only made great discoveries, but, when he became professor, set his pupils thinking and experimenting, and by his own example imbued them with a deep sense of how far mankind still remained from a knowledge of the true causes and connection of things'. The other was Joseph Priestley (1733–1804), 'who, he alleged, never was at any College, and, although engaged all day with his business of teaching and not possessed of means, yet made many noted discoveries'.

Haldane's selection of Black and Priestley shows how his own determined course in the study of gases was already set in place. In an unpublished, handwritten physiological textbook Haldane termed Joseph Black 'Black of Edinburgh', who 'discovered . . . carbonic acid or carbon dioxide (CO_2) in the blood'. Joseph Priestley shook off the harsh Calvinist doctrines of his upbringing and assumed a life as a dissenting minister as well as scientist. Using apparatus of his own invention in his private laboratory, he discovered ten gases including nitrogen, carbon monoxide, and on 1 August 1774 'a gas which he obtained by heating red oxide of mercury' which 'supports life longer than an equal quantity of air. Where a mouse was put into a glass vessel filled with the gas and inverted over water, it continued to live much longer than another mouse placed in the same vessel filled with air. A candle also burned with far greater brilliancy in the gas than in the air.'

The gas was oxygen. Priestley took his discovery to the French chemist Antoine Lavoisier in Paris, who 'placed a sparrow under a bell-jar inverted over mercury, and left the animal until it had died of suffocation. The air had not increased, but slightly diminished in volume . . . Lavoisier concluded that in respiration nothing is absorbed but oxygen, and no other gas is formed but carbonic acid.'[23]

Priestley's mouse had a glass vessel. Lavoisier's sparrow had a bell-jar. Haldane now sought to develop the findings of both scientists. Instead of a bird or mouse he used himself and his colleague Lorrain Smith, arrived from Edinburgh to work alongside him, as the experimental subjects. Instead of a glass vessel, they were contained in a wooden box.

Humans break down the carbon molecules in food, making use of the energy that holds those carbon molecules together to spur all the metabolic interchange in our bodies. As a part of that process our cells bind two atoms of oxygen to one of carbon, forming carbon dioxide, which we breathe out as a waste product. Haldane and Smith's experiments were geared to answer the question of how pure air is spoiled once it is breathed. Those single-roomed dwellings of

Dundee's slums were the inspiration for the wooden box, though its constrictions were more intense than any slum's. Six feet long and four feet square, the innards were lined with lead and the door fitted with rubber flanges. The box was as airtight as it could be. Observers peered in through a glass window, checking to see if the occupant had turned blue, passed out, or was in panic.

Haldane was never one to panic. After three or four hours observers noted he was panting violently. The panting became shorter and heavier. His head ached severely, though no observer could guess at that. Haldane made no show of pain. More obvious was the vomit that spewed from his mouth. The wooden box was opened at that point, the experiment ended, the lead walls cleaned.

Haldane and Smith took turns in the box, samples of air drawn out through a tube. They pushed up their levels of endurance till their stays in the box's tight confines stretched to 7½ hours without a break. By that time the oxygen level in the box had fallen from 21 to about 13 per cent. The carbon dioxide had risen to 6½ per cent. What factor had caused the panting, the headache, the nausea?

The experiment was run again. This time a tray of slaked lime and caustic soda joined Haldane in the box. This absorbed carbon dioxide as it was breathed out. The experiment could now focus on the effects of a human breathing oxygen in quantities that grew less, and less, and less.

Flames need around 17 per cent of oxygen in the atmosphere to keep on burning. Humans survive on less. Haldane struck a match inside the chamber after two or three hours. It fizzled but did not light. 'We found that in ourselves lack of oxygen began to produce a quite perceptible deepening of the respiration at about 12% of oxygen,' Haldane recalled.

With 10% this effect was more violent, and at the same time the lips became bluish, although the distress was still slight. At about 8% the face began to assume a leaden colour, although the uneasiness was not great. At about 2% or 6% there was marked panting accompanied by failure of the senses and the power over the limbs. The failure of the senses and muscular power came on without any marked previous distress, as would be the case with carbonic acid poisoning . . . Breathing an atmosphere free from oxygen, or containing only 1 or 2%, caused the subject to become unconscious and fall over within about 40 seconds, and without any perceptible previous distress. We thought it wiser on the whole not to push these experiments to the further stage of convulsions.

Instead of moving on to convulsions, the subjects decided to see what it was like if the carbon dioxide was not absorbed. They closed themselves into their chamber again, but this time without the addition of the soda lime.

Panting started when the carbon dioxide content hit 3 per cent. The loss of the same degree of oxygen had had no effect. It became clear that carbon dioxide was the cause of the panting.

At 5.8 per cent 'the panting had become severe and was rather exhausting,' Haldane reported.

The feeling was just like that experienced after making any considerable exertion. Along with the panting there comes on also frontal headache, and this also was found to be due to the carbonic acid. The headache had the peculiarity that it often became intensified for a time after one leaves the vitiated air. We investigated still more highly vitiated air by breathing and rebreathing the same air from bags; and found that with about 10% of carbonic acid the panting became so distressing that it was not possible to continue the experiment.[24]

Increasing the oxygen content in the air above normal, accumulation of carbon dioxide still made Haldane pant severely. Lessening of oxygen on its own did cause him to pant, but not to the same degree. Most likely because he did not have time. Haldane simply became blue and fell down unconscious.

Most significantly, if the carbon dioxide was continuously removed from the chamber, and the oxygen that was used up was replaced, Haldane was able to stay in the otherwise sealed place indefinitely.

If such a chamber could be made portable, might a man survive in such lethal atmospheres as the aftermath of a coal-mine explosion? Clearly in such situations more gases came into play than in regular open air. Haldane was set to put himself through two of the most significant self-experiments of his life.

The first would expose him to every possible cocktail of gases that might be met with in the deepest seams of a coal mine.

The second was marriage.

6

THE HOME FRONT

From Edinburgh, Kathleen Trotter wrote to Haldane about a certain 'Prof C.R.'s' reaction to the news of their coming marriage. 'He was much excited, & jumped almost, saying "This is the *very* first I'd heard about the engagement! Haldane, dear me! I'm very glad to see you, I'm sure! But, dear me, *Haldane*!" The next time anyone expresses such unbounded astonishment I shall say, "I quite understand your surprise. He was a very difficult fish to hook. I assure you, it took me *years* to land him."'[1]

This was very pleasant, and of course quite artful. Haldane had twice proposed, and twice been rejected, before she changed her mind. Kathleen had wanted to train as a doctor, but as an only child whose landowning father was devoting himself to life as an invalid, her role was becoming prescribed as her mother's companion. She felt a mixture of respect and profound irritation for Haldane, both of which she was canny enough to realize would increase with the intimacy of their living together. The engagement was preceded by 'months of correspondence and some rather agitated interviews'.[2]

While the debate around Home Rule for Ireland dominated intellectual discussion, Kathleen and Haldane managed to bridge what for some would have been an impossible divide. Kathleen's mission in life was to promote the interests of the British Empire, which she saw as being a hugely beneficient force for all its members. Her grandson Murdoch Mitchison recalls how different Kathleen (known to him as 'Maya') and his grandfather were both in temperament and in what interested them. Maya was 'an imperialist of the old school; a liberal nationalist. The colonies were a good thing because black races were culturally and morally different and needed leading by whites.'[3]

Such an opinion was the antithesis of the political views of the Haldanes. This opposition between the two camps crested a wave each time Kathleen and Richard Haldane found themselves close together. Assessing his own life from near its close, Richard noted his own immense capacity for hard work, even though 'I was gifted with but a poor voice and with only a dubiously attractive personality . . . I think that there were few mental or physical undertakings of which I was much afraid. Perhaps I was unduly confident in my capacities. At least, looking back, I think so now. But that is a matter which has ceased to be important.'[4]

Its importance may have ceased for him, but even seventy years after her marriage Kathleen recalled that 'his omniscience, his self-satisfaction and his sneers at the ideas and loyalties of people who disagreed with him, were enough to account for my dislike. Nothing, however, but realization of the harm that he and his party were doing to the country would have accounted for and justified the extent of my antagonism. But for his politics he would not have been interesting or important enough to command such intense dislike!'[5]

The brothers Richard and John remained firm friends. Their fiercest argument had been years earlier. Driving to a tennis party the young men entered a huge debate about Zeno's paradox of Achilles and the Tortoise, a conundrum in which a tortoise sought to prove that however fast Achilles might run, the tortoise would somehow remain ahead. Such was the brothers' passion for pursuing the various points involved that their vehicle left the road and they landed in a ditch. This was one of those rare philosophical debates that reach a conclusion agreed by both parties: they should never quarrel again, at least while driving. Kathleen recognized that her antagonism towards Richard spoiled her chances of intimacy with her mother-in-law Mary Haldane. This was a sad sacrifice she was obliged to pay for her political beliefs. She consoled herself by running the Oxford branch of 'The Victoria League for Commonwealth Friendship'.

Haldane's mother Mary had conceived a true 'love match' when young. The man she loved was an appropriate fit as regards social and financial standing, and was indeed a devout Christian, but her parents felt that his religious beliefs and their daughter's were incompatible. They prevented all thought of marriage. Mary decided to remain single. 'In my youth a married woman had no more position than a cat,' she later told a friend. 'But when Mr Haldane wished to marry me I felt it was my duty to obey the nearer call and devote my life to him and his motherless children.'[6]

Though his parents' marriage offered a successful model of the institution, Haldane did not see marriage as part of his own future. In 1890 his brother Richard, known to the family as 'Bo', became engaged. 'Lady Helen . . . & Bo sat together on a sofa most of the time,' Haldane wrote to his mother, 'so I didn't have much opportunity of conversation!

However, I have no doubt that they will get on excellently, & that she will get on well with us all. It all seems very curious. I had somehow made up my mind that if any of us married it would be Willie.'

It is notable that while not expecting to marry, Haldane maintained on the basis of no evidence that his prospective sister-in-law would get on well with the entire family. This notion of enfolding any spouse into the Haldane tradition was strong.

The engagement of Lady Helen and Richard would be called off, by rumour because she was in love with another woman. Haldane was keen to overcome any obstacles to his own wedding. From the night of Monday, 7 December 1891, he offered his mother a rare glimpse into his private emotional world. 'You and Bay [the family name for his sister Elizabeth] know Kathleen so well now that I know you feel that our marriage is just the best and truest kind of marriage both for her and for me. Loving her has from the beginning brought a world of new strength and faith into my life, even when I thought that she might never be able to love me in return. It seems strange to me to look back at this time last year. Things seemed just about at their worst for me.'[7]

This snatch of letter is a touching insight into the power of his love for Kathleen, as well as into the loneliness and unhappiness of recent times. Poor health had likely been part of that issue. Rheumatism and rheumatic fever had been plaguing him for years, consultations with various doctors bringing little respite. As part of a recovery programme he regularly jumped on his tricycle and headed out for many miles along country roads. In April 1890 he tricycled off to the city of Bath to meet up with his sister and mother. Mary Haldane had come down to take the waters of the spa.

Brother and sister took the opportunity for mounting natural history expeditions out into the surrounding countryside.

Haldane's battle with the Edinburgh professors had consumed much of the passing decade. On firing his last shots of that battle in 1890, Haldane perhaps suspected how little he might have achieved. He thought his teaching load at Oxford would stand him in good stead in his academic career. Such an academic career was not helped by a fulsome quarrel with the medical faculty of his alma mater. His job was onerous and ill-paid, his uncle paying him an additional £200 per year 'out of his own pocket, as the laboratory costs do not even cover the present expenses'.[8] Oxford was a hard place for an outsider to fit in, and the Physiological Laboratory in constant straits as regards funding, as well as facing attacks by antivivisectionists. Teaching extra classes to cover for his uncle's illness, fixed to an agenda of microbial research more in line with his uncle's interests than his own, the prospects for a Haldane life of true glory had apparently been diverted into some backwater.

Clearly his mother was concerned for her son's spirits even at the point of his marriage, for Burdon Sanderson wrote to her: 'I do not think that you need in the least fear that John will not develop sufficient energy. His marriage may have a considerable influence on the direction in which this development will take place and I think that it may be in the *right* direction – that in which I myself am interested.'[9]

With her light brown hair tied back in a severe central parting and bound in a low bun, Kathleen had a keen intelligence which informed her beauty. Soon she would trim back her hair and keep it short. Her face and chin were strong enough to carry a large nose. John felt quite able to give her free rein so far as her political interests were concerned, while pledging to take no active part in politics himself. He was thirty-one, Kathleen was twenty-seven. He would accept any deal to secure her.

In August 1891, accompanied by Lorrain Smith, Haldane set off to visit Kathleen's father Coutts Trotter, then convalescing at the Hotel Hof Ragatz in Zurich. Acceptance of Haldane's marriage proposal had already come by letter. 'I feel greatly touched and moved by what you say of your feelings towards my daughter and I can well understand her interpreting such feelings in a man of honour and intelligence, and I have from them not a shadow of doubt of their absolute sincerity and that she is exceptionally capable of judging for herself in such a matter that I believe she has chosen wisely in accepting your offer.'[10]

His daughter was set to inherit £10,000 on marriage. On top of that 'I do not see my way to allowing my daughter more than £300 a year at the outside.'

Haldane had stated his own annual income at £500, of which £300 was earned. 'I think we ought to do all right really,' Kathleen assured him. 'I shall have no clothes to get the first year, so we can save!' Their life together would mix duty and play. 'We'll have a lot of looking after our friends to do in all the rest of our lives,' she asserts, while, 'We'll go to a lot of plays, won't we?'

Plays were no problem. Haldane was a true enthusiast for the theatre when time allowed, and would later introduce his daughter to the works of George Bernard Shaw and John Galsworthy. More awkward was the matching of his views on the Empire with his fiancée's. He worried about one such comment he had made in an earlier letter. 'Dear,' she consoled him, 'don't get into your head that it could make me love or trust, & *absolutely* respect you less – I think you know, at least I've tried to show you how utterly I do the latter.'

From Haldane we hear of love, from Kathleen mostly of respect. Above the top of this letter, sent to meet up with Haldane as he arrived to meet her father in Switzerland, she wrote the bold assurance: 'I want to make you happy, my John – Kathleen.'[11]

Mary Haldane selected a travelling bag as the wedding gift for her daughter-in-law, and a sofa for the couple. The imminent wedding 'seems like a milestone in our lives,' she told her son – that 'our' particularly striking. 'I trust however that it *will* draw us nearer to each other than keep us further off.'[12] Kathleen was stepping into an intense and intimate family grouping. Would she fit in or smash the small world apart? 'I hope that now we shall all be just closer than before,' Haldane suggested. 'Kathleen's having no brothers or sisters of her own makes it in some ways easier.'[13]

Kathleen was not particularly enamoured of becoming a Haldane. The very fact that she would need to change her surname proved 'irritating and inconvenient', while 'among other things I strongly objected to the farce of being "given away"'.[14]

Mary Haldane took rooms at 28 Atholl Crescent, Edinburgh, in preparation for the big day. The love she bore down with her was an intense one. 'Nothing I know will change that love and affection which is deep and strong with us both toward each other,' she assured her son, 'and I feel that dearest Kathleen . . . will dovetail everyone together. I do not and cannot speak about what lies deepest in my heart, but you know what I feel. God will bring about everything we desire, which is according to his will.'[15]

Both mothers rather hoped for a ceremony in the drawing room of 17 Charlotte Square. The Trotters fancied an Episcopalian ceremony. The couple fixed instead on the nearest available Presbyterian church of St George's. Its bold porticoed front and dome stood just to the left of the palatial frontage of 17 Charlotte Square that the Trotters had taken over from the Haldanes.

A friend of Haldane's, the minister of Glen Devon just south of Cloan, sent Kathleen a short form of the service he proposed to conduct. She duly struck through it with a blue pencil. The ceremony would be brisk and to the point. Haldane had bought himself an 'umbrella, night things and razor', his mother at his request seeing to 'the other things . . . I suppose we're sure to have some rush at the end, more or less, & I'm pretty safe to forget something or other.' Indeed he did forget his umbrella, delaying the wedding a fraction while he returned to the house to fetch it.

The congregation was gathered when John and Kathleen walked in through a side entrance. Kathleen was arm in arm with her cousin Lady Glasgow, whom she had caught trying to make a discreet early exit. John came in with Lady Glasgow's brother Jock, Lord Abercromby. The bride wore a dress, jacket and muff of grey cloth, with a belt and inverted lapel of mauve velvet, all under a three-cornered grey hat. Those friends who were not invited to the wedding watched from the shop window of Vallance's as the couple marched past on their way to the Caledonian station, the bride's stout shoes splashing through the rain. Plans for an 'At Home' the day after the wedding were scrapped out of respect for the recent death of Professor Fraser Tytler, a close family friend of the Trotters. The congregation was locked inside the church till the newlyweds were well clear, then 'herded' next door to have their piece of wedding cake and be done with it.

'The first time we are quiet together,' Kathleen had written to her fiancé that summer, 'you must tell me more how you got metaphysics into love of humanity.' It was a game attempt on her part, even if of doubtful sincerity. Spending ten days over the following Christmas at Cloan, Haldane hurried her upstairs to take dictation of one of many drafts of a forthcoming book on Vitalism. 'He thought that dictating helped him, and he was obsessed by the theory, and spoke as if nothing else in the world was of so much importance and interest. If accepted, it would revolutionize the teaching of physiology, and explain much which perplexed men of science more and more as knowledge of the life and growth of cells increased.' In seeking the right words he would enter spells of silence. Kathleen held her pen ready, trying to read a book of her own while waiting. This was unacceptable. 'He wanted me to follow his thoughts and tried to make me feel how important it was and to say things which would show that I was not only interested, but convinced and in complete sympathy.'

The visit at an end, Kathleen took the train the 40 miles back to Edinburgh while John walked the same distance. The wedding seems to have been a perfunctory business matter for Kathleen, the best available route out of limited domestic circumstance. Happiness was no part of the equation, and she found it hard to sustain any vestige of bridal glow. 'We had a big reception to show the wedding presents and to drink healths,' she wrote years later. 'I tried to make it something of a festive occasion for my cousins, the children at Colinton, but it was no good; they were as depressed as I was.'[16]

★

Kathleen and her mother had come down to rented rooms in Oxford the previous January, searching for a home. Number 11 Crick Road was 'crammed with furniture,' Haldane wrote to his mother, but Kathleen 'thinks we might be alright there for the present'. Brother Willie travelled down to arrange the deal, the house was rented at £60 per year, and John moved in. 'It is semi-detached and has a garden front and behind. There are two sitting rooms and a kitchen on the same floor. Upstairs there are four good bedrooms and two good attic rooms, and a bathroom. The house is as nice a one for its size as is to be had in Oxford, and is in very good condition.' He sought a £200 loan from the family trust to furnish it, and now expected to 'do very well on £600 a year'.

Kathleen remembered the house as 'little': 'the sanitary arrangements were rather primitive, but there were two Burne-Jones lights in the drawing-room bay window, and the dining-room opened into a perfectly charming little garden, which must have been carved out of an old orchard. It was half-filled with the best bearing apple trees I have ever had to deal with.' When Kathleen pulled out the drawers containing Haldane's clothes, a cloud of moths flew into her face.

Crick Road was near the Burdon Sandersons at 64 Banbury Road. Ghetal Burdon Sanderson loaded dinner invitations on the newlyweds like a burden, the Haldanes finding them tedious. Her generous introductions to Oxford society brought little more success. These visitors left their cards with the Haldanes' parlour maid, who was consumed with religious mania. Believing Mrs Haldane had more than enough visitors already, the maid thrust the cards away in the back of a drawer. A local cook and a young boy, Willie Ball, who came to do the boots and shoes in the mornings, made up the rest of the Haldane household. Young Willie was paid 5 shillings a week plus his breakfast, considered lavish reward at the time. Growing under Haldane's care from laboratory boy to laboratory man, Willie Ball would eventually move out to the university of Texas as the assistant to Julian Huxley.

Coutts Trotter held the notion that his daughter was something of a delicate flower. 'I think in my daughter's case the maintenance of health would depend a good deal on a certain standard of physical comfort,' he warned Haldane, 'and also, to some extent, on climate – I think it very doubtful that Oxford would suit her, without a good deal of leave of absence.' She was certainly in robust form when the vicar of their new Oxford parish paid his courtesy call. He was saddened that the couple had not visited his church, and hoped that if Kathleen was in any spiritual difficulty she would open her heart to him. Each sentiment he expressed added to Kathleen's distaste for the 'fat and familiar' man.[17]

'Dear, dear, oh dear, really,' he lamented, on learning the couple had not yet settled on a local church. He wondered to which branch of the Church they belonged.

'My husband is an Original Seceder,' Kathleen stated, 'and I am an Anti-Burgher.'

The parson scuttled away, never to return. While John did his best to secure his footing in Oxford academia, Kathleen was securing their private domain. She was also pregnant. Just before the birth Haldane brought T. H. Huxley and his wife to see her, from their stay with the Burdon Sandersons. A visit from Huxley, the most phenomenally charismatic of the century's scientists, a man who had espoused Darwin's cause and lectured the young Haldane in Edinburgh, was the most splendid gift Haldane could bring to his wife. Whether she felt the required thrill or not slipped her mind in later years.

The real impression was made by Mrs Huxley, 'a charming old lady with a cap tied under her chin like an early Raeburn portrait, who talked encouragingly about the unpleasant aspects of child-bearing. She was a dear.'[18]

A tumbled mass of Haldane's unfinished scientific papers lay on many of the surfaces of 11 Crick Road. Rob Makgill, the son of Haldane's half-sister Lady Isobel Makgill, gathered these stray papers together and began to sort them. Fresh with a medical degree from Edinburgh, Makgill was able to trace lines of logic across the jumble of sheets. He wrote and rewrote the papers to achieve the proper degree of coherency. Through clouds of tobacco smoke, Haldane listened as the young man read his own findings back to him, and eventually nodded his assent. These were his early papers. He no longer had any pretext to refine them through further experimentation. They were ready for publication.

Makgill became Medical Examiner for his native Auckland, but always looked back with pride on his time working alongside the man he called the Senior Partner. The name became the fond term for Haldane used by generations of young physiologists.

In November 1892 Kathleen gave birth to John Burdon Sanderson (JBS) Haldane, known to his parents as 'Squawks'. By New Year's Eve she was up and about, coping well with temperatures that plunged to -11 °C. She and Haldane saw in the New Year by skating for a couple of miles up the frozen river Cherwell. By May Squawks was growing fast, the scientist in him already emerging as he was 'becoming much more amenable to reason in all sorts of ways. He spends most of his time out of doors either in the garden or in the park in his perambulator.' By June, untroubled by the cutting of his teeth, he is 'getting more rational'.[19]

By the end of May 1894 Squawks, though flourishing, 'still refuses to speak, & bursts into tears when anyone asks him to do so'. Perhaps some difficulty lay in the vocabulary required of him. At the age of two he was already donating blood for his father's analysis. Before he was four, he is said to have examined the blood pouring from a cut to his forehead. 'Is it oxyhaemoglobin or carboxyhaemoglobin?' he asked.[20]

For Haldane, blood relations meant blood donors. Anyone close to him was invited to provide a blood sample for some investigation or other. In the young boy Jack, he had an accomplice to train into ever more extreme sacrifices on behalf of science.

GULPING DEADLY GASES

'I . . . err . . . mm . . . A very delicate matter.' The gentleman visitor stood in the Oxford Physiology laboratory of Burdon Sanderson, hesitating about how he might continue. 'The fact being that my wife's cat has been lost . . . and we thought that possibly . . . er . . . it might be here?'[1]

While not an antivivisectionist himself, the gentleman's wife was. On her behalf he had entered the lion's den. Such was the common perception of the Oxford Lab that its workers were deemed to prowl the streets and gardens, snatching unsuspecting pets. Vivisection featured prominently in the *Handbook for the Physiological Laboratory* that Burdon Sanderson had edited in 1873. The book gave fodder to the 'Society for the Protection of Animals Liable to Vivisection', an increasingly effective political pressure group led by Frances Cobbe. Burdon Sanderson became their *bête noire*, and their protests focused on his new laboratory. The Oxford authorities provided funding for the new physiology lab and its running costs, but more in defiance of outside pressure than in wholehearted support. Vivisection was not banned as the pressure groups wished, but it did become liable to regulation under an Act of 1876.

'Yesterday the vivisection inspector was here,' Haldane wrote to his mother. 'He says I shall probably want a licence for my work. It seems illegal even to take an animal's temperature without a licence!'[2]

Kathleen's cousin Jock, Lord Abercromby, who had shepherded Haldane to the altar for his wedding, was one of the couple's first visitors at Crick Road. He overheard Kathleen suggest that John take some food to the laboratory 'for your cat in the bottle'.

Jock was horrified. 'O, you don't really put cats in bottles, do you?' He and other family members had been bombarded with leaflets from the RSPCA when the wedding to Haldane was first announced. Now it seemed his cousin was in intimate contact with the shocking tales of vivisection he had read.

'Come and see,' Kathleen suggested. 'We'll take our tea down at the lab.'

Curled in sleep inside a big beaker, the cat roused itself slightly when it sensed the tea preparations. Haldane placed a saucer of milk near the neck of the beaker. The cat uncurled itself, reached out its forepaws, drank the milk, and then curled back into sleep. Jock caught a sense of the fond relationship that can exist between vivisector and animal, but a clearer demonstration emerged that evening. The cat followed Haldane from the laboratory to his home, stalking him from behind the park railings. Kathleen disliked cats in kitchens, but outside was cold and wet and inside was warm. The cat moved in for the night.

Haldane's son believed his father 'might have become a bacteriologist. But he found experiments involving injury to animals distressing. And through most of his lifetime bacteriologists were largely occupied with taxonomy rather than the physiology of bacteria or their hosts.'[3] Haldane did experiment on animals. However his experiments were designed to bring benefits to human welfare, so the most appropriate animal on which to experiment was a human one. The most articulate of those was himself. When dumber animals were used, they were cast in the role of unwitting colleagues.

'The worst of any new experiments,' Haldane wrote to his mother in 1888, 'is that they take a long time before everything comes right.' With his colleague M. S. Pembrey he developed a gravimetric method for determining the amounts of carbon dioxide and moisture in air. Colleagues on the invention of a new type of calorimeter, a device measuring the amount of energy given off as heat, included the physician William Hale White, whose father's writings as Mark Rutherford had impressed the young Haldane. This field of calorimetry was annexed by the publication of another scientist's, Max Rubner's, classic work in the field. Haldane returned his attention to human respiration in hazardous conditions.

How do different gases bind themselves to haemoglobin? If you can measure the percentage to which blood has been saturated by a gas, you can measure the effects of gas on a human body. Just this one element of the experiment Haldane had in mind required a significant advance in the understanding of science. To help achieve it, in December 1893 he and Lorrain Smith set out for the Copenhagen laboratory of Dr Christian Bohr.

Kathleen accompanied him for the first few days, the Bohrs becoming firm family friends. Christian Bohr, the

Professor of Physiology at the university of Copenhagen, was pioneering research into respiration. His wife came from the wealthy Adler banking family, and Haldane's Christmas was spent at the home of her mother Mrs Adler. Not only the adults but almost all the children spoke English, including the young Harald, who would grow into a first-rate mathematician, and the future Nobel Laureate Niels. The eight-year-old Niels received a carpenter's bench for Christmas. Haldane, Lorrain Smith and Christian Bohr each received a 'cigar' which Bohr promptly lit. The cigar was in fact a container for an enormous pencil with a highly inflammable celluloid top, which blazed wildly. Thus Niels Bohr received an impromptu demonstration of the basic laws of physics.

Christian Bohr's recent experiments suggested oxygen entered the blood by active secretion from the lungs, a theory in support of which Haldane would commit much of his life gathering evidence. His visit gave him invaluable experience of observing Bohr's methods of gas and blood-gas analysis.

It also provided the introduction of the game of golf to Denmark.

'We are still very busy trying to finish our work before Tuesday week,' Haldane wrote to his mother on New Year's Eve, 1893,

> but had to stop yesterday on account of the gas engine at the laboratory having broken down, & the consequent stoppage of the electric motors we were using. We all took advantage of the time to go out into the country and play golf. It was the first introduction of the game into Denmark. Prof Bohr had got clubs & balls from England, & Lorrain Smith gave instruction as to playing. Of course we had to make our own holes,

& find a place to play at. The ground we chose was in a deer park belonging to the king, & did very well, although probably people mayn't be allowed to play there. We were all very bad players, but one or two very much worse than others. Bohr played rather well for a first attempt. It was rather windy & cold, so we had a race round a tree & back . . . I was first, & Bock (who was at Cloanden)* last. Bohr is going to speak seriously to the latter about being too fat.[4]

This new tradition would gain a flourish in later years. Haldane accompanied Niels Bohr (known to the Haldane children as 'The Great Wild Boar') back to Copenhagen after his visit to Britain, and the two men chanced a game of golf. A ball sailed over the palace walls and the two scientists climbed in after it. In more uptight countries this might have caused a fuss. In Denmark, King Christian simply stepped from his palace and joined in the game.[5]

In 1815 Sir Humphry Davy presented to the world his first wire-gauze lamp, the 'Davy lamp', its gauze being a 'metallic tissue, permeable to light and air, and impermeable to flame'. The invention stemmed from Davy's discovery that explosion would not pass through small apertures or tubes. 'I value it more than anything I ever did,' he declared. 'It was the result of a great deal of investigation and labour; but, if my directions be only attended to, it will save the lives of thousands of poor labourers.'[6] The Davy lamp did indeed save many lives initially, and mines that had been closed as too

---

* Mary Haldane renamed the estate Cloanden. Richard turned the name back to Cloan after his father's death, so I have kept to that name throughout for consistency.

unsafe to work with the illumination of naked candle flames were reopened when this new style of lamp was introduced. However the lamps also allowed mines to sink ever deeper, accessing previously unattainable seams, to fuel the rapacious demands of the industrial revolution. The deeper the mines, the more dangerous the situation, as previously unknown mixtures of gas seeped into the workings. The gauze screen and small apertures of the miner's lamp were no longer valid protection. Explosions, and deaths, increased.

Haldane brought back from Denmark the information he needed in order to devise appropriate methods of blood analysis. He could measure amounts of gas absorbed by blood. After the sewers and slums, he now sought to understand the nature and effects of the air breathed by miners. The only question now was, which gas?

News of a mine explosion at the Albion Colliery in South Wales offered Haldane hope that he might collect evidence, even perhaps a sample, of the lethal 'afterdamp' that occurred in the wake of explosions. On Saturday 23 June 1894, just before four o'clock in the morning, an explosion had devastated the workings, killing 281 men and boys. Many bodies brought to the surface were so badly burnt they were unrecognizable, and some corpses were delivered to the wrong households. By the time of Haldane's arrival five days later, all the men had been brought to the surface. The rescue workers now had the job of bringing the carcasses of 123 working ponies to the surface. Haldane entered the pit to note how one of the ponies had fallen.

'It was lying in such a position that it must have been in the full blast of the explosion; but its coat did not seem much singed, and the hairs of its tail were not brittle.'[7] The pony was drawn up, giving Haldane the chance to perform a thorough examination. The blood drawn from cuts in its organs was the normal dark venous colour. The evidence of his new form of spectroscopic analysis also gave no sign of carbon monoxide poisoning. This simple apparatus would develop into 'The Haldane Haemoglobinometer', the standard commercial instrument for blood analysis, in which a blood sample suffused with gas was placed in dilution in a tube next to one with a regular blood sample and their colours compared. Discovering that light tended to dissociate a mixture of carbon monoxide and haemoglobin, its pink colour no longer showing when shaken, Haldane came to add a drop of carmine to both samples.

From his work with Lorrain Smith in the lead-lined wooden chamber he had conceived a breathing apparatus which he was longing to test in afterdamp. Exhaustive blowing of glass and manoeuvring of tubes, bladders and metal evolved into a machine deemed to be both portable and inexpensive. To give a desperate miner an hour to effect his escape would require 60 or 70 litres of oxygen, costing 6d (in today's value about £2), compressed into a steel bottle of half a litre capacity. His experiments had proved that this oxygen could be rebreathed again and again, as long as the carbon dioxide was removed. A layer of coarsely granulated potash-lime in one compartment of an oval metal box performed this job, a valve or exposure to the open air releasing the carbon dioxide. The other compartment contained the cylinder. A short piece of tube connected the oxygen bottle to the breathing tube. 'To use the apparatus it is only necessary to turn one of the oxygen taps, put the breathing tube to the mouth, and breathe in and out through the tube. With most persons it is advisable to also clip the nose.'[8]

*

Under the guidance of W. N. Atkinson, the Inspector for Mines in North Staffordshire, Haldane began a series of on-site tests into the air of coal mines. After staying the night with Atkinson in October 1894, the two men descended a series of pits together. The manager of the first pit led the men to where a tunnel was closed off by a 'stopping, through which an iron pipe had been set with a tap to let out the "chokedamp".' It was commonly thought that 'chokedamp', known for putting out or 'choking' lights, was pure carbon dioxide. Haldane needed to collect a sample to test this supposition through laboratory analysis.

The chokedamp snuffed each of the lamps, which could not be relit due to the presence of firedamp. Haldane now carried the only light against total darkness, a small electric handlamp made by the Lithanode Company. He set to collecting samples of the 'damps', breathing through a tube to draw the mixture into a lean, dry sampling bottle – and of course in consequence breathing the same toxic air into his lungs. A rubber band held the cork stopped in place, otherwise the drop in atmospheric pressure during the ascent to the surface could have seen it burst free.

The samples collected, Haldane shifted to direct experimentation. He closed his lips around the tap drawing the gas from the seam, and sucked at the undiluted gas. A connoisseur of such gases from his laboratory experiments, he recognized at once the sensation in the back of his mouth. It was the same as air containing 8 to 10 per cent carbonic acid. Atkinson and the manager held the electric lamp close to study his face. After the first couple of breaths Haldane was panting. After thirty seconds he felt 'so queer and confused' he had to stop. His face had turned blue.

His two observers kept looking as he breathed the normal

air of the tunnel again. His face turned back to red. 'This was very interesting,' Haldane observed, 'showing that want of oxygen, and not carbonic acid, was the source of changes.'

This was all too exciting. Haldane turned back for some fresh gulps from the tap. The men watched as his face turned from normal to blue to normal again. And then, like a wine lover on a cellar visit to Bordeaux, because he was deep underground after all and such opportunities are intensely special, he closed his mouth round the tap, just one more time, 'to be sure'.

The men's next pit visit took them much deeper, to a place so very hot that they left their coats and waistcoats at the bottom of the shaft. A walk of a mile and a half led them to a point where firedamp was coming off the coalface very quickly. Miners were working beneath a big air-pipe supposed to carry the gas away. 'It was rather a nasty place, I thought,' Haldane told his mother.

This firedamp was essentially methane, also known as marsh gas, the most common of the gases in British mines. Methane explodes when mixed with seven to sixteen times its volume of air. Lighter than air, it tends to rise and be captured in cavities in the tunnel roofs. When ventilation is good there can be a very clear line between the gas and the pure air running beneath it.

The Manager put up his lamp to see whether there was a 'cap' on the flame, & before he had time to see the 'cap' the gas exploded in the lamp. This is what is called very 'sharp' gas – the most dangerous kind. It was surging and crackling out of the coal, & came out quickly from a pipe which had been driven in. From this pipe I got the samples. Altogether it didn't seem to be very safe. If this gas had exploded, probably the explosion would have run through the whole mine, as there was a great deal of dry dust along all the roads. It seems extraordinary that explosions are so rare as they are.

Samples of gas were next collected 'from some fires in heaps of waste on the surface. These fires are much the same as fires which occur in the mine, in the rubbish which accumulates in the "gobs" or disused workings.'[9]

Preparing the apparatus and methods of analysis for the expedition had taken days. Subsequent work on the samples led amongst other findings to the discovery that 'chokedamp', thought to be pure carbon dioxide, was in fact only 13 per cent carbon dioxide, the rest nitrogen.

From a Staffordshire colliery on 28 December 1894 Haldane wrote to his mother: 'Today we finished with the work in pits. We were down there today, which is hard work, & were experimenting with blackdamp on ourselves.' From all these visits Haldane chose the gas of choice for his series of experiments: carbon monoxide (carbonic oxide).

In certain seams the coal is very apt to 'heat' or undergo spontaneous combustion in the pit. I recently examined the gas given off from heated coal and found it to contain sufficient carbonic oxide to render poisonous a very large volume of air. This poisonous air is known in some districts by the expressive name of 'gob-stink'. In other districts it is called white damp. It is naturally much dreaded by miners, since a lamp may give no warning of the presence of the poisonous air.

Haldane had developed blood tests to show the presence of carbon monoxide. 'Unfortunately the blood test is not available by the dim artificial light of a safety lamp.' Some other means had to be discovered to alert miners to the presence of carbon monoxide in the atmosphere. 'On thinking the matter over while myself engaged collecting examples of white-damp,' Haldane told an Edinburgh audience, 'I hit upon the plan of simply taking a mouse or small bird with me and watching its symptoms.'

The final element for one of the most dramatic series of self-experiments in science history was now in place.

— Whole of I – VI ?

By experiment VII the mouse was allowed an honourable withdrawal from Haldane's classic sequence of experiments, and the carbon monoxide now flowed directly towards his own mouthpiece. The percentage of carbon monoxide was 0.21 per cent and the experiment lasted 71½ minutes. The blood sample was 49 per cent saturated with the gas. 'Vision dim. Limbs weak. Had some difficulty in getting up or walking without assistance, movements being very uncertain.' After two minutes Haldane found he 'could walk fairly straight across the room. Could write on black board, but letters not formed as usual, and some mistakes in spelling etc. Felt confused.'

He appeared to improve, then 4 minutes later the account gathered drama once again. 'After walking four or five times up and down the room I staggered and nearly fell. On going on I was very unsteady, often nearly falling, and grasping uncertainly at various objects for support. Vision also very indistinct. I seemed to see things, and yet not recognize their details . . .'

After 12 minutes: 'Said over German numerals correctly up to 25. Still rather unsteady, and nearly fell when turned round.'

After 13 minutes: 'Attempted to walk along the line of one of the boards on the floor. Did so with much difficulty and great staggering and waving of arms.'

At this point oxygen was administered. It brought immediate and distinct improvements. Haldane had survived for experiment VIII. His life was entrusted to apparatus of his own invention. This was a little like strapping yourself into a home-built aircraft and launching it off a cliff. The model on the drawing board suggests a clean flight and a happy landing, but if just one strut is loose reality can be a downward spiral. In experiment VIII Haldane placed the valve to his mouth. Unknown to him a tube became disconnected. The experiment lasted 35 minutes. For the last ten of these, 0.43 per cent of carbon monoxide was flowing into his system.

At the end of the experiment a sample of his blood was taken. *Saturation 56 per cent.*

That figure could quite reasonably be the stated cause of death on a death certificate. 'At the end of the experiment I could hardly stand, and could not walk alone without falling down. Neither breathing oxygen for a minute, nor lying down with legs and pelvis raised (which in a former experiment had seemed to cause improvement) had any immediate good effect.'

A bad headache persisted through the following morning. Haldane went back for experiment IX, a light dose of .027 per cent of carbon monoxide breathed for just 3½ hours. This experiment simply left him with a headache for the following 12 hours. A relatively light day at the office.

At a recent explosion at the Lannerch Colliery in Wales, 'nearly every man had penetrated a long distance, probably over broken doors and timbers, towards the downcast shaft.

One or two had apparently retreated; and five or six had tried to get out by the return air way. Nevertheless most of the men are certified as having been killed by burns and injuries. It seems only too clear that they were nearly all suffocated while attempting to escape.' He was blunt in his verdict: 'It seems to me to be nearly certain that the usual cause of death from after-damp must be simply want of oxygen.'[10]

Armed with a mouse so that he could penetrate deep inside the hell-realm of the next underground explosion, he was set for one of the most significant surprises of his life. The 1896 explosion at Tylorstown in Wales set the course for mine safety regulations in all the years to come. How soon would it be before his recommendations took effect?

Thirty-five men stepped on to the first of the ladders and started their descent inside the mountain. The lead mine was fairly primitive, sunk into the flank of Snaefell on the Isle of Man. The younger men were first on to the ladderways. Fit from a Sunday's rest they aimed to reach the lead ore at 130 fathoms (238 metres) within 15 minutes.

This Monday, 10 May 1897, was a date to carve on the island's tombstones. The shaft dropped like a well inside the mine, the ladders to its centre, pipes for the pumps and compressed air to one side, the ropes for the winding system the other. At six o'clock in the morning the air in the mine was hot, but the men saw no flames. Thirty-five men climbed down into darkness. It was some time after their descent that the first man reappeared at the surface. Two other men followed him up the ladder, barely making it to safe ground, exhausted by their brief climb and the effects of what turned out to be noxious air below. The return of these three men raised intense concern about the condition of the mine and the health of those men still below.

Captain Kewley, his full white beard displaying his sixty-five years but still a powerhouse of energy, immediately assembled a rescue party. He punched holes into the twin lines that normally carried compressed air down to the boring drills, giving rescuers a chance to make short dashes without falling unconscious themselves. Some men were hauled up by ropes through manholes on the platforms, a tight squeeze of 22 by 19 inches. Others were laid inside 6-foot-long wooden boxes which were hooked on to a winding mechanism normally used for the 'kibbles', tubs used to carry lead ore, and wound up to the surface. The last survivor was brought up at five o'clock that afternoon. All the rescuers could hope for now was to reclaim corpses before they putrefied in the heat below.

By Wednesday evening eighteen corpses lay in the carpenters' shed. One rescued man never recovered consciousness and died in hospital. That left the body of Robert Kelly lying below. Her Majesty's Inspector of Metalliferous Mines, Dr Clement le Neve Foster, arrived to take charge of this final recovery. Aged fifty-six, his gentlemanly air even when down a mine in pit clothes, and the fine bristle of his full moustache, have led his photographs to be mislabelled as Haldane's. Alert to Haldane's recommendations for mine safety, Foster took time before catching the ferry from Liverpool to buy a supply of mice.

Extracting the mouse's exercise wheel, turning it on its side, and placing the mouse inside it, he had a new contraption for testing the air in the mine. Attached to a hook on the kibbles' windings, the mice were lowered one by one down the shaft and examined for any effects on their return to day-light. The air seemed not so bad at 115 fathoms down. At 130 it was deadly. Two dead mice along with samples of the poisonous air were sent to Haldane at Oxford for analysis.

The mouse supply was running low by the Saturday morning, one animal still collapsed on its return from 130 fathoms. Foster judged that a ventilation door at that level needed shutting. Hopefully he and his team could recover the last body on the same venture. For want of mice, a tame white rat now tested the way, lowered in its improvised cage with a candle stuck horizontal to its lid to supply illumination. Progress was steady and careful. The men could now see Robert Kelly's body just 10 feet below them.

The white rat was lowered, Foster checking his watch to time the creature's stay. As the cage reached the body, the candle went out. Foster took the warning. He ordered that no man go down. Instead a ladder was moved, clearing the way for grappling irons to grab at the body.

The movement of the ladder stirred the air below. 'I am feeling bad,' Captain Kewley said. After ten rescue trips in the worst of the air, for the old man to admit to illness was drastic. 'I must go up.'

'All up at once,' Foster shouted.

The first task was climbing 80 feet of ladders back to the 115 fathoms level, where Kewley was loaded into a box and drawn up the shaft. A link of its chain caught between two planks. The box was stuck.

Three men were left with Foster. Stupor was setting in. Walk a dozen steps and they would be the other side of a partition, where they knew a current of better air was flowing. Nobody moved though. They sat on the floor at the foot of the ladder and waited, carbon monoxide numbing their legs and their brains. Foster took out a notebook and started writing. An hour later the box was still stuck above them, and Foster was still jotting out notes. It was time to say goodbye to his family. 'I fear we are all dying. No help coming . . . The box does not come . . . No real pain. Goodbye. I feel as if I were sleeping. Again, goodbye, all!'

His recorded notes show frequent repetition of words, another sign of the poisoning of his brain. He put his mouth to the compressed air-pipe and sucked in occasional lungfuls, knocked on it three times as the 'ringing' signal, calling in help from above. The first timing recorded in his notes was 2 pm. By 2.15 pm: 'We are all done. Oh, for the box! It is hell in the shaft.'

Captain Kewley's son joined a rescue party, releasing the box that held his father by 2.25. 'It is strange to write notes while we are dying,' Foster persisted. 'While there is life there is hope. Good old proverb! Send a note for more brandy.'

The empty box was lowered back to them. One by one the other men were raised clear.

'2.45. I have written pages. Kewley is a good fellow. There is life in the old horse yet. I feel as if I could sing. God is helping us; he has heard our prayer. My turn to go.'

The local doctor awaited him at the top. Foster insisted he first take a specimen of his blood, for Haldane's spectroscopic analysis. The doctor tried, but could draw none. Foster turned back to his diary, marking in the time. 'Dr Miller says I must be quiet,' he wrote, 'but I won't.'

Such belligerent moods were one more display of the poisoning. Foster was persuaded out of walking the 4 miles to Laxey and travelled by trap. 'I became unconscious for a few minutes; it was not a true fainting, but something of the nature of epileptiform seizure, as I am told that I was a little

convulsed, though I never had anything in the nature of a fit
before. Dr Haldane has pointed out that seizures of this
description are not uncommon after carbonic oxide poisoning.'[11]

'On no occasion,' Foster remarked after Haldane's analysis
came in, 'has a sample of such a terribly poisonous character
ever been taken in a mine.' The haemoglobin in one of the
dead mice Haldane had been sent was 80 per cent saturated
with carbon monoxide. 'The composition of the sample,'
Haldane declared, 'corresponds to a mixture produced by
the combustion of wood or other similar material. Inhalation
of air of this composition would produce helplessness (in a
man) within about seven or eight minutes at most, and would
soon cause death.'

Haldane had one sure way of knowing more. Paying his
own way, as was customary for gentlemen physiologists of the
time, on 16 June he took a very stormy passage from
Liverpool across to the island. The same afternoon he started
the descent down ladder after ladder, stopping at the 130-
fathoms level. Regular deployment of mice had shown that
the air was now clear, and the last body had been removed on
7 June. About 630 yards north of the shaft Haldane and his
companions found the way completely blocked by rubbish
fallen down from the workings above. The supporting timbers were charred by fire. Haldane's analysis was proved
correct. The gas was the result of an underground fire, most
likely caused by a candle stuck to a beam and poorly snuffed
out.

Clear and tragic evidence of death by carbon monoxide
was highlighted by Haldane at the following day's inquest
into the deaths. Foster's substitution of a white rat, ten to

twenty times as heavy as a mouse and taking two or three times as long to show its responses, had been the one near-fatal twist in the rescue procedures. Twenty men had died at Snaefell, but mice and small birds were now set to stop those figures soaring in subsequent rescue attempts.

UNDERGROUND REALMS

Point Haldane at a fallen cross-beam caught at an angle across a black chasm, and he would skip lightly across it. So long as it was underground. He had no head for regular heights, but the fiery landscape of a post-explosion tunnel saw adrenalin pump him into a veritable trapeze artiste. Heading for a pit near Birmingham to collect gas from a couple of coalfaces, he reckoned it would be 'a change of air and somehow the climate of a coal pit seems to suit me particularly well'.[1]

Much as a tree drops roots that deepen as the tree grows, so the growth of city life above ground sank tunnels that stretched and expanded into a series of different networks below. Haldane twinned his early investigations into pit conditions with on-site experiments during the construction of the Rotherhithe tunnel under the Thames, discovering why workers in the compressed air were injured on coming out. Elsewhere in London tunnels forged their way through the clay, annexing for themselves the level below the drains and the sewers.

When the rail tunnels were built the plan was to run

'hot-water locomotives' along the tracks (then called 'roads'). Now known as 'fireless locomotives', the steam to drive them was created at fixed points, their boilers charged at high pressure at each end of the route. These failed their test runs and coal-powered trains took over. Sulphurous clouds instead of water vapour poured from the engines, but the necessary ventilation was never provided. The worst stretch of all was between King's Cross station and Edgware Road. Along this line the station of Gower Street, known since 1909 as Euston Square, had the most poisonous reputation. A chemist by the exit kept a brew called 'Underground Mixture' to help resuscitate those passengers overcome by the fumes.

'The road now began to be uphill,' a journalist wrote of this stretch in 1893, 'and at the same time the air grew more foul . . . By the time we reached Gower Street I was coughing and spluttering like a boy with his first cigar. "It is a little unpleasant when you ain't used to it," said the driver, with the composure born of long usage, "but you ought to come on a hot summer day to get the real thing!"'[2]

Some 539 trains a day used that section of line. In the short run between Baker Street and King's Cross, 38 trains an hour consumed 15 hundredweight of coal and evaporated 1,650 gallons of water. Haldane's renowned expertise in tunnels saw him appointed to the Board of Trade inquiry into conditions on the Metropolitan Railway in 1898.

Out came his measuring bottles, his six-year-old son Jack accompanying him on the Underground trains as Haldane leaned from the open windows to snatch samples of the air. The foulest air was predictably found on the platform at Gower Street – 0.89 per cent carbon dioxide, 0.066 per cent carbon monoxide. Haldane's report advocated intermediate systems of extra openings for ventilation, but beyond that an urgent switch from coal to an electrified railway system. This electrification was finally in place by 1905.

Jack's day out through the sulphur clouds of the Underground was one in a run of trips out with 'Uffer', his name for his father. Jack joined in an excursion down a pit in North Staffordshire, man and boy sitting together in a large bucket which was slung on a chain and lowered down a shaft. This section of the pit was closed, though air came through a part that was still being worked.

Their party walked a little way, crawled further, then reached a point where the roof was high enough for them to stand. A man raised his safety lamp above his head. It filled with a blue flame and went out with a pop. The lamp had reached into a stratum of firedamp, methane that would have exploded had the flame in the lamp not been shielded by its screen of wire gauze.

'Stand up straight,' Haldane said to his son, 'and recite that speech of Mark Antony from *Julius Caesar*.'

Jack was adept at delivering such literary quotations so duly obliged. 'Friends, Romans, countrymen,' he began, 'lend me your ears.'

He was good at amateur dramatics, performing in school plays, but his delivery started to falter. Soon he was panting. Around 'the noble Brutus' his legs buckled and he fell to the floor. With his face against the surface of the road, his senses returned. He could breathe again. Two lessons were learned. Firedamp was lighter than air so floated above it. Breathing it you might well drop senseless, but into the lower breathable air, so ultimately it wasn't dangerous.

★

A birthday letter swooped down from Perthshire. 'My Dearest Golden Eagle,' it began. 'I am hoping my Golden Eagle may fly in some day soon, but I know he has many demands on his time, and also that he never forgets his old mother. Nor does she ever forget him although she would often like to write more letters to him.'[3]

Family friends liked to call Mary Haldane 'the Eagle', her room at Cloan something of an eyrie from which she looked out on the world. Illness kept her increasingly in bed, but her mind, her prayers, her reading and her pen kept racing. Her letters flew around the globe.

In 1895 her brother John Burdon Sanderson was elected Regius Professor at Oxford. It was a high honour, which also freed him from some teaching duties and gave him time for more visits to his older sister. As always throughout his life, it was worth staying in her good graces. He wrote to her of his care for her son. 'Jonny is working for the XXth century and you may I think be quite sure that he is doing so with extraordinary abilities for that end. What I hoped some four or five years ago was that he would work also for the XIXth. But even in 1900, he will be only *forty*. When I was his age, I had done much less scientific work than he has. What I want is that he should now make his plans so as to ensure his position in 1900.'[4]

The letter glosses sublimely over the actual events of that year. His appointment as Regius Professor made Burdon Sanderson's current post as Waynflete Professor of Physiology available. The post had three main applicants. The most senior was Professor John Newport Langley of Cambridge. The others were Haldane and his former colleague in the laboratory, Francis Gotch.

Langley had just taken over the editorship of *The Journal of*

Physiology from its founder, Michael Foster. He wrote to let Haldane know that if appointed he would immediately divide the Chair, keeping the anatomical part for himself and leaving Haldane the chemical side of the teaching, 'in equal partnership'. The prospect was most agreeable.

Among the impressive testimonials Haldane drew to his application was one from 'Friends who have carried out Original Researches with Dr Haldane': 'His great characteristics are his fertile originality, his laborious, but at the same time successful striving after accuracy, and his enthusiastic devotion to his work,' they wrote. 'He is in fact a genius from whom no slipshod or inaccurate results escape.'

Beyond that, these friends remarked on Haldane's extraordinarily supportive presence in the laboratory. Burdon Sanderson had a reputation for claiming credit for work done by others in his laboratory, a far from unusual tendency in the competitive world of academic science. Haldane was singularly striking in the extent to which he promoted the careers of others.

We know from personal experience that his gift of raising others to his own level makes it a privilege and an honour to work with him, while at the same time his charming kindness, unselfishness and geniality render it a pleasure ... It must be remembered that, owing to his generosity to those who work with him, he is really responsible for much that is not published directly under his name; but still it will be seen from what he has published that his work is especially important, as it deals with subjects that have been but little investigated in this country.[5]

The electors for the Chair let it be known that the choice for his successor lay with Burdon Sanderson. He feared the appointment of Haldane would be regarded as nepotism. 'But,' said an elector, 'if you don't support your nephew everyone will think that you have something very serious against him.'[6]

Ostensibly, Burdon Sanderson's final statement was: 'If I don't support Gotch, it may go to a Cambridge man!'

Burdon Sanderson's biographer is more candid about his role in promoting his protégé, stating that he 'worked behind the scenes to get Gotch into the Royal Society and made sure Gotch followed him as Waynflete Professor'.[7]

Such behind-the-scenes manoeuvring had been distinctly lacking in Burdon Sanderson's failed attempt to have Haldane elected to the Royal Society. Haldane had already threatened resignation from his post at Oxford, after drafting and signing a petition by all the demonstrators for better pay and conditions. He refused his uncle's offer of a rise in pay and improved conditions for him alone. Burdon Sanderson now arrived at Crick Road to deliver the news of Gotch's appointment. He sought Kathleen's help in inducing John 'to take a reasonable view of the position'. Would she make him promise to give his 'full support to Gotch, and to carry on at the laboratory exactly as he was now doing'?

She was delighted to announce that Haldane had already submitted his resignation as a demonstrator. Fists clenched, the old man stormed around the drawing room. 'There's nothing further I can do for John,' he declared. 'So what does he propose to do now?'[8]

Tighten his belt, was one answer. Continue his revolutionary work on blackdamp, which even his uncle deemed 'excellent'.[9] And appreciate the support that immediately came his way from Cambridge. The first Professor of Physiology there, Michael Foster, wrote to say that if any

Cambridge position should come up that Haldane might deem worth accepting, he should have it at once.

In many ways Burdon Sanderson had been playing catch-up with Sir Michael Foster all his life, one reason he guarded his old professorship from going to 'a Cambridge man'. Foster pioneered teaching through laboratory experimentation and research. Many of the leading biologists of Britain and America in the early twentieth century were former students of his. Haldane's first visit to Cambridge was at the beginning of December 1888, staying with Hugh Anderson. His association with Oxford was an accident of birth, which gave Haldane his relationship with his uncle Burdon Sanderson. Cambridge would have fitted more closely with his own views on education. While he would remain in Oxford for the rest of his life, it was Cambridge interests that secured him a Grocers' Scholarship of £400 per year. This lifted the Haldanes to financial security. His election to the Royal Society in 1897 came through sponsorship and influential backing from Cambridge. When Burdon Sanderson hotfooted from the train station with news of the election, Kathleen was able to deflate him once again. They already had the news, she told him. A telegram had arrived from Cambridge.

From Oxford Haldane wrote to his friend Wilson out in Sydney: 'I should have liked the chair here, & think I could have helped to make something out of the school & evolve a race of physiologists less densely ignorant than the present of the relations of Natural Science to its own history & to other branches of knowledge. Oxford seemed to be the place for such a school – but these are dreams of the past!'[10]

Heading to Belfast to team up with his friend Lorrain Smith was an option for a while, but his wife's rigid stance on

Home Rule ruled that out. She would have liked him to take a post in the 'Dominions' but for the fact that her mother would miss her too much. It is doubtful that Haldane ever took such a suggestion seriously. He kept seeking ways to bring his friend Wilson back from Sydney, suspecting any reputation garnered so far away would not carry back to Britain where it mattered. Oxford at least had a splendid library, which for him was a prerequisite of successful research.

Michael Foster's eminence as a teacher at Cambridge came at the expense of his own original science. Lack of a professorship saw Haldane spared such a fate. He was always averse to administrative tasks in any case. Now he could run a solo model of how Britain could emulate Germany, linking academia and industry. From within academia, he would produce superb physiology. Within industry, he would prove the practical value of scientific research.

An 1897 birthday gift of money from Haldane's mother provided parts for new gas-analysis equipment, which was put to immediate use in Haldane's work for the Water-Gas Committee. A method for creating hydrogen gas by passing steam over hot coal was developed in America in 1873. Businessmen alert to the commercial opportunities soon set up gas plants along the eastern seaboard. Known as water-gas, this was widely distributed in America, and suppliers sought the authority to extend the provision to British homes. When he engaged with the work, Haldane soon realized that he had 'to be most careful about statistics and conclusions, as there are very large financial interests involved, and apparently a good many clever and unscrupulous people ready to seize on any weak point in the conclusions, or to make an unfair use of them'.[11]

Haldane's conclusions, both in the laboratory and from analysis of American statistics, led him to report how dangerous wide usage of water-gas would be. 'Roughly speaking the loss of life arising in one way or another – accident, suicide, or homicide – appears to be fully a hundred times greater with water-gas in America than with coal-gas in this country,' stated his report.

Co ?

Assuming that Boston has a death rate equal to that of London, about one in every three hundred deaths is due to accidental water-gas poisoning. This represents an annual death rate about the same as that of 'child-birth' or of 'suicide' as returned in the official statistics for England and Wales for 1880 to 1890. The total death rate for poisoning of every kind in this country, whether accidental or suicidal, and whether by solids, liquids, or gases, is only about half the average death rate from water-gas poisoning in Boston, New York, San Francisco and Washington.

The effects would be all the more catastrophic, given that the people of Britain used four times as much gas as the average American. Haldane calculated that the 'reckless' distribution of water-gas in America cost 800 lives a year. If the same distribution methods were introduced to Britain, 1,600 people would die every year.

The experiments involved leaking the different gases into seven different rooms. Whereas five were in the physiology building at the university,

Room C, in which a short experiment with gas and a number of experiments with candles were made, is in my own home . . . There is one window, and a fireplace. One wall is an outside one, of brick. The walls and ceiling are papered. There is no gas in the room, and gas was therefore brought through India-rubber tubing from a gas-jet in a neighbouring room, and allowed to escape at the floor level.

Room G, also in my own house, is an attic room of very irregular shape, and of 786ft capacity. It has one window, and no fireplace, and the walls but not the ceiling are papered.

Kathleen decamped to her parents' home in Edinburgh for the birth of their daughter Naomi in 1897. The arrival of the baby meant they had outgrown the home in Crick Road, yet still space was found to render a room into a gas chamber (the attic was simply used for experiments on the effects of smoke from candles). Once gas was released into a room to mix with air, how did it disperse? Despite the obvious dangers of such a general release into the homes of the world, such investigation was entirely new. Haldane's method of detecting the gas is unlikely to have been used in households before or since. Climbing ladders to reach the air near the ceiling, stooping to the floor, reaching into corners, he probed for the gas with a miner's lamp.

The trick was to keep watch on the lamp to see if the ordinary flame ever received a conical cap of slightly luminous flame. Rooms were dimmed appropriately, the hydrogen flame from a Clowes lamp offering a detectable cap with as little as 0.1 per cent of gas. At 7 per cent of carbon monoxide the Oxford gas gave Haldane the chance to notice the 'cap' flame and get down from his ladder before giddiness set in. Air was whisked away in bottles sealed with paraffined corks for analysis in another room

Defending Britain against an invasion of water-gas meant doing so in court. 'It was necessary to do the work,' Haldane assured his mother, 'as we have to deal with a number of "skilled witnesses", chiefly Professors of Chemistry. The first of them broke down hopelessly under cross-examination yesterday, and I have no doubt the rest will do the same. The whole thing seems rather discreditable, but I think we shall get to the bottom of it, as the chairman, Lord Belper, is now getting very keen on the subject.'[12]

One by-product of this work was proof that no ordinary room of its day could be rendered gas-tight. The most sealed of his experimental rooms had its air replaced by leakage in five hours on a calm day, more quickly on a windy one, the air permeating the brick. Another by-product was Haldane's appointment to a new and remunerative post. He was made one of three Metropolitan Gas Referees in late 1899.

The small office in 64 Victoria Street where the Gas Referees met for a day every week or two brought together two of the great individualists of British science. W. J. Butterfield took care of the administration and much of the engineering, leaving Haldane in charge of the chemistry and Charles Boys of the physics. Boys picked up his physics from the Royal School of Mines, and found his first employment in a colliery before returning to the Royal School of Mines as a demonstrator. This mining background was reason enough to twin the two scientists, but Boys brought with him a talent for invention that made him an ideal playmate for Haldane. They kept their apparatus locked in a side room, gathering coats of dust, so that no cleaner might damage it. In a *Boy's Own* method of science, Boys invented a machine based on a toy bow and arrow which shot out long strings of quartz filaments. He subsequently used these to estimate the mass of planet Earth. Boys took on calorimetry, while Haldane was responsible for the quality of London's supplies of gas for heating and light.

The job might well have been short-lived. From his early twenties Haldane's correspondence carries news of illness, rheumatism, and pleurisy cured by the air of Switzerland. A doctor's examination at the turn of the century declared he had heart disease. His only chance for a prolonged life was to spend it as an invalid. The doctor went on to suggest a cure: the mineral water of Bath was 'valuable because it contained hydrogen, carbon, nitrogen, oxygen, and sulphur, like a protein'.[13]

The advice let Haldane cast the doctor as a quack. He sought a second opinion from James Mackenzie, and was told to carry on. Though Mackenzie was later knighted for his services to medicine, his advice was perhaps as medically unsound as the doctor's advocacy of protein-rich mineral water. For Haldane 'carrying on' meant further trips into the aftermaths of explosions, further lungfuls of poisonous gas, sealing himself in pressurized chambers, grappling with the atmosphere in the depths of the sea and on the highest peaks. He substituted incredible stamina for health, and became the most enduring invalid on the planet.

'Illness of different kinds (such as 'flu) leave one's nervous system in a depressed state,' he advised one correspondent, 'for which the shortest remedy is usually a good change of some kind; and I should advise you, if possible, to go off somewhere, taking some of your work with you. I have at least found this very effective myself, and that I was quickly quite up to work again.'[14]

'There are few more contemptible figures in the world than those men who spend all their energies in looking after their own health,' was the opinion of J. S. Haldane, MD.

'Those who spend too much of their time in looking after other people's health are apt to be terrible bores. A sane and whole man or woman wants to do a man's or woman's work, and not to exist simply for the benefit of his or her health, or for the sake of making money. That is a piece of psychology which I learned from my mother and my old Scotch nurse.'[15]

At the end of 1899, 4 St Margaret's Road was a stark choice of new home in north Oxford, composed of blocks of dull bare stone, tall and functional with little pretence of beauty. In October 1899 Britain had launched itself into war – an imperial war after Kathleen's own heart. Kathleen's spoken marriage contract, which required Haldane to keep his political views quiet, now annoyed her. She needed her husband to talk, needed his agreement, yet it seemed the Haldanes had scarce an imperial bone in their entire massed bodies.

The British High Commissioner to South Africa, Sir Arthur Milner, sought citizenship rights for the flood of 'Uitlanders', non-Boers most of whom were British, who were magnetized by vast potential profits from the discovery of gold and diamonds in the country. Milner's negotiations with Paul Kruger, President of the South African Republic (an area also known as the Transvaal), were a sham. His demands were so excessive, his willingness to compromise so non-existent, that a breakdown in talks was inevitable. This provided Britain with the moral high ground for the war Milner had desired all along, which would pit almost half a million soldiers against the Boer forces of around 88,000. As with many such wars, the true reason lay in mineral deposits. In 1821 Britain was the first country to adopt the gold standard, switching from silver. Germany, France and the United States made the full switch themselves in the 1870s. Gold deposits in the western United States saw America claim 27 per cent of global gold production. More than half the world's gold in 1902 still originated from the British Empire, 24 per cent of that total coming from Australia, 7 per cent from Canada, yet even in the throes of war 12 per cent came from the Transvaal.[16] Britain could not afford to lose control over its gold supply, which formed the very basis of its monetary system.

On 11 August 1900 Haldane was called to the parade ground of the military headquarters at Aldershot. It was a Field Day. The army had suffered casualties from heat exhaustion the previous month. With thermometer and stethoscope in hand, Haldane kept pace with the troops and monitored their condition. He subsequently gave advice on the nutritional value of army rations. The consequent expertise let him ride with all guns blazing into the most nefarious aspect of that Anglo-Boer war.

Though heavily outnumbered, the Boer resistance was effective. They were defending home territory, of a roughness and expansiveness which stretched the British lines of communication. Names such as Spion Kop, Mafeking and Ladysmith were branded on the British mind as redolent of sieges and defeats. Lord Kitchener and Earl Roberts took over control. The relief of Mafeking in May saw Kathleen take her children by the hand to join the Oxford crowds celebrating 'Mafeking Night'. British troops were in control of the major cities by the end of 1900.

Effective guerrilla warfare still left large swathes of rural areas under Boer control. To combat this, Kitchener embarked on a scorched-earth policy, razing the farms of both Boers and Africans. The twentieth century still drawing its first breaths, Kitchener then inaugurated what would become the century's greatest horror. Boer women and children, and just a few men, those called 'the hands–uppers' who had surrendered, were rounded up and installed in the world's first concentration camps.

In the summer of 1900 a women's rally in London raised the plight of the distressed women of South Africa. It was led by Emily Hobhouse. Her younger brother Leonard Hobhouse had worked as a pupil in Haldane's laboratory in 1888, 'a Fellow of Merton, who wishes to do some physiology for the sake of philosophy, which is his subject. He works three or four hours a day here. I am of course very glad to have him. He seems a very able man.'[17] Four years Haldane's junior, Leonard Hobhouse grew in reputation to become a leading sociologist and philosopher, teaching at Oxford and the London School of Economics and writing regular leaders for the *Manchester Guardian*. Emily largely kept to their Cornish home till the death of their father in 1895, when she set sail for Minnesota on a mission to help the Cornish miners who were working there. That relief work was focused on helping miners deal with alcoholism. The problems she encountered when she sailed to South Africa in December 1900 were of a different degree.

When embarking on her voyage she knew of only one concentration camp, in Port Elizabeth. She came to learn of thirty-three more, across the Transvaal and Orange Free State. As farms were razed, more and more of their occupants, mostly women and children, were herded into the mass of tents.

From the spring of 1901 she recorded her eyewitness accounts of Bloemfontein.

I saw families huddled up close to the railway line near Warrenton and Fourteen Streams. I saw an overcrowded train crawling along to Kimberley throughout a whole long night. I saw people, old and young, bundled in open trucks under a scorching sun near a station building without anything to eat. At midnight they were transported to empty tents where they groped about in the dark, looking for their little bundles. They went to sleep without any provision having been made for them and without anything to eat or to drink. I saw crowds of them along railway lines in bitterly cold weather, in pouring rain – hungry, sick, dying and dead. I never had any doubt that every female countryman of mine would feel just as I did at the sight of all this – with a profound feeling of compassion, burning with the desire to alleviate the suffering.

Well, not quite. 'When the troubles in the concentration camps were reported, John refused to listen to reasons why the camp was created,' Kathleen reported. 'It seemed as if he were deliberately closing his mind to any reasoning on that matter, and could only talk about "inhumanity" and "starving women and children".'

The government sent a commission of investigating ladies in the wake of Emily Hobhouse's report, which Haldane was sure was only meant to discredit it. From a visit to his brother at the House of Commons Haldane told his mother: 'Feeling has got very bitter over the concentration camps evidently. It is a terrible thing to think of. Mr Balfour's [the prime minister] reference to it in his speech of yesterday seems to me thoroughly contemptible.'[18]

Kathleen felt that 'the army supplied the concentration camps with much which it could well have used itself in the matter of food and equipment, of tents, doctors and nurses'. Women and children were signalling troops from their farms, supplying their men with food and ammunition. Burning the farms and imprisoning the women was our 'very "Christian" method of conducting a war'.[19]

'Soap was an article that was not dispensed,' Emily Hobhouse reported. 'The water supply was inadequate. No bedstead or mattress was procurable. Fuel was scarce and had to be collected from the green bushes on the slopes of the kopjes by the people themselves. The rations were extremely meagre and when, as I frequently experienced, the actual quantity dispensed fell short of the amount prescribed, it simply meant famine.' The worst plight for the women was the way their undernourished children fell to epidemics of measles, bronchitis, dysentery, pneumonia and typhoid. In such close confines, with at least one sick child to every crammed tent, there was no way of keeping a child healthy. More than 20,000 people died in the camps. That figure is likely to have been multiples higher were it not for the action of Haldane.

He may have had no ready audience for his views at home, but his colleague C. G. Douglas remembered how 'in his lectures Haldane spoke with contempt of the ignorance and stupidity of some woman (a member of a commission of inquiry) who proposed to rectify matters by substituting an equal weight of jam for part of the fat ration, oblivious of the fact that the jam would have less than half the energy value of the fat which it replaced so that the already deficient diet would become still more inadequate'.[20]

Haldane wrote letters to the papers which itemized the number of calories needed by each woman and child, and declared his readiness to head for South Africa to see his advice put into place. His brother Richard had worked his network of political connections as an MP to the extent that he would take office with the next Liberal government. Out of the public eye, he helped John Haldane carry his demands for improved rations behind the scenes of the political arena. Mr L. G. Wicham-Legg, editor of *The Dictionary of National Biography*, recalled:

> My authority is Fisher who one day soon after the Boer War said in my hearing that Haldane had done more to save human lives than (I forget what phrase: like 'the whole medical profession put together') and said that when Miss Emily Hobhouse (was it not?) began her campaign, Haldane went to Richard and said that there were things in Miss Hobhouse's report which indubitably showed that there was something very seriously wrong. R.B.H. after listening to it said: 'Go and see Chamberlain, he's a very sensible fellow' and armed with an introduction from R.B.H., J.S.H. went and the result was that orders were sent out for the effecting of the improvements.[21]

Joseph Chamberlain was then Secretary of State for the Colonies. Once a Liberal and a social reformer, his imperialist urges had seen him cross over to the Conservative Party. Britain's role in the Boer War was increasingly notorious on the international scene, and especially vilified in Germany. Haldane's private pleading, doubtless impassioned and informed, found the right moment and the right sympathetic ear. Douglas added the following sentence to his *Dictionary of National Biography* entry for J. S. Haldane: 'During the South African War Haldane's influence was largely responsible for the improvement of the inadequate diet at first provided in the concentration camps and thus abolished a serious menace to health.'

Haldane subsequently gave evidence before the War Office Committee on Canteens about insufficient quantity in the soldiers' rations. 'You no doubt saw,' he told his mother, 'that the death rate in the concentration camps has gone down to a tenth of what it was when the food was insufficient.'[22]

Mary Haldane coaxed descriptions of plants out of her granddaughter Naomi, then troubled to show her how these might be improved. As Naomi Mitchison she would come to include science fiction in her novelistic career, a woman pioneer in the genre. Novels were one way of containing and balancing all the stark contradictions of her early years. Her father's lap was a place of refuge, where she could curl her body against his warmth, and reach up to stroke his thick brown moustache or hook her finger on to his ear. Sometimes she would adopt imperialist statements from an era before she was born, lines her mother took delight in repeating. If these pleased her mother, then her father would like them too. His obvious shock and upset at the little girl's words frightened her. Years later, with her own political stamp now established as way to the left, father and daughter took a walk in the hills around Cloan. 'You can imagine what was said,' Haldane noted, 'when I married an Edinburgh Tory.'[23]

Naomi was welcomed into the Oxford laboratory, which 'was full of fascinating things: balances, tubes, lovely little blobs of mercury, and houses – as I thought of them – in process of construction, among them, no doubt, the Haldane gas-analysis apparatus . . . Sometimes it came home with my father for further work in his study.'[24] She found a particular rapport with the lab's guinea pigs, learning to speak their language. One summer in a later home the gardens would fill with cages of the creatures, she and her brother breeding them to establish a new genetic principle. Naomi's name joined her brother's on the subsequent published scientific paper, for she was adept at fitting in.

'My brother was five years older than me but I tried so hard to keep up and often succeeded,' she later wrote.

> Things seemed to be always cheerful and in the everyday world with my brother Jack – Boy for me. Certainly he did testing things sometimes like making the water in the basin live – off the ordinary household electricity when we finally got it – and putting in pennies for me to snatch. Often he teased me till my temper went and I stamped and screamed, feeling furiously helpless. I hated him for minutes then suddenly it was all over. But this wasn't the kind of thing which really worried me. This was alive.[25]

Her father would take each child's head in his hands and kiss the head goodnight, a touching and unusual gesture for fathers of that era. In Naomi's old age her father would ghost the comfort of his presence to her in dreams, but the love of her life, her true passion, remained her brother Jack. In childhood she was granted a level of freedom that was positively wild for a girl of her class and time, the only girl among the boys at the Dragon School. With the first sniff of puberty she was dragged from her school and attempts were made to put the lid on this seething girl. Jack would get to join in his father's experiments. She, instead, had the task of standing outside her father's private gas chamber, peering in through the observation window in case her father should pass out, when she was to pull him clear and seek to resuscitate him.

Hers was a relatively passive role, but an electric presence in the background of Haldane's life.

'You come in,' Naomi said to a six-year-old friend passing their home. 'My father wants your blood.' The friend ran away screaming. Naomi, of course, had already donated a sample. Science required such sacrifices. It held the status of some uproarious god in her life, always set to drag humans through pits of smoke and fire and disaster, yet honouring their submission by returning them unharmed. Whenever news of a mining explosion was relayed to their Oxford home, Kathleen pulled the mining clothes and helmet out of a bottom drawer and Haldane set off for the first train.

After a bit, a telegram would come: 'I am alright.' Then, an hour or two later, another, in the same words, and we at home would know that he had been breathing too much carbon monoxide, which would have affected his immediate memory . . . I was never afraid that anything would happen to my father, even though I knew he would be in the most dangerous part of the mine: science would be with him.[26]

HEAT, SWEAT AND LARVAL WORMS

Accidents aside, Haldane claimed that the average miner lived a healthier life than a barrister. One exception was Cornwall. The county's tin miners suffered from 'Dolcoath anaemia', named after the tin mine where it was most endemic.

The deeper a mine sinks beneath the Earth's crust, the higher the temperature. In Cornwall the average rise was 3 degrees for every hundred metres. Mines plunged to depths of more than 1,000 metres, where the temperature of rock equalled the body temperature of a man. If air from the surface caused the temperature to drop, oxidization of iron pyrites made it rise still higher. Many miners had worked mines as far afield as the Transvaal, West Africa and Malaya, and these Cornish mines could seem as tropical as any of those.

Mines provided many varieties of working environments that science had yet to explore. Haldane described the first stage of his Cornish work as 'a somewhat unsavoury subject'.[1] The mines had 'no underground sanitary receptacles of any kind, and the men are in the habit of relieving themselves at any convenient place. The consequence is that the ground is extensively polluted.'[2]

Temperatures in these tunnels were a constant minimum 70 degrees Fahrenheit and often much higher. Haldane scoured this ground-covering of faeces to collect his samples, as well as working through the faeces of infected men. He found the same larval eggs in both sources. Doctors in Puerto Rico might have rubber-stamped their diagnosis at this point, since at one time 20 per cent of deaths on the island were attributable to one disease: ankylostomiasis, with its infestation by hookworms. Find this in Malaya and West Africa and you wouldn't be so surprised. In Cornwall it was entirely unexpected. Haldane had been brought in for his expertise on respiratory issues. Luckily he had the skills and free thinking to range much wider when necessary, at this point extending our knowledge of the biology of the larval Ankylostoma.

The hookworms flourished inside the constant temperature of a man, sending eggs out in faeces to extend their territory. Cornish miners returned from far-flung mines, carrying their infection with them. Deposited in a Cornish chamber pot or beside a Cornish lane the larval Ankylostoma soon perished. The warm conditions of a Cornish mine, however, provided a sanctuary. After nestling in faeces on the underground floors, warmed to a life-enhancing temperature, larvae hatched and looked for their next home. Miners worked close to each other, many without clothes to survive the extreme heat. The larvae burrowed through human skin. A breeding colony of up to 1,000 hookworms could take up residence in a miner's duodenum, the first section of his small intestine. Half an inch long, they attached themselves to the living membrane of the bowel, abstracting blood by suction.

The diagnosis of this 'worm disease' took months of painstaking research. Throughout that period Kathleen was quite sure her husband would be infected. Instead that honour fell to Haldane's assistant A. E. 'Teddy' Boycott. His wife, a Sister at St Thomas's Hospital, had to nurse him alongside their two baby boys.

If tropical Cornwall was a strange concept, tropical Westphalia in Germany was absurd. In north-west Germany, the Ruhr Valley had recently become the most industrialized region in the world. When Haldane accepted a British government commission to make a comparative visit to Westphalian collieries, rife with a similar disease, he knew what to expect.

The British consul in the region, Mr Mulvany, was unusually adept at providing Haldane with the necessary introductions. His father had done much to develop the coalfields of the region around forty years earlier. The names of collieries, such grand Irish words as Shamrock, Erin and Hibernia, gave clues to the origins of these early miners. Haldane was surprised and touched by the warmth of his welcome into the German mining area. Managers, mine inspectors and doctors knew his pioneering work on mine gases, had studied and applied it, and were set to celebrate the man.

British newspapers had picked up the story of 'worm disease' in the area and run with it, as though a severe epidemic were set to reach across the North Sea. The reports were exaggerated. Haldane went underground at several collieries. Few men were truly ill, and none had died. Many were infected however, and well capable of spreading the disease.

The authorities there had undertaken a radical method of curing the outbreak. They examined the faeces of every coal miner. If they found any eggs from the worms they treated the carriers with male-fern extracts. Men objected. They generally felt well, but the medicines were unpleasant and compulsory. Some were forced into hospitals and so received almost no pay. At least, Haldane noted, these measures were 'most energetic, and on the whole effective'. As with his view of German universities, Haldane found superlatives hard to avoid. He was 'immensely impressed with the progress made here,' he wrote to his mother, on completing his trip. 'The men at the collieries are very well looked after by the government. There are, for instance, lots of baths for everybody, whereas at home there often isn't even a bath for the manager. The managers, inspectors, etc. who I have met are most capable men – all of them properly educated and the machinery appears to be extremely good. Yesterday I went to see the Principal of the Mining School at Bochum. It is a splendidly equipped place.'[3]

Haldane's son recalls his father's visit differently, so maybe the ferry ride across the North Sea gave time for a critical view to ferment. The fern-extract treatment forced on the German miners blinded many of them, many others lost their jobs, and the costs of the operation were vast. Haldane made friends with a German mining engineer, G. A. Meyer, but his appreciation of Germany's industrial progress was diminished by what he saw as 'German authoritarianism' that 'was dangerous and inefficient'.[4] Such drastic treatment actually caused the infected men to move to other mines and spread the disease.

In Cornwall Haldane worked to have underground sanitation installed. He then persuaded the men to use the facilities, and treated the sick men with thymol, which was effective without rendering them blind. The epidemic disappeared from the Cornish mines and Haldane proposed the same regimen for the Westphalian mines.

Back in Cornwall, it was time for his investigations to move on. A new problem had arisen.

Dolcoath, near the town of Penzance, was known as the 'Queen' of Cornish mines. Active as a copper mine since at least the mid-eighteenth century (Dolcoath translates from Cornish as 'the old pit'), when its deposits of copper were exhausted, shafts sank deeper to reach rich lodes of black tin. By 1914 a network of some 70 miles of levels would reach out towards the various mineral deposits. One world war later and cheap international tin made working these Cornish lodes uneconomic, but in 1895 confidence was such that a new shaft sank the 1,000 metres to connect with the latest vein of extractable tin. The mine was recognized as the most progressive in the region, importing new equipment from California. It used that same spirit of innovation to call in a medical research scientist. Haldane solved the problem of anaemia. The cause of a more severe one, a lung disease known then as tubercular phthisis, was still unknown.

For coal and iron miners, 3.4 men in every thousand aged 35 to 45 died of lung disease. For tin miners the figure was ten times greater. In post-mortem examination a lung of such a 35-year-old would be almost stony hard to the touch, feel gritty when the knife sliced into it, and contain no apparent cavity. Squeeze it and a dark, ink-like fluid poured out.

Most experts put the cause down to poor ventilation. Others blamed the lack of sunlight in a miner's life; the extreme demands of ladder climbing in a tin mine; infective bacteria; particulates from the drilling or the smoke from explosives and candles; high temperatures and the sudden switch from the heat of the mines to the cold of outdoors; and the general insanitary conditions of a miner's domestic life.

Such theories came from guesswork. For Haldane, foot-work was just as important. It was foolish to conceive theories about an environment without experiencing it first-hand, in each of its many manifestations. Equally impor-tant was the ability to distinguish one environment from a seemingly related one. Haldane kept gathering first-hand knowledge of coal mines. The lead mines of the Isle of Man gave him one distinctive comparison, and new trips to iron mines in the north of England gave him another. Now he needed to explore the furthest reaches of the Cornish tin workings.

The Levant mine was deep, and hot. You descended it on a 'man-engine', an early and primitive form of escalator. Matching your pace to that of the machine, you stepped aboard as the platform passed you by, making sure to stand in the middle of the narrow strip of wood, stepping nimbly off again as the need arose. The descent took three-quarters of an hour. 'I think I am going to dream about it all night,' Haldane wrote to his young son.[5] The party got lost among the dis-used workings, turning back again and again till the mine manager found them an exit. Haldane's temperature reached 103. Once out of one mine, he would go straight back down another.

Haldane snatched samples of air in the wake of detonated charges, took further air samples at different heights and in areas where gases might have caught, measured air currents and rock and air temperatures. Point by point, he was able to discard many of the current theories. Iron and coal seams were worked horizontally, whereas tin mines were worked on slopes. Cooler air passed naturally down through the workings, the warmer air rising. Tin miners had a great many more ladders to climb, but reduction in this brought no lessening of lung disease. Whereas coal miners neither had nor wanted pithead baths, tin miners washed and changed in a heated building on site.

While men stood on the slopes working rock drills into the mineral faces, Haldane would observe alongside them. About the size of a man, these drills were driven by compressed air and churned up clouds of stone dust. Haldane measured the dust, and then asked for a set of health statistics. In the one district, 142 of those who died had worked rock drills. Ninety-four per cent of these died of lung disease.

By process of elimination, Haldane now had his last piece of evidence. He knew the cause of 'phthisis'. It was the breathing of stone dust, the disease later to be labelled silicosis or more generally pneumoconiosis. The soft dust of coal or iron workings choked a miner's lungs but did not prompt tubercular disease.

Discovering the cause of environmental illness should be enough for a medical research scientist. It was never so for Haldane. He was a jack of all trades. As a doctor, a biologist, a physiologist, a chemist, he first sought the correct diagnosis. That was step number one. Next was to find the prevention and the cure.

Each experiment called on Haldane as inventor and engineer, as new apparatus was modelled and refined. Glass receptacles and tubing of the necessary dimensions could seldom just be bought, they needed to be blown. Haldane remained something of an amateur at glass-blowing – an expatriate German named Rittershaus became his resident expert – but with blown glass, mercury and rubber tubing to hand he was in his element. *The New York Times* in 1894 acclaimed him in his role as an inventor for a device to 'allow miners to live from one to three hours in afterdamp. The invention consists of a steel case holding compressed oxygen and a respirator, the whole no larger than a safety lamp.'[6]

Investigations at Dolcoath had already called for new apparatus for measuring dust. Haldane's skill at manipulating his delicate apparatus was especially exquisite considering his reputation otherwise as a clumsy man. The next step in preventing rock drillers' death from lung disease called for apparatus of a different magnitude. Haldane the engineer now came fully into play.

A shed was set up in which Haldane, alongside the manager of the mine, worked a drill to simulate conditions underground. Together they developed a high-pressure jet water delivery system, driven by compressed air, to wet the dust as it was drilled. The system was then put into use in the tunnels below.

It was effective in ridding the atmosphere of stone dust. It also left drops of water falling from the roof on to the men. They were reluctant to make use of it. Haldane the educator then came into force, teaching the men the health issues involved, the stark choice they faced between a little damp and petrified lungs. Then Haldane the advocate went to work, persuading the authorities to regulate some form of water dampening as compulsory.

From this south-western tip of England, measures were

now in place to spare the lungs of miners in the fast-developing tin mines of the world. For tropical conditions in Cornwall it was necessary to go deep underground, but while Cornwall sucked in rains from the Atlantic the peninsula was also hugged by the Gulf Stream. It was a prime holiday spot. Haldane the physiologist, the biologist, the doctor, the engineer could bloom afresh as the family man.

Sennen Cove tucks into the south-western tip of England, just above Land's End. Obliged to work in Cornwall, Haldane took the chance to bring his wife Kathleen, son Jack and daughter Naomi down on a series of Easter vacations. 'Why in the world do they choose such a name?'[7] wondered Ghetal Burdon Sanderson at Naomi's birth in 1897, apparently oblivious to the weirdness of her own Christian name. Cornwall was a fine chance to escape such opinionated family dynamics for a while.

A carriage brought them from the railway station in Penzance to the house of a Mrs Pender. She took a few lodgers into her two-storey home, among the houses that studded the hillside above the sea, while also keeping the Ship Inn for the fishermen of the village. Lamps lit the rooms, painted glass rolling pins and spiritual texts adorned the walls, and for the toilet you stepped outside to an earth closet. Somehow the context of the sea allowed Kathleen to let go of her class prejudices and relax into the place. A non-swimmer, she donned a plain white cotton gown and stretched her arms wide in the very shallows of the sea, bobbing gently as the waves pushed at her sides.

Large trunks of barnacled timber marked the point where the Atlantic cable entered the ocean, linking Europe to the Americas by telegraph since 1858, when President Buchanan had responded to Queen Victoria's greeting. Two rock break-waters withstood the power of the waves as the Haldane family walked the shore on Sundays. A straw boater was pinned to Kathleen's short hair, perhaps with cherries on it, since this was a Sunday. Naomi had on her knitted tammy, a round flat cap sporting a tassel. Jack wore his school cap, while Haldane's cap was made of tweed to match his tweed knickerbockers and thick woollen stockings.

Sunday found the Methodist villagers gathered in the tarred-wood Mission Hall. One stricture among these working folk involved keeping the Sabbath. Working for pay on that day was unforgivable. One fisherman did the unforgivable, however. His wife was sick, they were poor, and he needed money to pay for a doctor and medicine. He sold his Sunday catch. The village refused to speak to him. Haldane and his wife heard the story. The fisherman had acted out of necessity. He deserved exemption. Starting with their landlady, Mrs Pender, they visited each house around the Cove to persuade the villagers to change their minds. Haldane worked some of these holiday days himself, assuming the role of doctor and administering to the sick who were too poor to pay. The nearest regular doctor was 7 miles away, in St Just.

Puffins darted low across the water while black shags and gulls flew screaming over the great twin Brissons rocks out in Sennen Bay. A lifeboat was stationed in the village, and once a week a boat went out to the Longships Lighthouse.

'Now now now,' Haldane said, as a swell came in on one such outing, and one of the rowers smashed his oar against the lighthouse rocks. It was the same caution he uttered when his son Jack grew overheated in the pursuit of laboratory experiments. 'Now now now, go easy.'

The boatmen were none too keen on Haldane's discomfort. The next time their boat was heading out, they threw a handful of gravel up at Kathleen's open window. 'We won't call the doctor as 'tis fairly rough,' they explained, 'but you and Missy us'll fetch along and welcome.'[8]

The courage Haldane showed in his scientific pursuits seems sweeter when you know that bravery wasn't his default setting. Kathleen had to restrain him from nagging the children whenever they approached a cliff, trying to instil them with his own intense fear of such drops. Haldane only overcame his vertigo by shrouding it in darkness such as is found in a pit. To balance the cliffs of Sennen, there were the caves. Haldane thrilled to such sniffs of an underground world, taking special delight in leading his family down an old mine on the point of Cape Cornwall where an occasional wave would submerge the entrance and pour along the floor.

Son Jack was given an exceptional hands-on education in the working life of a field scientist. He was taken down Dolcoath mine, and then in order to gain some points of comparison was taken by Haldane to the Glencraig Colliery near Loch Leven in Scotland. This was 1902. The new century was revving up with a vengeance. Mr Wilson, the mine owner, took father and son on a very early car ride through the Yetts o' Muckhart. 'We didn't break the law badly,' Jack noted in his diary, 'as we only once, I believe, reached 24 miles an hour! However we averaged about 17 on level ground.'

Life with his father was set to get much more dangerous that that.

Striding through the hills of his native Scotland, Haldane knew that tantalizing feature of mountain climbing: you

reach one apparent summit only to find higher ground in
view. His progress through science was much the same: espy
one new challenge, tackle and conquer it, and you simply
find a fresh challenge staring you in the face. Working at the
interface of man and extreme environments brought Haldane
up against the nature of working in excessive heat. The situation would be of active interest to him right up to the end
of his life. For Cornish miners, he noted, 'the heat is probably as trying as in any place where men have to live and
work'. He studied not only their working conditions, but
their methods of coping with them. Horses would often die
of apoplexy in the hottest mines, but then they had few
options of adapting. Haldane found that the miners, on the
other hand, even in the very hottest places, did not allow
their temperatures to rise 'more than very slightly. What they
did was simply to come out and rest in a cool place as soon as
they felt that they were getting too hot. In fact they seemed
to be nearly always resting in this way! At a wet-bulb temperature of about 27 the amount of work done by a miner
begins to fall off, and as the wet-bulb temperature rises further the work done gradually diminishes to a vanishing
point.'

Unlike the pit ponies, miners were 'perfectly free to follow
the promptings of nature – for instance, to take off their
clothes, stop working, or go into a cool place or even into
cool water when they are too hot'.[9] Haldane's work on a
commission for the ventilation of factories had also shown
him the extreme heat conditions of the cotton and flax textile industries. In a resultant paper, published in *The Journal of
Hygiene* which he co-founded and edited in 1905, he told
how his research applied to 'many other occupations, such as
work in the stoke-holds and engine-rooms of steamers, in

drawing the ovens used for firing potteries, in the drying of salt, etc. where men are exposed to high temperatures'.[10]

The first two of Haldane's heat experiments happened down the tin mine in Dolcoath, his son Jack beside him. Being just eleven years old, Jack had something of a canary's role, succumbing to the effects of mild exercise at high temperature much more quickly than the adults. One of the principal differentials of Haldane's tests was between wet-bulb heat and dry heat. Wet-bulb heat was discovered by wrapping a piece of wet cloth around the bulb of a thermometer. In very dry conditions a dry bulb may measure 110 ° degrees while the wet bulb measures just 70°. Wet-bulb heat is the hardest to work in. When the air is saturated with water, it means that though we sweat, that sweat does not get a chance to evaporate. It merely runs down our bodies. To evaporate a gram of water at body temperature takes about 576 calories. Evaporating 5 litres of sweat could get rid of 2,900 calories a day. Talking to a group of students, Haldane later recalled:

In Cornwall, near Land's End, there is a mine which runs under the Atlantic, and there was excessive moisture, which to the unwary stranger was like a death trap. An old manager at this mine never went underground himself, but welcomed all visitors at the office. This man said to me, 'The one thing you have to take care of is that you don't get cold coming up, and you must put on thick flannels.' That first time I put on thick flannels, but never afterwards. I had a thermometer with me. My temperature was 104. The miners there had practically nothing on, and did very little work. They were quite happy, healthy, and knew the mine. That mine had rich lodes of tin, and they could afford to do things in that way. Acclimatization is largely a matter of learning not to do too much.

The students laughed.

'I'm not joking,' Haldane persisted, though of course he had won the laughter deliberately. 'You have to learn, and on noticing symptoms of discomfort, stop working. I know when my temperature is about 103 I get sick of what I'm doing. The miners also got to know that pretty well, and consequently their temperatures did not go up.'[11]

Charles Blagden (1748–1820) was an early pioneer in surviving heat-filled rooms on behalf of science. In January 1774 he and some colleagues were invited 'to observe the effects of air heated to a much higher degree than it was formerly thought any living creature could bear. We all rejoiced at the opportunity of being convinced by our own experience of the wonderful power with which the human body is endued, of resisting an heat vastly greater than its own temperature.'[12] Blagden took a steak into a room heated to 260 °F and stayed in it for over three-quarters of an hour, by which time the steak had been baked to hardness. Haldane's own experiments saw him locked at high heat in the moist atmosphere of a Turkish bath. Dry air he could withstand to an astounding high of 300 °F, though if he moved about too much his hair began to singe.[13]

On 19 July 1905 Haldane worked alongside his young colleague C. Gordon Douglas. After half an hour's work in a temperature of 99 °F dry bulb and 88 °F wet bulb, Douglas gave up, with a rectal temperature of 102.4 °F. Haldane continued for a further half-hour. The previous month Douglas had lasted for 22 minutes in a room at 165 °F dry bulb and 98 °F wet bulb. Haldane worked on for 55 minutes.

His work showed that air movement played its part in controlling a body's temperature. Some movement helps to evaporate sweat. When the air is very hot, just the slightest breeze has the required effect, whereas a wind will in fact heat a body. His conclusion that, in still air, it is the wet-bulb temperature that makes hard work practicable or not was a groundbreaking physiological observation on which subsequent safety regulations for workers in hot environments have been based. It is a prime example of Haldane's belief in the interaction of an organism with its environment. The wet-bulb temperature does not simply give a bald statement of what a temperature is, but states how it feels. It provides a measure of the stress of working in hot conditions which is as relevant to military exercises as it is to deep mines. As the wet-bulb and dry-bulb temperatures draw closer, the strain of the heat increases. Different physical activities cause different effects. Air movement makes a difference, as does clothing. Nothing can be seen in isolation.

If workers in hot surroundings lose interest in their tasks, find it hard to stay focused, want to move somewhere more comfortable and grow irritable because they cannot, they are not simply being moody. They are showing early signs of heat stress. Such stress reduces work rates, makes accidents more likely, and ultimately can lead to heat stroke. Haldane entered zones where the interplay between human physiology and the environment was at its most extreme. He faced a world in which men were treated as machines. His deeper insight into the human condition introduced practical measures for improving health, productivity and safety. Military personnel, exercise physiologists and industrial engineers now implement something called the Wet Bulb Globe Temperature (WBGT) to gauge heat stress and set firm boundaries on what they require of those people under their care. The National Weather Service in the USA uses a 'Heat Index' to alert citizens to the actual risks of hot weather. These all stem from a century of physiological work building on Haldane's early insights.

Physiology was blind in so many areas. As regards metabolism, for instance, Haldane found:

> One gets the oxygen into the lungs, & the food into the intestine, & then there is a huge gap, or rather series of gaps, in the physico-chemical theory, till the CO_2, urea, heat, & mechanical work leave the organism. It is like trying to make a single map from a series of surveys, each starting from a different point, the relation to one another of these different points being quite unknown, & the different surveys never quite succeeding in meeting.

He drew guidance for his own map-drawing from 'the great central fact that an organism maintains & asserts its identity in exactly the same way in the domain of physiological activity as in that of anatomical structure'.[14]

For Haldane: 'The aim of the science of physiology is to deliver general principles which shall enable us to *predict* the behaviour of the living body under varying physiological conditions.'[15]

One aspect of 'why we breathe' was known. We do it to absorb oxygen and discharge carbon dioxide. But what triggers that breathing? Why does the brain keep pulsing the message 'Breathe!' along the nerves to the breathing muscles?

To answer the question, Haldane came up with one more invention. He built a wooden box shaped like a coffin, indeed termed 'the coffin', and one of the first occupants of the coffin was son Jack. A rubber collar allowed the occupant's head to be outside the coffin while keeping the box itself airtight. As the man or boy inside breathed in, his chest expanded. This pushed air out of the coffin through a tube, which made a drum outside rise. When he breathed out, the chest deflated and air was sucked back in. This lowered the drum. A lever attached to the drum inscribed the effects on smoked paper. For the first time, records were kept of exactly how much air a man breathed. And it could be seen how different mixtures of gas administered to the experimental subject affected the process.

Add just a touch of carbon dioxide to the mixture, and the recipient is unlikely to notice. The measurements of inhalations in the coffin, however, were much more sensitive. That extra touch of carbon dioxide stimulated deeper breathing. Take away some small degree of oxygen, on the other hand, and the coffin measured no change to the breathing whatsoever. The conclusion? Breathing is stimulated not by oxygen, but by carbon dioxide.

In 1885 the German physiologist F. Miescher-Rüsch had guessed as much, using currently available data. A brief poetic flight closed his discussion: 'So carbon dioxide spreads its protecting wings over the oxygen needs of the body.'[16] Haldane's work twenty years later was designed to give the first quantitative description of carbon dioxide's role. With his colleague J. Gillies Priestley he took his equipment to the top of Ben Nevis in the Scottish Highlands, the highest mountain in Britain at 4,406 feet (1,343 m). The aim was to test the air deep inside the air pockets of the lungs, known as the alveolar air, working on the assumption that the carbon dioxide pressure there was the best expression of its pressure in the arterial blood. Carbon dioxide is a small molecule and highly soluble. When blood flows through a lung the transition of these molecules from capillary blood to the air pockets in the lung (the alveoli) is rapid. Testing the air from these lung pockets for carbon dioxide is therefore equivalent to testing the blood. Sampling from close to the mouth, Haldane's apparatus snatched the last of the air from a full expiration, this being the air from those lung pockets, the alveolar air. Having found the carbon dioxide levels in this air to be constant, though the levels of oxygen varied, he wanted to test it at different atmospheric pressures.

From Ben Nevis they took the same test at 2,042 (622 m) feet below sea level down Britain's deepest mine, Dolcoath. Comparing the statistics from both, alongside test results from Oxford and from a low-pressure chamber in London's Brompton Hospital, they found the same weight of carbon dioxide in a given volume of alveolar air whatever the barometric pressure, though the percentage was larger in the thin air of the mountain top. From this they could judge that the amount of carbon dioxide dissolved in the blood also was a constant, and recognize that it was carbon dioxide that triggered the brain to send its 'Breathe!' message along the nerves.

A sequence of tests in a closed box and with breathing apparatus saw Haldane test the limits where breathing was affected not by excess of carbon dioxide but by lack of oxygen. Further work on especially constructed exercise machines saw Haldane and Priestley begin to grapple with the problem of what causes an increase in ventilation during muscular work. Achievements in science were never a crowning glory, but steps along a continuum, building from the work of earlier scientists, and opening the way for scientists of the future.

not the same thing

Haldane considered the resultant paper he published with Priestley to be his most important. His work in this field would become known to science as 'The Haldane Effect', the rule that increased oxygenation of haemoglobin promotes dissociation of caarbon dioxide.

Essential to the investigations were his inventions of new apparatus, including that for measuring gas inside the lung. In 1963 it would be recorded that for half a century his 'blood-gas techniques – the Haldane gas analysis apparatus, the Haldane haemoglobinometer and the ferricyanide method for estimating oxygen (and carbon monoxide) in blood – have been in use throughout the world, and the total amount of useful knowledge which has been accrued through them must indeed be incalculable'.[17]

As his father worked to broaden the known parameters of his science, young Jack alongside him was gaining the sort of education Haldane had been driven to Germany to find. Later in his own career he would pick up his father's baton and work on how carbon dioxide acts on the blood to trigger breathing. Perhaps it made the blood more acidic. If acidity in the blood changes the breathing, then make the blood more acidic and test the results. One ruse was to drink hydrochloric acid. More effective was drinking a solution of ammonium chloride, not so strong that you vomit, and not so much that you die. 'An ounce or two of ammonium chloride liberated enough acid to make me very short of breath. I panted for several days on end, and a number of curious things happened in my body with which I need not trouble you.'

As well as a taste for poisons and self-experimentation, his father demonstrated what wild fun could be found in taking physiology into fieldwork. 'If we want an answer from nature we must put our question in acts, not words. And the acts may take us to curious places . . . that is one of the things I love about science research. You never know where it will take you next.'[18]

For the young boy Jack, it was about to take him to sea.

10

BUBBLES IN THE BRAIN

Family hunting parties at Cloan found great sport in clubbing rats and chucking their bodies into the sty of the sow. That great creature crunched their bones while their tails hung from the sides of her mouth.

From the joys of rat-bashing on the Scottish estate, Haldane's pursuit of the creatures went global. A particular concern was possible invasion of Britain by plague rats, evacuees from plague-infested areas of India. In 1900 Haldane examined the holds and corners on ships of the P&O line for possible rat hiding places. Since they could easily swim ashore or run out along the mooring or anchoring ropes, or conceal themselves in the cargo, these were near-impossible creatures to control.

The plan was to attack the rats with carbon monoxide as plague-infected ships came into dock. By October 1903 the French government had an alternative plan in place to release sulphur dioxide, and Haldane was invited to report on the procedure. The outing became a family jaunt, Kathleen and Jack joining in for a trip from Tilbury to Dunkirk on the

SS *Bavaria*. Haldane told his sister the trip was 'a great success. There was rather a bad storm the night we started, but we got into a sheltered corner in the Downs and anchored there. K. and Boy weren't even slightly sick.'[1]

The SS *Bavaria* was a cargo ship from Calcutta carrying jute, linseed and poppy seed. Her captain and officers were all from Glasgow, her crew Indian. A yellow flag flew to denote her infectious origins as she entered port, where a member of the Institut Pasteur came on board. Haldane's brain assured him he had crossed to mainland Europe, so he switched to his default language. '*Ach mein lieber Kollege!*' he exhorted the Frenchman.

A rubber hose joined the ship to a barge, on which an iron furnace had been specially constructed to burn sulphur. Sulphuric acid accounted for 15 per cent of the resultant gas, together with residual nitrogen and sulphuric acid in suspension. The latter made it white and opaque, heavier than air so that it dropped down into the further reaches of the hold space. A return hose brought air from the ship back to the furnace.

After an adequate interval, the hatches were opened. Jack joined the Muslim crew in a competition: hold your breath against any sulphuric clouds, enter the forecastle, and see how many dead rats you can collect.

Jack was paying his way through his friendship with the crew, able to report on their psychological reactions to having their home at sea gassed. They seemed quite cheered by the fact. His next highly unofficial job was to test the quarantine system. The boy dodged the fat sword-brandishing gendarme on guard duty, and ran down the dry dock. Now the ten-year-old boy experienced the especial power of French when heard on French soil. '*Ventre du diable!*' screamed the gendarme from on high.

Haldane stayed on board, checking for the effects of the gas not just on the rats but on mice, cockroaches, different forms of pathogenic bacteria, and the merchandise. Cockroaches and bedbugs stayed immobile for a while, but tended to revive. Some rats had found haven in the lowest reaches of the ship. His official report, published the following year, foresaw such gassing being used only in critical cases where plague had occurred on board, and recommended the addition of a little carbon monoxide to the mixture.

As with all such issues, Haldane never fully let them go. A family story remembers a plague rat that travelled back with him from the Lister Institute to his Oxford home, sheltered in a paper bag in his pocket. After plague rats were reported at the Grand Hotel in Glasgow, Haldane insisted on staying there whenever he passed through the city, on the slight but ecstatic chance that a rat might expire in his bedroom.

For Jack the precedent was set. When Haldane was invited by the Admiralty to conduct work on the ventilation of their new submarines he needed an assistant, but the work was top-secret. Someone had to look after the soda-lime necessary for experiments, but he couldn't simply trust the matter to a regular laboratory assistant.

As his father mused aloud on the difficulty, Jack stood first on one leg, then another. His mother frowned to keep his excitement in check, and raised a finger to her lips. Finally she asked: 'Why not take Boy?'

'Eh, what? Is he old enough?' Haldane turned to his son. 'What's the formula for soda-lime?'

Jack took a deep breath. His mind flashed across the constituents of the white granules: majority calcium hydroxide. Small parts of sodium hydroxide and potassium hydroxide. He rattled out the formula.

'Well, that would simplify matters,' said his father, after a moment's appreciation. 'But remember, you mustn't even *look* as if you know anything about it.'

Jack's bag was packed and father and son set off for Portsmouth.

When Haldane and his sister Elizabeth were treading through the shrubbery at Cloan, sampling the air above the plants, they moved in the scientific footsteps of Stephen Hales (1677–1761). As with Haldane after him, Hales was an experimental physiologist, chemist and inventor. His career shifted from measuring the air to measuring the 'force of blood', and on to designing a 'ventilator', in effect a modification of organ bellows, to bring a flow of air to the likes of the holds of a ship.

Now Haldane, young Jack beside him, turned to the novel problem of bringing adequate ventilation to submarines. The mission was secret, but his brother Richard was soon let in on the nature of its success. Richard Haldane was regarded as the one prominent Liberal politician with truly considered views on the military, so with an eye to the future should his party come to power, leaders of the armed services sought to keep him informed of developments.

Sir John Fisher, an admiral and first sea lord, was busy overseeing radical changes in the fleet which included the development of submarines. Richard accepted an invitation to visit the admiral in Portsmouth, from where he wrote to his mother how he found his host to be:

a remarkable character, very original and very outspoken. He doesn't suffer fools gladly, and has plenty of enemies, but a devoted band of followers in the Navy. He took me to see one of the new submarines. Sir John Fisher was proceeding to tell me with pride about the white mice they had in the boat to indicate the presence of bad air when the commander said: 'Ah! Sir, you needn't tell Mr Haldane about bad air and mice. His brother at Oxford has taught the British navy all it knows on the subject.' I found Jonny to be greatly esteemed by the experts. Just what these new boats are going to mean nobody really knows. The young enthusiasts talk about eliminating the battleship, the old men wag their heads and say that the battleship had survived the torpedo discharged from a boat on the surface and there is no reason to suppose a torpedo discharged under water will make any difference. Clearly this new invention is only at its beginning, and as the French are hard at work developing them we must do the same, and I am proud that Jonny has had a hand in making this possible for us.[2]

Haldane himself found great relief in the Admiralty's readiness to speed his recommendations into effect. He was used to having more of a battle on that score. His work with Priestley led to their 1905 paper in which it was shown that regular breathing depends on the carbon dioxide pressure in the respiratory centre. One obvious application of this new knowledge was in the unexplored area of diving. Haldane proposed to the Admiralty a commission to investigate diving, and readily accepted their 1906 invitation to lead it.

Haldane's colleague from the Dolcoath investigations, A. E. 'Teddy' Boycott of the Lister Institute, was made his medical deputy. Haldane had taken his work to mountaintops and down the deepest mine. Here was the opportunity to investigate man's interaction with his environment at record depths underwater.

★

Deep-sea diving was not yet a sport. The Admiralty needed maximum work effort from men trained to drop towards the seabed. Their divers working at depths of 12 fathoms (72 feet) frequently reported exhaustion after 30 minutes work. In extreme and not uncommon instances they were hauled back unconscious.

Haldane suspected the symptoms might be due to an excess of carbon dioxide. From personal experience he knew that at such excess the gas was a narcotic and depressant. Taking samples from divers' helmets, then known as 'hats', after vigorous work at depth off Portsmouth, he did indeed find surprisingly high levels of carbon dioxide.

The French physiologist Paul Bert's (1833–86) work on the physiological effects of air pressure provided the platform for Haldane to build on. Bert highlighted not the physical but the chemical effects of pressure, in that it changed the proportions of oxygen in the blood. It is not pressure that damages the body, but differences in pressure, for example between inside and outside a diver's lungs.

At sea level, atmospheric pressure stands at 1. As you ascend, it drops into fractions. Descending through the sea, this figure rises. Following Bert's principle of partial pressure, Haldane pointed out that the carbon dioxide level would rise in proportion to the fathoms by which the diver drops below the surface.

Air reached the diver through a hose that connected him to a pump on the surface, worked by six men turning a capstan. Testing the pump, Haldane discovered a 57 per cent leakage of air. Any air that did get delivered tended to be hot and reek of oil. The engineer in Haldane turned to redesigning the pump for increased efficiency. He also showed how the amount of air pumped into the diver's helmet and suit had to increase in proportion to the absolute pressure, so the further below the surface, the more air was needed. Appreciating that the current pumps were not powerful enough for adequate performance at the greatest depths, he added a carbon-dioxide-absorbent canister to the diver's helmet.

One problem dealt with, a more serious one remained. Paul Bert had been mostly concerned with the effects of low atmospheric pressure on balloonists, but saw the value in comparative study of higher pressures underwater. Twenty-one dogs gave their lives to the research, as Bert exposed them to pressures of between 7 and 9¾ atmospheres then decompressed them quickly. He discovered that the cause of death was gas collected in the body tissues and the blood, and further analysis identified this gas as nitrogen.

Breathing compressed air (and air had to be compressed to be delivered through such pressure), the diver took in more oxygen and nitrogen than usual. The oxygen was burnt up, but the nitrogen was very soluble and dissolved into tissues, blood, and even bones. Fat is especially absorbent, and the oil in tissues like the brain and nerves allows nitrogen to dissolve easily. When pressure is lowered or released too quickly, the nitrogen emerges as bubbles. Bubbles in nerves cause pain and sometimes paralysis, the 'diver's palsy' in which the knees become paralysed. Bubbles in the blood can block lung or heart vessels, bringing loss of consciousness and, fairly quickly, death. In the most extreme cases, fragments of exploded brain had travelled up to the surface through the air pipe.

These symptoms were popularly known as the bends. Haldane used the analogy of uncorking a bottle of soda. Removing the cork lowers the pressure and the carbonic acid effervesces. The same happens to the nitrogen in the blood and tissues of a diver, the pressure lowering as he emerges to the surface. The hardest part of his job was learning how to unplug the cork without provoking the fizz. Regulations already called for a slow ascent of 5 feet a minute, believing that would give time for decompression. It didn't.

The Lister Institute of Preventive Medicine in London, founded as a British counterpart to Paris's Pasteur Institute and the Hygienic Institute in Berlin, offered one venue for the work. Ludwig Mond (1839–1909), a German-born chemist and industrialist who took British citizenship, ironically made part of his fortune through a process of developing the water-gas that Haldane had shown to be so dangerous, a gas Mond branded with his own name. Some of that fortune bought the Lister Institute a large experimental steel chamber that could hold several animals or men at one time. Haldane and Boycott needed divers on their team before beginning their series of experiments. Haldane 'did not want publicity-seeking "human guinea-pigs" but experienced divers with brains, courage and patience'.[3] He would find them on board HMS *Excellent*.

Born on the Isle of Wight, Lieutenant Guybon C. C. Damant joined the Royal Navy as a red-headed thirteen-year-old in 1895, and made his first dive in 1904. Diving was the province of gunners at that time, little more expected of them than freeing a caught propeller or scraping barnacles from the bottom of the ship. The Admiralty was just growing aware of the need for divers to do more, to go to the assistance of the newly invented submarines that tended to fall to the seabed.

The *Excellent* served as both a gunnery and a diving school. Damant's diving instructor was Warrant Officer Andrew Yale Catto, whose brother Lord Catto was to become head of the

Bank of England. Damant and Catto formed the diving team. Damant remembered his instructor as 'modest, shrewd and tactful. Haldane, a fellow Scot, took to him at once, and in all the underwater experimental work relied on Catto's practical knowledge to ensure that accidents, outside of physiological ones, did not occur.'[4]

The Navy worked on a 100-feet limit for its dives. The new team's first step was to gather records of deeper helmet dives achieved elsewhere. Greek and Swedish divers had reached 190 feet in Greek waters in 1904, inspecting the wreck of the sunken destroyer *Chamois*. This opened up the bounds of what was possible. The main task now was to work out how to reach such depths regularly, and safely.

Pigs have the closest physiology to humans, but a supply of goats was far more available in the London area. A goat's ratio of body mass to cardiac output was fairly close to that of a lean man. They were placed in the large steel chamber of the Lister Institute. Exposed to a high pressure of 6 atmospheres for a long time followed by sudden decompression to 2.6 atmospheres brought no ill effects to the goats. Few fared so well in a corresponding series of tests when the pressure dropped from 4 to 1.1. One benefit of goats to the observers was that they could show some signs of distress, slightly lifting a leg. Seeing this, onlookers could guess that bubbles had entered at the joint, causing some pain. The animal now needed to recompress from the bends.

Haldane attended relatively few of these experiments, which went on to feature men as well as goats. Sooner than teach him something new, the experiments were set to confirm his theories. These were informed by reading papers and data, talking to divers about their experiences, and that little flip of genius that seizes on one simple factor that others have neglected and therefrom extrapolates a universal theory. Many extended dives had happened in atmospheres of 2¼ or less, down to 42 feet, divers subsequently making rapid returns to the surface. None of those divers had reported the bends. It was therefore fair to suppose that the body could withstand saturation with nitrogen to this degree.

One step beyond that: take the observation that whatever the pressure, halve that pressure and the same volume of nitrogen gets dispersed. So if there is no problem for the diver when moving from a pressure of 2 to 1, thereby halving the pressure, might there similarly be no problem moving from 4 to 2? From 8 to 4? Rather than the slow ascent as practised, would divers not be safe with a staged ascent, stopping for a while at each point where the surrounding pressure has halved?

The revolutionary concept of underwater staged decompression, so vital for the safety of all divers, began as a logical deduction in Haldane's brain. Shifting the tests from the Lister Institute to open water found him thoroughly engaged in the experiments once again. A compression chamber was a known environment. The deep sea was a magnificent unknown. Besides such obvious factors as pressure and buoyancy, how did the cold affect a diver's ability to perform such delicate manoeuvres as might be necessary in rescue operations? Attached by a safety line, how could a diver maintain any control when his body was snatched and pulled by the currents and tides that swept and tugged at the British shores? Breaking all depth-diving records was one thing, but the Admiralty had no use for such records in themselves. Indeed when such records were broken by the Haldane team, again and again, they were never publicized. Divers were not only testing human physiology and man's powers of endurance, they needed to show how work could be achieved at great depths, how missions could be accomplished. Could they do so with almost no visibility? How could they avoid getting tangled in the boat's anchor line? How could those on board pump air against such intense pressure? The variables placed Haldane in his element, a study of how the human organism shifted and adapted to accord with the ever-fluctuating conditions of its wider environment.

In August 1906 HMS *Spanker* motored out off the Isle of Bute. Damant had never dived below 110 feet (33.5 m) before. On his first test dive he followed his instructor, Catto, down to 138 feet (42 m). The following day they sank to 150 (46 m). The *Spanker* moved on in search of greater depth, out through the Kyles of Bute to the entrance to Loch Ridden.

Haldane incorporated an extra factor in the tables he designed for the test. He divided the body into five separate 'compartments' or groups of tissues that released the nitrogen at different rates. Each of these compartments was given what he termed a half-time, either of 5, 10, 20, 40 or 75 minutes: the time it took in the same ambient pressure to become half saturated with gas. Those tissues that absorbed nitrogen most quickly would release it most quickly. The decompression tables had to take such factors into account.

The third day of dives saw Catto and Damant sink to 162 feet (49 m), then 174 (53 m), Catto then trying for 180 (55 m). Haldane had set tasks for the men to accomplish each time they reached their record depth. A special valve was sunk into their helmet, to which a rubber tube could be attached and air drawn off to gather a sample inside a glass collecting bottle. Haldane could then calibrate the various constituents of the gaseous mixture. The divers also had to simulate work conditions at depth. At 180 feet Catto took hold of a rope that had travelled down with him and pulled away at it. The action was similar to a bell-ringer's, except that the rope rose much further than the highest church tower. At the surface the rope curved round a block and was attached to a heavy weight, which Catto was required to lift, again and again.

The men on board struggled to turn the capstan to maintain the supply of air down to Catto as he pulled and pulled at his rope. They could not stop pumping for a moment, so others had to deal with desperate concerns. Catto's safety line had tangled with the lines of the *Spanker*. He was stuck on the seabed, pulling at his rope. They had to disentangle the line and haul him in. Somehow.

Twenty minutes passed. Catto maintained his exercise, panting now, his breaths growing shorter, his mind beginning to lose focus. He was breathing his own expired air, feeling the effects of carbon dioxide poisoning. After 29 minutes Damant finally managed to unravel his instructor's safety line. They hauled him in, by degrees, Catto hanging in the cold for each of the pauses in his staged decompression.

Man needs time to recover from such an ordeal. Tell that to a diver engaged in the most dramatic trials his profession had ever endured. Catto was back overboard the next day.

It was a novelty for Haldane to have his experimental test subjects encased in rubber clothing and a copper helmet. Besides the encumbrance of that outfit each boot weighed 20 pounds, and 40 pounds of weights were attached to the chest and the back. The total weight of gear was 155 pounds, heavier than either of the divers. With no tender as yet in the Royal Navy, the men had to carry this weight down the side of the *Spanker*, one rung of the ladder at a time, before the sea took on the burden of weight.

One recommendation of Haldane's committee was the use of a hoist to transfer divers to and from the water. Other changes to the diving regimen were introduced as the tests proceeded. Instead of the chest and back weights, Damant substituted a leaden belt. To prevent the suit from ballooning he added laces at the back of the legs.

In Loch Striven Damant achieved the deepest dive of the whole venture, which was of course the deepest dive of all time, a record that was to stand for the next eight years. He sank to 210 feet (64 m), where the pressure was over 100 pounds a square inch. Thirty-five fathoms down he worked the valve in his helmet to gather Haldane's air sample, and signalled to be pulled back to the surface. At 110 feet he paused and hung for a while, decompressing as Haldane had taught him, releasing some of the air from the sample bottle so that it did not burst under pressure. Man and sample returned safe to Haldane on the deck. The scientist's radical safety measures had been proven to be sound.

For Jack the trip up to the open-water tests in Scotland was to be a family excursion with his mother and sister. For two days he and Naomi explored the burns behind their hotel at Colintrave on Scotland's west coast, pushing up through dwarf oaks and birches, heather and high bracken, looking for the hillside sources of the trickles of streams. Then Haldane appeared. Without the necessary tables. Could Jack create such tables and graphs showing the rate at which nitrogen entered and left the various tissue groups?

Jack had no table of logarithms to simplify the matter, but set to the task on the hotel's drawing-room table. It was quite an exam for a thirteen-year-old boy. He passed. As a reward, Haldane promised to let him dive.

actually drew up the log tables?

'Jonny' Haldane in the girl's attire customary for infant boys, with brothers George (left) and Richard

Brothers George, John and Richard with their Edinburgh tutor Hugh Wilson

J. S. Haldane's birthplace and Edinburgh home, 17 Charlotte Square

Cloan, the family's Perthshire estate, home to the first private Haldane laboratory

Mary with her children Richard, Elizabeth and John (standing) in the doorway of Cloan

D'Arcy Wentworth Thompson, pre-eminent zoologist and lifelong friend

Ernst Haeckel of the University of Jena, one of many superb scientists Haldane encountered in his German University studies

J. S. Haldane (right) with Professor Thomas Carnelley investigating the air of Dundee's sewers, 1886

J. S. Haldane carrying son Jack (J. B. S. Haldane) in their Oxford home used for gas experiments, 11 Crick Road

Tylorstown Colliery. Haldane descended into the aftermath of its 1896 explosion to find why miners died

Haldane in action, using breathing apparatus of his own invention down a coalmine

Haldane introduced canaries into mines and invented this 'canary box', whose handle was an oxygen cylinder to revive the fallen bird

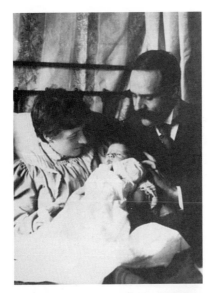

J. S. Haldane with his wife Kathleen and baby daughter Naomi, 1897

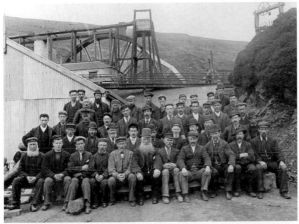

The Snaefell lead-mine disaster rescue team of 1897, white-bearded Captain Kewley at the centre

Drill workers in Dolcoath tin mine in Cornwall, prone to silicosis before Haldane's onsite investigations

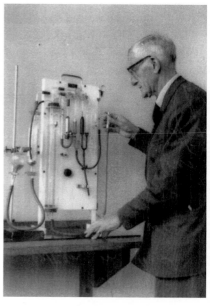

Haldane (right) down Britain's deepest mine, Dolcoath, where he found a lurking tropical disease

Haldane's gas analysis apparatus, demonstrated by his mining colleague J. Ivon Graham

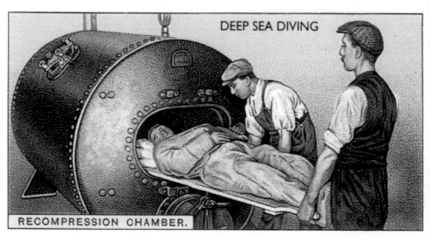

Haldane's great breakthrough in deep-sea diving, pioneering staged decompression and devising diving tables, helped spare divers from the bends and recompression chambers

The Oxford–Yale Expedition gathering high altitude data atop Pikes Peak, Colorado, 1911, C. G. Douglas wearing his 'bag'

Haldane was the Allied scientist sent to First World War trenches to investigate poison gas, and developed the first gas masks

Mary Haldane, bedridden and saintly in her old age at Cloan

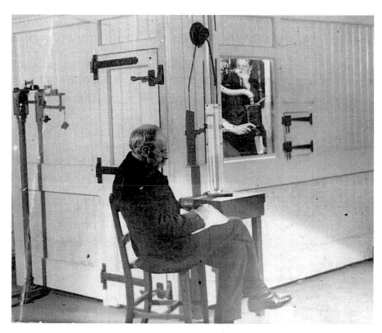

Haldane in his sixties, taking notes outside his experimental chamber

J. S. Haldane at Cloan,
Whit Monday 1933

J. S. Haldane and sister Elizabeth flying
the Middle East on the 'Hengist',
conducting heat experiments in his last
months alive, 1936

Haldane was always into improving efficiency of work as well as safety. Staged decompression, ascending to the point where the previous pressure has been halved, allowed for rapid ascent in the early stages, giving the divers more time to conduct their work at depth. So much had now been proved. Now Jack was to be offered up in the cause of increased naval efficiency. Naval ratings at the time were not allowed to go down 40 feet (12 m) without a month's training. If a thirteen-year old boy could sink to that depth on his first attempt, surely the training schedules could be shortened?

The Navy was also wasting valuable divers' time, in Haldane's studied opinion, by insisting on a slow descent. To disprove this need the final diving party would plunge as fast as possible. Increasing the test basis for this final lunge, Haldane added himself to the diving party.

Before watching Jack get thrown overboard into the fray, it is worth noting that his father was the first over the side. It was to be expected. This pioneering physiologist was never shy of experiencing new environments for himself. How could he appreciate the experience of a diving suit without diving in one himself? One factor makes this particular feat stand out. Haldane never learnt to swim. As a non-swimmer, he donned helmet and suit and stepped into the sea to prove it was safe for a man to sink fast.

Jack was placed in a compressed-air chamber on board first of all. Inside the human ear, a tube from one side of the eardrum leads to the outside world. From the other, the Eustachian tube leads down to the throat. It is important that this is unblocked when diving. In the chamber Jack was taught the technique of clearing his Eustachian tubes. Then he dropped into his diving suit, and climbed down into the sea. Since the purpose was to show the safety of rapid descent by untrained people, he was rushed to a depth of 40 feet.

His ears in fact hurt fit to burst, but didn't do so. Exploring the bottom for 30 minutes, he wrote to his grandmother of his discoveries, 'the same beautiful light green from the sky down to the dust clouds, or as one should say mud clouds, that one kicked up'. He failed to mention the gathering chill. The diving suit was an adult's. Jack's body was that of a thirteen-year-old boy. The suit was meant to be sealed at the cuffs, but his wrists were too thin. The sea water streamed inside. He worked the valves as well as he could, and was saved from drowning by the air pumped down to his helmet and chest. He was hauled up and the sea came with him, caught in his diving suit and lapping around his neck. Wrapped in blankets he was given whisky to warm him and laid down on a bunk.

Perhaps the speed with which the Admiralty put Haldane's recommendations into effect stemmed from his fury when incompetence brought a diver up too quickly. One such diver went black in the face and lost consciousness when he reached the surface. His helmet was screwed back on and he was thrown overboard again. This gave a chance for the bubbles to dissolve. Communication with the surface happened through an underwater phone line, or failing that through the tugging of your support line. The diver was soon able to answer the phone, and returned after waiting the required time.

The Deep Sea Diving Committee, of which Haldane was the scientific member, published Haldane's diving tables in 1907. The following year saw the Admiralty adopt the tables for all their divers, and publish them as a Blue Book for public use. They awarded Haldane an array of inscribed silverware that graced the sideboards at Cherwell. A more personal gift from the *Spanker* team was a pipe, its bowl shaped like a diver's helmet.

The townsfolk of Auchterarder, as ever, had a chance to be ahead of the game. On the evening of Monday 6 January 1908 the Secretary of State for War, Richard Haldane, came down from his home at Cloan to preside at the Auchterarder Literary Society. Guest speaker on 'Deep Sea Diving' was his brother John, who told how divers now felt no discomfort working at a depth of 210 feet. 'Great Britain now possesses a means of carrying out her diving operations such as is unequalled by any other country.'

In rounding off the evening, Richard noted how 'Dr Haldane has shown yet one more instance of the application of science to practical work, and of how necessary it is to prosecute the higher branches of science in the Army, Navy, and commerce, and all other spheres of practical activity. Work such as has been described results both in increase of efficiency and in saving many lives, and we are not yet aware of how many lives are being unnecessarily lost through lack of knowledge.'[5]

The US Navy adopted Haldane's dive tables in 1912, and used them till 1956, and all subsequent international dive tables have been based on Haldane's original. As with each element of his career, once Haldane was engaged with an issue he stayed hooked. With Sir Robert Davis of the diving manufacturing company Siebe Gorman he helped develop a submarine escape apparatus, and experimented with cylinders in which divers could carry supplies of air, the aqualung, or mixtures of oxygen and nitrogen.

In the last year of his life he would discuss with Damant the extension of his tables from one hour to infinity, allowing for a possible extension to eight hours for a caisson worker's shift. The discussion prefigured the introduction of saturation diving, where divers stay at depth for twelve hours or more.

Estimates of the number of divers currently active in the USA range from 1.6 to 2.9 million, with between 7 and 9 million divers active throughout the world. Haldane's work made every one of their dives possible. Each one of these divers was trained in the use of dive tables that derive from Haldane's original. Outside of its military and industrial uses, diving has created its own industry. Fifty thousand people work in the tourist trade related to the Great Barrier Reef alone, generating A$4.3 billion and hosting 4 million day trips a year.

Another booming leisure industry is wreck diving. While the scientist's work never stops, it's fair to let the sun set on this tale of Haldane at sea with a story from August 1919.

The 15,000-ton White Star liner *Laurentic* set out on her maiden voyage from Liverpool to Montreal on 29 April 1909. Triple steam engines drove the two outer propellers while a steam turbine drove a central propeller to give her a powerful turn of speed. In 1915 the needs of war saw the liner converted into an Armed Merchant Cruiser. In January 1917 she set sail from Liverpool for Halifax, Nova Scotia. Sailing around the north coast of Ireland on 25 January, she struck two mines laid by the German U-Boat U-80. Of the 745 men on board, 345 men were killed.

Guy Damant had retired from the Navy in 1911. The adventures with Haldane propelled him into new interests in life, which included work with J. B. S. Haldane on mine rescue equipment, and physiological experiments undertaken with A. E. Boycott. The war called him back to salvage duties. In the wake of the sinking of the *Laurentic* he was summoned to Whitehall and a meeting with several admirals.

These worthies doubted the Germans knew about their U-boat's success in sinking the *Laurentic*. They certainly did not know the Admiralty secret that made this ship's loss one of the most devastating blows of the war. Stored in a second-class cabin on board was £5 million worth of gold bullion (a present-day value of about £200 million). This was destined for munitions payments to America. Without that payment, the supply line of arms from America might well be shut down. The British economy could not sustain such a loss. Could Damant possibly lead a dive team to reclaim the gold bars? This was January. It meant dives of 120 feet in the rough winter storms of the Atlantic.

'I walked on air,' Damant remembered. 'I knew just what I wanted, and where to find old diving allies. It was quite a change for a dug-out lieutenant commander to be responsible to the Admiralty only.'[6]

The salvage operation set sail six weeks after the sinking, though bad weather meant regular delays. The *Laurentic* was located but found to have its back broken at its bilge. Its decks lay at an angle of 60 degrees, too steep for booted men to walk on.

A diver named Williams was one of the first to enter the ship. He was climbing down a staircase to the saloon when something bumped against him. 'It was a human body, and as my eyes grew accustomed to the light, I saw other bodies. It was a terrible sight. The unfortunate seamen's bodies were swollen, their eyes glaring and their hair drifting about.'[7] Worse was to follow. Observers on the diving vessel, the mooring lighter *The Volunteer*, spotted a German submarine. One man's life was not worth leaving the whole boat at risk.

Williams was dragged for seven miles as the boat raced for harbour. Hauled aboard unconscious, he recovered to be back diving just a fortnight later.

On the fifteenth day of diving a heavy latticed gate was blasted aside. Working in total darkness, Ernest 'Dusty' Miller used a chisel to prise open a steel door and entered the strongroom. His feet kicked against wooden boxes, 6 inches high and a foot square. In air they would weigh 140 pounds, and even underwater they weighed 85. Miller crawled and pushed a box to the portside opening, and attached it to a sling. He got the bends for his trouble, recovering in a decompression chamber, but the gold hunt was on. In two weeks they had recovered £32,000 worth.

A storm blew in from the north-west that forced them to port for a week. Damant looked out at the shore. Red and white rubber floor tiles washed up among wreckage piling up on the beach. Damant called in the boatswain rescued from the *Laurentic*, who identified them. They had come from the second-class smoking room. The *Laurentic* was breaking up.

Back at the wreck the team's mooring buoys had been swept away. The pressure gauge showed the first diver sinking ever deeper. The *Laurentic* had collapsed in on itself, the steel decks falling into each other. Damant put on his diving suit and went down, squeezing through the narrowed entry corridor till he found it fully blocked by torn steel.

Five decks now lay between the divers and the gold. For weeks the divers burrowed and blasted their way down, the gold room now resting on the seabed. From 120 feet, way beyond the Admiralty diving limit before Haldane introduced new procedures, the telephone report finally came back. A diver had reached the strongroom. 'The gold's not here, sir! It's gone. The deck is full of holes.'[8]

The gold bars had slipped to port and vanished as the boat's innards were torn apart. A new tunnel was needed, the divers blasting again, ropes hauling steel plates high enough for explosives to be slotted beneath them. After ten weeks of diving, hauling, blasting and burrowing the divers began to recover more ingots. The team worked for nine months, bringing £800,000 of gold to the surface. An urgent call to reclaim a sunken submarine pulled them away. The recovery operation lost some urgency when America entered the war, but gold has a strong call.

In 1919 the operation was revived, under the command of Guybon Damant, now with the rank of Captain. In August that year, thirteen years after their joint expedition that had made the wartime salvage possible, Haldane sailed out to observe his colleague's rescue operation. From Donegal he wrote the tale home to his mother.

We are on a steam yacht attached to the salvage ship from which the diving work is conducted. The wreck of the Laurentic is about a mile off the mouth of Lough Swilly, and the two ships run out there every morning if the sea is not rough. So far, we have had beautiful weather, though there is a pretty heavy swell at the wreck.

There is only room for three divers to be down at a time, and they grub about for gold ingots at one part of the wreck. It is more or less broken up, and a good deal of blasting has to be done to open out the plates, and they don't normally get more than 5 or 6 ingots a day, worth about £1500 each. One day last summer they got 220.

So far there have been no accidents causing serious trouble, but of course various things are always happening. Yesterday, for instance, a man was blown up from the bottom, and his pipe got foul of the propeller of a steam launch. However, he was got free very promptly, and sent down again before any harm came to him from his sudden rise to surface.

All the work is being done according to the regulations which I drew up about ten years ago, and which have proved very successful, so that all concerned have complete confidence. Work like this would have been quite impossible before, and attempts at it would have been excessively dangerous.[9]

Over 5,000 dives led by Damant ended in 1924, without any accident. All but twenty-five of the bars had been brought to the surface. Five of those bars were found by a salvage team in 1932. Twenty gold bars remain to lure twenty-first-century divers to depths Haldane first opened for them a hundred years before.

LIFE ON THE CHERWELL

On Sunday evenings at Cloan the Haldanes put on a performance for the servants. It was a play called 'Family
Prayers'. Whatever the private religious feelings of the
family, Sabbath-keeping was deemed a way of maintaining
the proper household order and keeping the servants'
respect. As Kathleen in her more agnostic Oxford household
used to say, religion, like the popular press, was for the
servants.

The large gong would resound from the entrance hall, and
benches of deep purple plush were brought in as seating.
Being the most senior of the servants, Mrs Cook the housekeeper entered first, wearing dark satin. The butler was next
in rank, other staff appearing by rank till the youngest kitchen
maid had taken her seat.

The family kept to their chintz-covered chairs, padded
footstools at the ready for comfortable kneeling. A small
table of plants marked the space between audience and
performers.

Audience participation meant sitting for the Lesson,

kneeling to pray, and standing to sing sad hymns in minor keys as Elizabeth accompanied on a black upright piano. The most senior available Haldane male was the star turn, reading the Bible passage and improvising a prayer in the proper Presbyterian mode. Not caring for improvisation, J. S. Haldane read from written prayers but with such a tone of surprise that they sounded improvised. His biblical selections reached into the obscure parts of Ecclesiastes or Proverbs, and they were long so that his listeners could appreciate the full rhythm of the prose.

A door from the hall led into the drawing room, 'the real social centre of the family', which gave one regular visitor the sense of 'being very much alive; and it had a good deal to say about the past and present of the family who lived in it. Distinguished ancestors looked down from the walls, their portraits reinforced by engravings, sketches, miniatures old and new, all in some way connected with the family. There were framed photographs: they might be of a grandchild, or of some special occasion, or the autographed likeness of a vis- iting royalty.'[1] Mementoes of Haldanes who had served the state were on display in glass cabinets. On one table lay the latest books, on another the day's newspapers. Couches and chairs with chintz covers were arranged to encourage a range of conversations.

The room was filled with flowers, and Elizabeth kept plants in a miniature glasshouse at the garden end which spread a special perfume through the room. Pleased with a newly painted ceiling, Elizabeth was not so enamoured of a party trick shown off one morning by a guest. The writer J. M. Barrie was a regular at such country-house weekends around the country, despite being 'a quiet, shy man who spoke very little'. He threw a penny carrying a postage stamp up to the high ceiling, where it is still stuck and on show a century later.

You had to be born a Haldane for admission to the New Year's Eve gathering. When illness kept Mary Haldane to her bed, this meeting was convened in her bedroom. Her two long plaits were tied with pink ribbons, a knitted bed jacket covered her shoulders, while her head was draped in lace and a feather-light Shetland shawl. Richard would address himself to God, delivering to the Almighty an account of what each of the Haldanes had been doing or thinking through the previous year. Mary Haldane then called a blessing down on each person present, and received their kisses. Reminiscences for 1905 included the death of Mary's brother John Burdon Sanderson.

Haldane had taken the train to Marseilles and then the boat to Algiers, visiting his uncle in his final run of illness. He wrote of 'the closing of a great life nobly lived . . . It is not in length of days though that the best lies. It is what has been lived in them while they lasted; and he lived his life up to his ideals and the limits of his strength – the utmost limit. That is fine and one reverences it.'[2]

A book of reminiscence of his uncle, which Haldane helped to edit, included fond anecdotes. Long walks in nature always rendered Burdon Sanderson young again, his tall thin figure striding off in its soft felt hat and Scotch plaid, the plaid whisked from his shoulders and laid over any barbed wire that lay in the way of his route. Drawing a magnifying glass from his pocket, he would swoop down to examine any interesting moss or stone.

Burdon Sanderson provided a whole run of absent-minded professor stories. One saw his wife Ghetal ask him to go downstairs and conduct their guests into the dining room.

Instead of guiding them through for dinner, Burdon Sanderson confused the order of events and helped the newly arrived guests back into their overcoats, bidding them good-night.

Like uncle, like nephew, for tales of eccentricity soon gathered around John Scott Haldane. Kathleen was keen to impress at her first formal dinner in their new Oxford home. The guests, thirteen or fourteen of them clad in evening-dress, were settled around the table when Haldane entered the dining room. 'Ah my dear a few friends to supper!' he announced. 'I'll just have a plate in the library if I may.'[3]

His family were never sure whether the high, starched collars Haldane wore at dinner would render him bad-tempered or not. His stiff shirts creaked and bulged, he had the devil of a job fitting studs through the stud-holes, and try as he might his white ties were never tied to impress. 'One never knew in what attitude he would confront the guests,' Naomi recalled. 'One day he found a made-up dish in front of him and asked his guests: "Would anyone like any of this? It looks rather bad!" Luckily everyone laughed. Or was that his intention?'[4] At another dinner party he wandered in, late as usual, and announced to the guests that he would return shortly, having changed into formal dress. He failed to return. Kathleen went off in search of him and located him in his bedroom. Finding himself taking off his clothes he had taken the next logical step. He put on his night shirt, and got into bed.

John Burdon Sanderson, a radical figure blazing a distinctive path in the field of physiology, had provided a compelling model for his nephew John. Professionally the relationship between the two men was sometimes fraught. They did not lack mutual admiration, but academic politics can warp even good family relations. Haldane's election to a fellowship at New College, Oxford, in October 1901 lessened the strain on the relationship somewhat. The first such election under a new statute, it came with no teaching requirements. 'It is the college I would most have liked to belong to if I could have chosen,' he told his mother.[5]

Uncle and nephew took long tricycle trips into the countryside, both finding balance for their working lives in the natural world. The river was like an extension of the university in summer, for private boat-owners or members of boat clubs only. Haldane frequently borrowed the Burdon Sanderson boat for rowing up the Cherwell, Kathleen holding the twin ropes for steerage. Maids would then come running to find him, the boat locked back in the boathouse and the key forgotten in Haldane's pocket.

On Sundays in the hall at Cherwell a large urn with a lamp lit below it delivered streams of hot tea for visiting students, while hot buttered scones were snapped up from a silver tray. Chinese willow-pattern plates hung on one wall, tiles by William de Morgan surrounded the fireplace, while a prominent portrait of Sir John Burdon Sanderson gave due honour to Haldane's uncle. Haldane made use of the dim light in the hall to pass some students unseen, 'especially the changing herds of Rhodes scholars' taken under his wife's wing as children of the Empire, instructing Naomi to talk to them 'in case they were sad at living so far from home'.[6] More formal occasions saw use of the 'spacious drawing-room; its bookcases and heirloom china; its cosy hearth and log fire; the huge, well-worn leather sofa behind the hospitable tea-table in the hall, to which guests drew up odd chairs and others sat on the stairs; the dining-room hung with family portraits, its solid early Victorian furniture and its views over a green field with its Jersey and Ayrshire cows at pasture'.[7]

The early years of the century saw a change of attitude at Oxford. Groups known as the Bloods, typified by the then 50-year-old Bullingdon Dining Club, exhibited a 'class arrogance', Naomi later recalled, 'which was becoming less and less tolerable in a society like Oxford, which was slowly changing into something fairly mobile class-wise'.[8] Still going strong a hundred years later, when the Bullingdon was described as 'a top secret drinking society' which 'draws its membership from Oxford's super-rich, enticing them to a life of secrecy, champagne drinking and ritualised violence',[9] they were satirized as the Bollinger Club in Evelyn Waugh's novel *Decline and Fall*. Haldane heard tales of how they broke into the rooms of intellectuals, several of them ganging up against one individual at a time, destroying books and pictures and delivering physical beatings. Disliking one particular don, they tore up his manuscript, destroying years of work. Bonfires or 'bonners' were regularly lit in the quads, into which they threw whatever they disapproved of. Since many of the Bullingdon Club came from aristocratic families, wielding political, social and economic power, the authorities were shy of reprimanding them. Haldane had no time for such a timid response. At each piece of news, Haldane would come out 'black angry at their anti-intellectualism'.

An antidote to the behaviour of the club was offered by the welcome the Haldanes extended at Cherwell to Ruskin scholars, generally either miners or the sons of miners. Kathleen was able to surrender her usually rigid class distinctions for miners, in the way she was glad to do for fishermen. Such people were suitably 'different'.

Of Haldane's working life at Oxford, Burdon Sanderson noted: 'Actuated by the highest motives, he possesses the power of attracting to himself the sympathy of younger men so that his motives become theirs. In this way he has exercised a powerful influence for good here.'[10]

Perhaps the greatest professor of all in terms of absent-mindedness was the Reverend Doctor William Spooner. As Warden of New College where Haldane was now a Fellow, he and Mrs Spooner became close friends of the Haldanes. The term spoonerism was coined to described his tendency to switch around the opening letters to words, so that a tremulous desire might become 'a half-warmed fish in my mind'. The one Haldane reminiscence of the man is more to do with absent-mindedness than words.

Haldane was generally the last to leave a dinner, in fervent pursuit of some line of discussion with his host, even while his wife and the hostess were blowing out the candles. Discussion during this evening at the Spooners' was more feisty than most, given that Viscount Milner was a special guest. Also a fellow of New College, Milner had not only been High Commissioner in southern Africa during the Boer War, his refusal to accept Afrikaner rights to South Africa rendered him the man most culpable for that war. Where Haldane found his heroine in Emily Hobhouse, Kathleen had her hero in this man.

Dinner ended, the Haldanes' carriage awaited them in Queen's Lane, and Spooner came with them to the top of the stairs. 'Be careful,' he cautioned, 'they're very slippery. I'll turn the light on for you.'

The light was on. Spooner turned it off. Faced with a flight of stairs in darkness, the Haldanes waited. Noting the sudden silence one of the Warden's daughters emerged from the drawing room. 'Ah, he does that sometimes,' she said, and turned the light back on.

Happy to have remained in his St Margaret's Road house, the arrival of Kathleen's newly widowed mother forced a change on Haldane. The mother-in-law brought with her not only a maid but the entire contents of her Edinburgh home. These included many large copies of old masters requiring lots of wall space, alongside hundreds of books, plus tables, chairs, china and clocks.

A local builder got permission to build on land beside the Cherwell. The effort involved in arranging and signing a 100-year lease from St John's College was as much energy as Haldane felt inclined to expend on the business. Mr Gardner the builder was keen to rush ahead without the bother of an architect. So be it. Haldane preferred to stay clear of the business side of life, entrusting all such aspects to his brother William and the family firm of Writers to the Signet. 'Well, well, well,' he reasoned now, 'the man got you the land. You have to let him build on it.'

A large and somewhat shambolic square house struggled upwards, its siting determined by the location of three grand walnut trees. With the place half completed, the Haldanes decided to lower the roof by 20 inches. It saved £200, steps between the two bedroom floors joining the different levels together. The house had one bathroom, its bath made of lead on Haldane's insistence – he didn't have to clean it, and liked the physics of its heat retention – and two toilets. The one immediately across from the entrance was the gentlemen's toilet, which women weren't even supposed to cast their eyes at. The entire contents of the Trotter home at 10 Randolph

Crescent in Edinburgh, admirably packed by the Edinburgh company Jenners, arrived in three railway vans. The huge weight made such a magnificent mess of the approach lane that rather than repair it, the local authorities engineered a proper road as an extension to Linton Road.

Once the house was built, its extension began. Reaching into the garden, though leaving a south-facing wall perfect for apricots, was the new laboratory. In what would grow to a triple run of rooms, the first was Haldane's original study, a seeming chaos of strewn papers from which he could somehow pluck out whatever he needed. A long wooden surface filled much of the next room, where two Bunsen burners were mounted. Here was where most of the glass-blowing was done to make the necessary tubes and vessels for the latest experiments. Shelves and cupboards made the rest of the room a storage space for appliances and materials. One step down from this brought you to the main laboratory room. Its windows looked out on to roses and peonies, while inside were sinks, a gas cupboard, working tables, and two steel chambers in which investigators could be sealed away for respiratory experiments. These private gas chambers allowed just enough room for modest exercise. Small windows let observers peer in at the levels of distress displayed inside.

Two small rooms eventually built beyond that were meant for storage, though in practice what were stored there were Kathleen's apples. The scent of apples coasting through the house added a hint of freshness to whatever the asphyxiate of the day happened to be. In Kathleen, Haldane had a stalwart domestic partner. The addition of a private laboratory gave him some real investigative freedom. If the university could not give him the domain he needed, she could.

Funding sources for the laboratory remain somewhat obscure, though his mother's donation of 'a further £100' towards its construction costs in 1913 suggests a round of private donations. Government funding was unlikely, since the Home Office refused the new laboratory a licence for animal experimentation. Haldane was using guinea pigs at the time to see the effect on them of breathing in stone dust. With or without that licence, he announced his determination to continue. If he was jailed, he promised to deliver a strike among the entire body of the nation's metalliferous miners, topped with the support of some mine owners themselves. The Home Office allowed the experiments to continue. Those few mine owners probably offered the laboratory some early financial support. From 1906 to 1911 Haldane was a member of the Royal Commission on Mines, concerned with issues of miners' health and safety.

In early January 1908 Haldane headed out on a sociological survey, visiting miners' homes in Scotland to report back on their conditions and their views. In his time in Westphalia he had seen the wonders of pithead baths. Mine owners were not especially opposed to their introduction in British collieries. On his many home visits and talks on the issue with miners and their wives, however, he found 'an almost unanimous objection' to the idea. 'I had hoped that at any rate the wives would have favoured the baths on account of the work and discomfort caused by the dirty pit clothes. To my surprise, the wives seemed more strongly against the pithead baths than the men. They feared that their husbands or sons might take harm, and seemed also to resent the idea that anyone but themselves should see after the washing and the clothes.'[11]

What they couldn't speak of to the fine gentleman was the

erotic charge of water steaming by the fireside, and wiping your man down to the white skin hidden beneath the black. Miners' skin was especially white for being hidden from the sun all the time. In houses crammed with the living, baths were a rare time when flesh on flesh was more than a scramble in the dark. Miners and their women did not want institutionalized cleanliness. They wanted this intimacy of touch.

The erotic charge of the miner's bath is powerfully evoked in Emile Zola's realistic novel of French mining, *Germinal*. A young boy growing up in Tylorstown recalled the ritualistic element of the miner's bath, the whites of his father's eyes and the red of his lips 'grotesquely vivid' against the black of his face forming his earliest memory of life. On Fridays the ritual changed. With help from his wife or his eldest daughter the father 'would wash his back, until that was as gleaming white as the rest of his body. The back was washed only that once in every seven days',[12] as was the habit with most of the local miners.

The miners and their wives disappointed Haldane too with their attitudes to their own housing. How come 'a very intelligent class of persons should acquiesce in living and overcrowding and discomfort of every kind'? They earned enough, yet would pay no more than two shillings a week for a house. No proper housing could be provided at such a rent.

Back home in Oxford that one lead bath stood behind a lockable door. Haldane's thin slice of a bedroom, cloudy with his tobacco smoke, stood across the hallway from his wife's. In 1907 Naomi, forced as a girl to ride side-saddle, fell when some cows charged round the corner in the grounds of her new home and startled her pony. Her foot caught in what was supposed to be a safety stirrup. The ten-year-old was dragged along the ground till the coachman could catch hold of the reins. She suffered a compound fracture. Her bedroom overlooked the river, not far from a little pigeon-house. Haldane had a board put outside her window, so that the pigeons could come and feed.

When the girl subsequently contracted TB her bed was moved. Until the day she left home to be married, she would sleep every night in her mother's bedroom. Supposedly the switch was to give her the necessary fresh air needed for recovery from TB. Since she already had a view over river and fields, that logic is somewhat warped. Naomi reckoned her bed had another purpose. Her mother had borne two children. Where love drove Haldane in the relationship, Kathleen was powered by a sense of responsibility. She had done her duty by sex. While Haldane knew not to cross the corridor to her bedroom any more, and he was a decent man, he was still a man for all that. If she lay there alone he might be tempted. No temptation, however, would let the man disturb his own daughter. With Naomi in her room, Kathleen could sleep safe at night.

For a passionate relationship, Kathleen had her green macaw. Named Polly, he was forty when he moved in to Cherwell and their relationship began. The Poet Laureate, Alfred Austin, was among the diners who admired the bird's dinner-table manners. The arrival of finger bowls was Polly's sign to climb from his perch and stand on the floor beside Kathleen, coughing up little balls of half-digested food. She took them as tokens of love.

Polly and Haldane had a more combative relationship. 'Will someone come and take away this ferocious bird,'

Haldane shouted. He was in socks at the top of a stepladder. A wild bird had flown inside the room, and was flinging itself at the high panes of glass in the window, and Haldane was reaching for its rescue. Polly, calling out as loud as Haldane in the fun of the game, pecked mouthfuls from the man's socks and stabbed at his heels. 'The funniest thing I ever saw,' Kathleen remembered.

Sure that no one but she would care for Polly, Kathleen wrote a most peculiar instruction into her will. Polly must not be allowed to grieve for her. He must be killed, his body laid in the coffin alongside Kathleen's so as to share her cremation. Taking matters into his own claws, Polly anticipated her by many years. He took a fit and died in the early weeks of the First World War.

While Kathleen had Polly, Haldane had a mouse. A cake and a plate of biscuits were left on Haldane's study table at night. Knowing the custom, a mouse emerged from the wall and climbed the table leg. Taking a few bites from a biscuit, keeping Haldane company in his midnight feast, the mouse then nudged a piece of biscuit off the edge of the table. It fell on to the black sheepskin rug to be carried away for later.

The mouse took up some of the affections Haldane used to lavish on Esk, a Scotch terrier. The dog was so beautiful that thieves loved him. Several times he was stolen, once being sold as far away as Cambridge, but the police always managed to return him in a few days. The terrier committed one crime of his own, killing a white kitten. The four children whose kitten it was decided Esk should be executed in punishment. 'John took them all up the river and spoke to them so wisely,' Kathleen recalled, 'that they told me afterwards that they understood it wasn't Esk's fault, in the same way that it would have been a boy's fault. They adored John from that day onwards.'[13]

The dog was three years old when the family disappeared to Edinburgh for Naomi's birth. It puzzled at the baby's subsequent appearance into their family unit, growling and trying to climb on to Kathleen's lap. She called for the vet, who recommended taking out the dog's canine teeth under anaesthetic. The terrier was taken away, and chloroform was administered. The terrier's growls ceased. It died.

'Nonsense,' Haldane shouted, hurrying back from the lab at the news. Kathleen had had the dog sacrificed 'in a useless panic'. It was no threat to the baby, he was sure, and such action should never have been taken without his permission. 'You don't understand dogs, and as to that old woman who says he is a veterinary surgeon! You said you were fond of Esk, but you have been cruel to him!'

Haldane's mouse had to make do without its midnight feast when the Senior Partner was away. During one such Haldane absence, Kathleen and Naomi were both struck down by measles. Kathleen, half blind with the effects of the illness, heard the creature running around the room, squeaking and scratching. Twice it ran up on to her bed, scrabbling its legs through the tresses of hair that were spread on her pillow. She called for the maid. The mouse must be fed. Food was laid on a trap. Grateful, the mouse took the bait. The trap snapped.

Haldane returned. His cake and biscuits appeared on his table, but no mouse came to eat, or to nudge its piece of biscuit on to the floor. He asked around.

Kathleen made excuses. The mouse was in her bedroom. Even Haldane was not supposed to come into her bedroom. Why should the study mouse have found its way there? It must have been another one.

But guilt showed on her face. Haldane had his verdict. 'You killed my mouse,' he declared.

One regular colleague in Haldane's laboratory was C. Gordon Douglas. 'To me, John Haldane meant so much,' he would later write, looking back to their first meeting in 1905.

> I remember when I began to read the First School of Physiology, I knew at once that I had met the man who was to be my master and I determined there and then that I would work with and for him if he would have me. In those early days he taught me, as no-one else could ever have done, the real meaning of scientific enquiry, and if I have done anything of merit I owe it to his patience and forbearance when I was but a beginner, and to his constant inspiration and interest, for I have only tried to follow those principles which I learnt from him.

Haldane's working presence in his Oxford laboratory, as the 'Senior Partner', was a solid inspiration to many young scientists. Douglas has a good go at enumerating why.

> It was not merely his genius and the amazing qualities of his mind which appealed to me; there was far more than that. I think every one of us who has been privileged to work with him has been inspired by a devotion and affection that can have been won by very few men. His sincerity and kindliness, his pleasure in our successes, his sympathy and help in times of difficulty, all these endeared him to us, and from him we learnt something of those high ideals which really powered his whole life, ideals which we could attempt to follow each in his own humble way.[14]

The 'Senior Partner' never needed to overplay his natural authority. Two biochemists in a London laboratory, 'one much younger and one very much younger' than he, were used to him dropping round to discuss experimental work. One day an accident saw the laboratory floor covered with droplets of mercury.

> Just then the door opened and Haldane came in. After a characteristically long pause, and a still more characteristic 'Oh!' (which those who knew Haldane will well imagine), he dropped hat and handbag (neither, by the way, likely to be much the worse for such treatment) in the doorway, went down on all fours, and continued to help us until the mercury was recovered. His whole action – the simplicity and directness of it, the readiness to help – was so characteristic of him.[15]

Haldane's colleagues were the lifeblood of his environment. His work in the mines proved to him the immense value of 'comradeship'. 'I have often been present at a colliery during some time of trouble or danger,' he once remarked, 'and it was this comradeship, from highest to lowest, that impressed me most. But whether or not unusual trouble is present, one seems to meet comradeship as one enters the colliery premises or steps into the cage.'[16] These younger men and occasionally women brought to bear in his laboratory their own factors of experience, skills and perception. In the interplay between the 'Senior Partner' and the other 'partners', science evolved. One of Douglas's own contributions to science, a rubber bag from which different mixtures of gases could be breathed, stemmed from his childhood in Leicestershire. However, as he explains, it took the interplay of conversation in Haldane's Oxford laboratory to bring that childhood observation into the realm of practical science – an explanation which incidentally illustrates the scientific background to being 'in the limelight':

> As a child I sometimes went to lantern entertainments given by the vicar of a parish in Leicester and was accustomed to see two large gas bags, the one containing hydrogen (or was it perhaps coal gas?) and the other oxygen, which were appropriately weighted to furnish the correct mixture for the lime light. When therefore during casual conversation at tea time in the laboratory some question about the determination of respiratory exchange arose the suggestion that expired air should be collected for a known time in a gas bag was only natural.[17]

Teddy Boycott at the Lister Institute, another of those young colleagues, monitored Haldane through an experiment in 1908. For twenty hours Haldane closed himself into a chamber with low oxygen to simulate high altitude. On emerging his tests showed a substantial fall in his carbon dioxide level, still persisting two days after the test. His tests three years earlier had shown carbon dioxide to be the primary agent in regulating breath. Now a longer period in which he had breathed low quantities of oxygen had increased his rate of breathing. This proactive role of oxygen challenged his earlier results. It needed to be tested.

Haldane had conjured an intriguing set of results out of a young man, Joseph Richards, who he learnt was heading out from the Dolcoath mine in Cornwall for the high mines of Bolivia. Richards received expert training from Haldane, and a haemoglobinometer for his luggage. Pricking a finger of his left hand he tested himself on the journey through Lisbon and Buenos Aires, and then up to 1,500 feet in Bolivia. Other miners, the foreman, the cook, all succumbed to such tests so that results could be sent back to Haldane. Besides these results Richards also relayed symptoms of altitude sickness. 'Now breathing, I think, is a very important matter here. Generally speaking an Englishman doesn't care for others to hear him breathing very hard – but I have often noticed that these people here when walking uphill breathe very loud. You can hear them from quite a distance.'[18]

In 1910 Douglas went out to Tenerife to visit two physiologists, the British Joseph Barcroft and the German high-altitude specialist Nathan Zuntz. They were completing tests at the Altavista Refuge at an elevation of 3,270 metres (10,728 feet) on the summit of Montaña Blanca. Built for mountaineers in 1892, the hut was so hard to reach, and conditions so primitive, that the scientists had been forced to take little equipment with them. Other equipment was scaled down to make it lighter. The sequence of restrictions led to inaccurate results.

Haldane's experiences sampling alveolar air on Ben Nevis had been bad enough. Unsurprisingly given conditions on the west coast of Scotland, his party were already cold and wet when they reached the summit. Their exertions clearly affected their breathing and hence the results. And some of their equipment, made of glass and so fragile, broke en route.

In 1910 Douglas accompanied Haldane on a visit to the International Physiological Conference in Vienna. Professor Yandell Henderson travelled to Europe from Yale University. Perhaps passing through the Austrian Alps stimulated their conversation, for Haldane mentioned his wish for 'a nice comfortable, easily accessible, very high mountain with a fairly good hotel on the top'.

Remembering his correspondence with Joseph Richards, Haldane thought the Andes offered the best option. Perhaps you had to be North American, like Henderson, to come up with a better response. A cog railway carried visitors up to the summit of 'America's favourite mountain'. In 1893 a professor on a summer teaching visit to Colorado College, Katharine Lee Bates, took the variant way to the top and hired a prairie wagon. 'Near the top we had to leave the wagon and go the rest of the way on mules. I was very tired. But when I saw the view, I felt great joy. All the wonder of America seemed displayed there, with the sea-like expanse.' Back down on the plain she penned the verses of 'America the Beautiful', set to become the 'second anthem' of the United States.

'Come to America next summer,' Henderson said, 'and we will spend a month or two on Pikes Peak.'

The invitation gave a technician at the Oxford laboratory a lot to add to the conversation when Douglas and Haldane returned from Vienna. Mabel Purefoy FitzGerald had been in Haldane's orbit for some years.

Fifteen years his junior, they were neighbours for a while without ever meeting, when Mabel and her freshly orphaned four sisters moved in next door to the Haldanes at 12 Crick Road. In the absence of her parents, her local doctor, a man by the splendid name of Dr D'eath, became her enthusiastic mentor. He recommended a career in medical science to her, starting with informal lectures in physiology at Oxford under Gustav Mann.

Women at that time were not allowed to study at Oxford; indeed, it was not till 1972 that the centenarian Mabel FitzGerald finally received an honorary Masters of Arts

degree in a full ceremony at Oxford's Sheldonian Theatre.
Haldane's former colleague Mr S. Pembrey refused even to
lecture to a mixed class. He felt 'so strongly about this point
that any attempt to override my conscientious scruples will
compel me to throw up my work immediately. To be forced
to teach ladies, who moreover are not members of the
University, would deprive me of the chief interest I take in
the efficiency of teaching.'[19]

Other than as one of four brothers teasing their sister,
Haldane had been very open to the admission of women to
the medical profession. As a student he declared that women
would be better than men at teaching obstetrics. On 18
January 1913, when the Physiological Society met in King's
College, London, Haldane proposed that 'it is desirable that
women should be regarded as eligible for membership of the
society',[20] and the proposal was carried on 23 January.
Florence Buchanan, a laboratory colleague in the early years
of the century, was a scientific pioneer who worked on plant
physiology. To the Haldane children she was Aunt Florence.
'She belonged to the generation of women scientists who
cared nothing for their appearance,' Naomi wrote. 'In addition she had a detached retina, which frightened me: she
came to lunch almost every day and I hoped not to have to sit
by her.'[21]

Mabel FitzGerald's eyes were firmly in place, and blue, her
light brown hair was pinned neatly, her dress sense immaculate without being showy, her nose long and her chin square.
Her brand of intellectual honesty was the type that saw her
once return a note to Queen Victoria, marked up for errors
of phrasing.

As the lab technician to Haldane, FitzGerald's physiological interests switched to respiration. Using the Haldane

apparatus, practising by measuring her own breathing every day for over two years, she developed such expertise that in 1905 her name joined Haldane's on one of his papers. Naomi and Jack became her experimental subjects, along with a host of children from Oxford's Dragon School which they attended. Among the adults were FitzGerald's sisters and Richard Haldane. FitzGerald's experiments became gender-specific to an unusual degree for her time, and led to her findings that women and children breathe more than men.

In 1905 Sir William Osler (1849–1919) succeeded Burdon Sanderson as Regius Professor at Oxford. While Professor of Medicine at Johns Hopkins University in Baltimore, he pioneered a system of teaching through clinical observation and subsequent laboratory work of the sort that Haldane had fought for at Edinburgh. His classic medical textbook inspired the founding of the Rockefeller Institute of Medical Research in New York. Osler took an interest in FitzGerald and recommended her for a Rockefeller research grant. Having worked on bacteriology in New York, she began a tour of the United States which she had first visited in 1901. 'Oh I am having a glorious time,' she wrote on a postcard to Haldane from the mountains of Colorado. 'The Rockies are all that I anticipated.'[22]

Henderson's invitation to Pikes Peak was eminently sensible to her. She had already ridden to the summit at dawn, and was able to tell Haldane of her first-hand experience. Her suggestion very likely led to the inclusion of a new member of the exploratory party, Edward C. Schneider, Professor of Biology at Colorado College, who brought with him access to laboratory facilities in Colorado Springs.

FitzGerald was just completing studies in the breathing of women patients at the Radcliffe Infirmary. Her expertise in measuring breathing and haemoglobin in large groups of people made her a perfect fit for the scientific adventure to Colorado. Funds from Yale and a Royal Society grant made to Haldane would pay her travel costs. As a 'gentleman's profession', however, physiology expected scientists to pay their own living expenses. With only two weeks to go, she found her funding. The remarkable Anglo-American Pikes Peak expedition was set to commence.

PIKES PEAK

Lord Haldane worked all the official channels in his role of Secretary of State for War. The UK's US ambassador had authorization sent from Washington. US customs officials at Montreal bowed to the inevitable and forced the railway company to take aboard the ghastly consignment, but on one strict condition. Whatever Haldane brought in with him, he must also take out. Five cases were carried by hand, five in the hold, and all the contents were highly dubious.

What did America want with 11 one-kilo tins of something called oxylith, for example? Or with 14 pounds of mercury, some plasticine, bile salt solution, a tin of ferricyanide of potash, carmine solution and Hayem's solution, and four tins of soda lime? What respectable travellers carried with them a straight rubber mouthpiece, nose clips, wedge-shaped gas bags, a steelyard and seat, a wooden work machine, one enamelled iron and one copper water bath? How come so much of the equipment was classified under the traveller's own name, so that there were three Haldane gas analysis apparatuses, three Haldane–Barcroft blood gas analysis apparatuses, and three Haldane haemoglobinometers? As if continual references in the inventory to blood and gas were not enough, the man was set on filling bottles with sulphuric, nitric, formic and strong hydrochloric acids.

Stretching the immigration officials' bounds of acceptance to the limit was the travellers' destination. They were hauling this vast array of what a newspaper termed 'delicate instruments of a secret nature' to the summit of a Colorado peak.

Douglas and Haldane settled themselves into the Plaza Hotel in Colorado Springs. Based on the northern edge of the city, next to Colorado College, the view west across the plain presented the two men with the broad vista of their destination. This was the view yearned for by early pioneers heading west in their wagons, known as 'prairie schooners'. The pioneers of Californian goldmining headed for Ute Pass, which curved round the mountain's base, coining the phrase 'Pikes Peak or bust!' Lieutenant Zebulon Pike came across the mountain in 1806, his ascent falling short at 10,000 feet (3,050 m), from where he looked up, declared the summit unattainable for any human being, and bequeathed it his name. Colorado Springs already lay at 6,000 (1,830 m) feet above sea level. Pikes Peak reared up above that for a further 8,000 feet (2,440 m).

The plain shimmered in July heat, Haldane and Douglas striding across it in square-toed shoes, tweed suits, powered forward by their walking sticks. Mary Haldane's birthday money for her 51-year-old son bought him a raincoat for the variable weather atop Pikes Peak. Part of the men's routine for five days was designed to acclimatize them to what was already a relatively high altitude. Their walks took them through the Garden of the Gods, dedicated as a city park just the year before, where red sandstone rock had been carved by erosion through 300 million years. Paths led between these vast forms of natural sculpture, and onward to the town of Manitou Springs.

Long sacred to Native Americans for the healing powers of its mineral waters, replenished by snowmelt from Pikes Peak, 'Manitou' is a Native American word for 'spirit'. Towards the end of the nineteenth century America's new inhabitants started to come for the cures. Manitou Springs was especially noted as giving relief to tuberculosis. When this inter-nationally famous lung doctor arrived to conduct secret experiments on a mountaintop above the town, such were the expectations surrounding his visit that Haldane had to go into denial.

'Don't think that this exploration is merely to find a remedy for tuberculosis,' he reprimanded his inquisitors.

That is a mistaken impression. Our work is deeper. We wish to learn conclusively the effects that the changed pressure of the atmosphere has on the blood of the human being. You've noticed that when a person makes a sudden change to the atmosphere of lightened pressure, his face becomes blue and he breathes in gasps and jerks. Our object is to determine just why this is and what causes it. Scientists call the changed breathing the Cheynes-Stokes effect. The cause of this has always been a source of interest and wonder to scientists. In six weeks' time we hope to discover the reason for this and to make a satisfactory report – one that will stand – to the Royal Society.[1]

The route for their expedition was laid following a visit to Manitou by Zalmon Simmons, who ran the Simmons

Mattress Company, the largest of its kind in the world. A two-day mule ride took Simmons to the summit of Pikes Peak then back down to relax in a mineral bath, a great place for daydreaming. His daydream saw him wish that others could share the magnificence of the summit view without sharing the aches and strains of mule riding. Hearing of the possibility of building a cog railway, he embarked on an audacious round of fundraising. The summer of 1891 saw the first coachloads of visitors hauled to the summit.

Cog railways mesh a gear into a special rack rail, so as to engage with the steep gradients of a mountainside. The Pikes Peak and Manitou Railway tracks through 8.9 miles on its journey as the highest railway in the northern hemisphere, and the highest rack railway in the world.

Hummingbirds flew around the base of the railway when Haldane and company climbed aboard on the morning of 12 July 1911. They were guests of the railway, having been issued with free passes. A steam engine at the rear of the carriage shunted the party up alongside a mountain stream, and through the boulder fields of the early miles. Up through ponderosa pine and Colorado blue spruce and the gradient grew gentler for a time, the halfway point of the journey opening up the first sight of Pikes Peak, still up and over to the right. Aspen and Douglas firs shrank to ancient knee-high versions of themselves, and then the slopes were bare. Trees on this slope twisted and bent gnarled boughs. Some bristlecone pines gripping at life on this mountainside were more than two thousand years old. At 12,000 feet (3,660 m) Haldane and company had left the timberline behind, C. G. Douglas nursing the first stirrings of headache. They had entered a region of Alpine tundra, rock marked just occasionally by mosses, grasses and tiny flowers. Already they noticed the chill. For every thousand feet of their ascent, the temperature had dropped 3.5 °F. Even in sunlight the summit was 30 degrees colder than the Manitou base. The climb was now steep, the train managing its maximum gradient of 25 per cent. Yellow-bellied marmots, bulky ground squirrels as big as piglets, had time to break from gazing into the sunrise, cross the tracks and drop into their burrows.

The train pulled up beside Summit House, a two-storeyed stone building. Nowadays some low broken walls survive as a historic landmark, for the foundations of buildings on the summit sink into the permafrost. In 1911 an iron tower crowned one end, and beneath this were the four rooms assigned to the expedition. Owned by J. G. Hiestand, who also ran an establishment in Manitou Springs and doubled up as the Pikes Peak official photographer, Summit House offered food and occasional beds to travellers.

Before ascending, Douglas had laid out for reporters something of the scientific goals and methods of their stay. 'In olden times,' he began, in full storytelling mode,

when investigators wanted to test the blood of man for its thickness of color, they merely had the king issue an order for a guillotine subject. The unfortunate victim placed his head upon the block and shed his blood for the sake of science. Our method is new. A drop of blood pricked from the finger of any healthy man in the party will furnish all the material we need to take from the human body. This drop is carefully tested, analyzed and the results noted. Then the subject inhales the fumes of natural gas, in measured quantities, and another drop of blood is taken. By comparing the two we can find just what changes occur when the atmosphere affects the blood.[2]

If only, poor man, it had all been that easy.

The party reached the summit at 11 am on 12 July. Already the altitude showed its marks. Haldane, Douglas and Henderson displayed periodic breathing, and all became breathless on moving about or unscrewing the cases of apparatus. The lips in all of them were more or less blue. Mabel Purefoy FitzGerald saw the party settled in then travelled back down the mountain. Her parallel quest took her to communities around different heights of Colorado, reporting her findings back to the scientists before descending on further respiratory quests.

Douglas's headache grew over the first night. He woke early, his head throbbing at the temples, nauseous, throwing up twice, quite unable to eat. The following morning his headache and depression were still accounted severe, not lessening till midday. His chief contribution at this point was the daily blood sample, taken from each scientist before breakfast then sent down to Colorado Springs for analysis.

Haldane too felt nauseous on arrival, suffered from stomach cramps and diarrhoea and did not eat on the first evening. He slept well though, and woke feeling quite fit. His stomach stayed somewhat troubled, his breathing stayed periodic and he was prone to panting quickly, but the colour of his lips soon became better than normal. For Mabel FitzGerald's first return visit on 16 July they were all able to put on a fine show of good health.

Life on the mountaintop was far from being hermit-like seclusion. Haldane reported how 'hundreds of people of the

most promiscuous kind come up every day . . . Those on foot
and on donkeys arrive at all times of the day and night. Some
demand to be taken in without paying, and there are consequent rows, occasional windows broken.'[3] The expedition
was not set up to collect data on the emotional changes
wrought by high altitude, but evidence of an unusual mass of
unreasonable behaviour led the scientists to judge that altitude
had left the visitors 'psychically affected'. The authorities certainly worked on the basis of summit madness. A deputy
sheriff was stationed on the Peak through the summer
months. On a private level the manager of the hotel, Howard
H. Robinson, was deemed kindly and helpful yet kept a
Mauser pistol to hand in case of emergencies.

Robinson also served as the scientists' exemplar of an acclimatized subject. He held the record for the climb up from
Manitou, covering the 8.9 miles and rise of 7,485 feet in just
2 hours 31 minutes. To that record he now added a fresh one
and entered the annals of science. Live within easy reach of
Haldane and you were always liable to have samples of your
blood taken for inspection. Robinson's sample astounded the
scientists. He had lived on the mountain for each of the last
twelve summers. Compared with someone at sea level, his
blood was 40 per cent richer in haemoglobin, and still 25 per
cent richer than those living at 6,000 feet in Colorado
Springs.

One of the scientists' four rooms was fitted out by a carpenter to form a highly workable laboratory, with shelves and
benches all around. A stove kept this to a temperature which
allowed for the delicacy of some of the chemical experiments
involved. Barbed wire formed a barricade at the separate
entrance door to keep out inquisitive visitors. No blood samples are recorded from the black chef, though his cooking

was reckoned to be excellent. Robinson served the meals in a separate room, adding tales of his adventures for extra spice.

A neighbouring room was full of tourists as the scientists settled into their laboratory on their first working day. They were already used to lightning and cloud, no longer startled by lightning strikes that others took for granted. Fear did jolt those tourists though, as a ball of fire entered the room and burst. Nobody was hurt, though the telegraph and telephone wires were smashed. Throughout their stay the scientists had times when they noticed electrical discharges from their heads or from their hands when held upwards.

Katharine Lee Bates took the view from the summit down to Colorado Springs with her, where she reproduced it in words for 'America the Beautiful':

> *For purple mountain majesties*
> *Above the fruited plain!*

The mountains from on top are indeed purple. The Rockies extend northward. Southward, the Sangre de Cristo range stretches into New Mexico. Westward lies the Continental Divide, and to the east a near-featureless expanse of plain reaching into Kansas. The grid system of Colorado Springs patterns the nearby stretch, Denver visible some 60 miles away. In some curious way, however, the view tends to pale through the sheer height of the peak. What might seem mighty from below looks relatively puny when seen from above. Pikes Peak commands great distance, but more impressive is its sheer sense of altitude. Air travel has perhaps made us blasé about the ability to ride above the world for a while. Afraid of cliff edges and visible heights, some consolation for Haldane lay in this aspect of immense altitude.

And at night, of course, the sheer drops from the mountain became hidden. As with his time underground, drops that Haldane could not see did not disturb him. The air was now at its clearest. He admired the lights of Colorado Springs, Denver and Pueblo – these latter two 150 miles apart.

Each day's work was vigorous. While the *New York Times* hailed Haldane as 'the moving genius in the work', Douglas was more accessibly admirable. 'Prof. Douglas offers a sharp contrast to his deliberate, contemplative chief. He is a type of the young, athletic Englishman, full of the cheery enthusiasm that enables him to surmount immense difficulties. It is he who has taken the long, exhausting climbs, and who has done the most strenuous part of the work to determine the effect of exhaustion on the unacclimated individual at high altitudes.'[4]

Tweed cap protecting his head, new overcoat guarding against the chill, stopwatch in hand, Haldane kept pace as Douglas took a 'hike' of a mile at top speed up a 25 per cent grade of the cog road just below the summit. Douglas wore a tweed suit and tie, his head sectioned by a strap that supported tubes connecting his mouth to the bag on his back. The aim was to measure the difference in the lungs' consumption at work and at rest. During the walk his lungs raced at four to five times their normal speed, each breath logged to be counted back in the laboratory where the bag's contents were analysed. A span on the summit where the track ran flat for 50 yards offered a level variant for experiments during vigorous exercise.

Yandell Henderson, though excessive smoking had given him a 'tobacco heart' that missed one beat in ten, was the most successful at avoiding altitude sickness. Within six days of the team's arrival on the summit a local headline declared

'RISKING LIVES IN CAUSE OF SCIENCE: Drs Haldane and Douglas Ill on Peak As Result of Severe Personal Tests'.[5] Henderson had taken the scientists under his care, the paper reported, and 'tacitly admitted' that the illness was not all due to the high altitude but 'to the severity of tests to which they are subjecting themselves'. The paper was in 'no doubt' that the scientists were 'actually braving death in their quest for information that will advance science and benefit humanity'.

A statement issued from the summit the following day denied severe illness. The high-altitude stay and severe exertions made conditions 'uncomfortable but not dangerous'[6] and sickness was yet to stop their hard work for even a single day. Dangerous or not, this hard work involved a daily intake for Haldane of measured amounts of carbon monoxide. He entered an airtight glass chamber into which air was pumped or extracted. 'The subject registers his sensations up to the limit of human endurance.'

From this mountaintop Haldane proposed to answer questions on such limits of endurance. How far can a man travel beneath the ocean? How high can a balloonist soar? He had explained the objects of these air chamber experiments before his ascent:

The atmospheric pressure at sea level is about 15 pounds to the square inch and the barometer will stand at about 27.28 inches. On the top of Pikes Peak the barometer will stand at about 22 inches and the pressure will be about 11 pounds to the square inch. The question is at what altitude will human life be impossible on account of the removal of atmospheric pressure. Some balloonists have died when their balloons got beyond their control and went to great altitudes. The question is at what height did they perish and what were the sensations they underwent and the symptoms manifested. By means of the air chamber we mean to determine some of these questions definitely.[7]

The reporters, quite reasonably, deduced that Haldane would bring himself to the very point at which divers and balloonists might die so as to be able to relate what it felt like. The whole basis of his self-experimental life in science stood on the need for such accurate reportage from such physiological extremes.

Haldane viewed the local press as 'wretchedly bad', his Scotsman's impression not helped by their terming him 'typically English'. Reporters streamed to the summit like a plague, and he once had to climb down half a mile to the rescue of one who had collapsed from mountain sickness. He administered oxygen to revive the man and sent him on his way. One bonus of the flow of visitors was a steady supply of unacclimatized subjects. The scientists took care of many who were plainly not fit to have even taken a stiff long walk, let alone rise to such altitude. The symptoms of those who walked or came up by donkey were 'more general and severe,' stated the official report.[8]

The blueness was more marked, and nausea, vomiting, headache and fatigue were extremely common. Many persons walked up during the night to see the sunrise, especially on Sunday mornings, and the scene in the restaurant and on the platform outside can only be likened to that on the deck or in the cabin of a cross-channel steamer during rough weather. The walkers struggled in one by one, looking blue, cold, exhausted and miserable, often hurrying out again to vomit. Some lay on the floor, blue and faint. Others were able to swallow some coffee, but very few had the heart to look at the magnificent sunrise.

Reporters were especially dense on the summit on 1 August. As Haldane tested human survival at barometric pressures only then envisaged for balloonists, two 'birdmen' had ridden the cog railway to the summit to hold a press conference. Phil Parmalee, a blond and baby-faced 24-year-old, was a protégé of Wilbur Wright. One of the first three men trained by the Wright brothers for their aviation displays, he rented a plane at $300 a day to amaze crowds in rallies across the country. The new biplane for this Pikes Peak adventure was called 'The Pike' in the mountain's honour. The most powerful plane ever produced by the Wright brothers, its wings could be warped so as to turn and spiral in one-third of the angle previously required. Beside Parmalee stood J. Clifford Turpin, taught to fly by Orville Wright and holding the 1911 world altitude record of 9,400 feet (2,865 m). The young men were spinning their own 'Pikes Peak or Bust!' dream, breaking the world altitude record by flying over the mountain. From Pikes Peak they looked not only down but up. Their press conference was something of a mute affair, the two men gazing around them 'in speechless wonder'. Parmalee was an 'unassuming fellow'. Would Turpin top the Peak in his machine? 'I had rather save any possible boasts till the thing has been done . . . but we're going to try.'[9]

Ute Indians returned to the old Council Rock in the Garden of the Gods below to dance their sun dances. Like the scientists on the mountain top, their dance had become work concerned with issues of twentieth-century health. 'In former times the dances were given to appease the Great

Spirit and avert misfortunes from the tribe but the modern Utes keep up the custom for the general purpose of guarding against the White Death, the worst modern foe of the redmen.'[10] The 'white death' was their name for tuberculosis. What the white men termed 'birdmen', the Ute Indians called 'Eagle Men', joining a crowd and parade of 50,000 to watch 'the last word in modern miracles'.

In truth the script of modern miracles is continually being written. With his experience as part of Haldane's summit team behind him, Edward Schneider would go on to push the bounds of flight in his First World War work for the American Airforce. In years to come the United States Airforce Academy would base itself in Colorado Springs. In 1911 Haldane heard the buzz of the biplanes far below. Turpin was flying over the town while Parmalee flew over the Garden of the Gods.

Parmalee climbed from his plane and looked back towards the mountain. 'Flying around Pikes Peak, provided the air is still, is simply a matter of having the motive power,' he said. 'With the engine we are using – 35 horse power – it is a physical impossibility, as the flights yesterday and today have shown us, to mount above the surrounding mountains. Give me 25 more horse power and I *can* circle Pikes Peak. What's more, I hope to come back here some time and do it!'[11]

By the following year, the 25-year-old Phil Parmalee held the American endurance record for aviation. And he was dead. A gust of wind flipped at the tail of his plane and smashed it into the ground from a height of only 400 feet. Turpin had recently brushed with death himself, his plane crashing into a crowd in Seattle, killing one man and wounding fifteen. In grief for his flying partner, he quit the air and never flew again.

'Before long we will be using the higher powered engines in exhibition work,' Parmalee predicted after flying through the shadow of Pikes Peak. Technology kept breaking new limits and taking young men with it. The twentieth century already had the air of a rampant machine that spat out lives as it raced ahead. Haldane took another of his daily breaths of carbon monoxide, this task being unique to him on the mountaintop. 'The headache, throbbing, nausea, vomiting, fainting etc of mountain sickness are all experienced in carbon monoxide poisoning,' noted the expedition's report, 'all of the symptoms of which have been shown to be due to want of oxygen and nothing else.' The human body was an essential part of its ever-changing environment, and could be killed or sustained by it. Haldane had work still to do.

Joseph Barcroft's high-altitude work in Tenerife saw that rival physiologist plagued by mountain sickness. Haldane was struck by how very like sea sickness the illness was. The team's staying power, the reality of staying five weeks on top of the mountain, allowed them to assess the very marked process of acclimatization for the first time. After two weeks they had reached their main results, the remaining weeks still 'with a good deal to do, but mostly in matters of detail'.

Their first two days on the mountain had seen the whole team laid so low by the effects that they were unable to perform their whole battery of tests on an unacclimatized subject. A student, Mr J. E. Fuller, came up from Colorado College for three days following the aviation carnival. He knew from experience that he would suffer from mountain sickness, and duly obliged in doing so again.

The company was good, Haldane puffing out clouds of

tobacco smoke in the evenings to add atmosphere to the fire of scientific conversation. Five weeks before the ascent Schneider had travelled up to his alma mater, Yale, and been trained up by Yandell Henderson in the appropriate respiratory investigative techniques. Through this period of instruction, Henderson doubtless recruited him to the cause. These scientists were essentially reporting back from the field about the effects of sustained periods living at low barometric pressure. Their findings were expected to apply to balloonists and divers, to the treatment of pneumonia, but primarily to add to the physiological knowledge of breathing. Before meeting Haldane, Henderson had become absorbed in discovering the physiological effects of low levels of carbon dioxide and anticipated a change in 'pulmonary oxidation during vigorous muscular work'. Haldane had picked up Christian Bohr's theory of oxygen secretion and run with it. In work with Lorrain Smith he had already proved, against the run of science, the secretion of oxygen in fish bladders. Proof of oxygen secretion by the lungs would add welcome data to his ongoing quest for a holistic sense of life and environment as one self-regulating organism. Were Joseph Barcroft or Nathan Zuntz on his mountain expedition, those evening conversations would have been far from the 'lively and pleasant' experiences Haldane recounted.

This was the wet season, with frequent rain and storms, hail and snow often falling without settling. 'Sometimes we see nothing but a sea of cloud,' Haldane reported, 'the Peak being the only thing above them. The sunsets are often splendid, and the shadow of the Peak either travels out across the prairie to the East, or is thrown against the clouds, like another huge mountain.' The daytime temperature averaged 50 °F in the shade, plunging to freezing at night. With the warmth of their stove the team never needed to wear their winter clothing.

The high whistles and trills of the yellow-bellied marmots pierced the daytimes. Unlike Haldane, these were diurnal creatures. Haldane was grumpy for some days on arrival, then managed to rationalize his situation overnight. At breakfast he was cheerful again. His Colorado working day accorded exactly with the one he was used to seven time zones away in Oxford. Six o'clock in the morning in Colorado was one o'clock in the afternoon in Oxford, a fine and normal Haldane hour to start a regular working day that would stretch through the night-time.

The broken pink granite and boulders of the surface covered what was truly an ice cap to the mountain, a layer of permafrost in which only occasional flowers took hold. The surroundings became 'all very desolate – nothing but broken rocks and precipices here and there'. The scientists yearned to climb down the two or three thousand feet, drop below the timber line and be among green things for a while. However the air was too rarefied, the oxygen too little, and time too pressed. On 5 August they did make the first such foray, stepping down 3,000 feet to where the dwarf trees grew above knee, then waist, then head heights, offering a forest to wander through, clusters of Alpine flowers, groupings of bright red amanita mushrooms. The return to the summit took 1¾ hours, all the men panting even though they were acclimatized, and ravenous for the evening's supper.

Still visitors came in their hundreds, men, women and children, with a 'venturesome spirit that is extraordinary'. People fainted without much attention given to them, since they were bound to come round fairly quickly, though one young woman climbing in the wake of the aviation carnival collapsed unconscious. Rushed down the mountain in a special train, even she soon recovered.

Results confirmed that low oxygen rather than low carbon dioxide caused the symptoms of mountain sickness. Haldane's team monitored breathing through sleep in the night in addition to their daytime observations. Repeated administration of oxygen overcame what was otherwise a mixture of short, gasping breaths around gaps in breathing. Their report recommended oxygen treatment as a cure for mountain sickness, especially the pneumonia to become termed high-altitude pulmonary oedema. Two other Haldane recommendations, to raise oxygen levels by the use of pressurized chambers or stimulating ventilation through breathing small amounts of carbon dioxide, saw him well on route for pioneering successful deep oxygen treatment.

Taking exercise on the broad flat surface of the Peak, or forced-marching up and down its cog road, required just as much oxygen as the same exercise at sea level. However with the lack of oxygen in the atmosphere its effective delivery took a great deal more effort of breathing.

Arrival on the Peak meant that water was lost from the blood. This concentrated the red cells. More slowly, new blood cells entered the circulation to increase the haemoglobin total in the blood. Speculating on the future, working on results achieved in their air chamber in addition to those on the summit, the scientists projected upwards to more than double their current altitude. Now they were fully acclimatized at 14,100 feet (4,298 m), could they conceivably mount to 29,028 (8,847 m) feet without supplementary oxygen? This was the height of Everest, the ultimate quest of mountaineers. Most physiologists doubted that such an oxygen-free climb was possible. Haldane decided that it was. Just. Man could, with care and preparation, attain the ultimate height of his known environment, his body adjusting itself accordingly.

Already he had stretched his own findings to shift from the effects of carbon dioxide in regulating breathing, to seeing the effects of oxygen. He had done so by moving his human test subjects, himself included, to high altitude and keeping them there. In extreme need of oxygen, he supposed, surely the lungs would not simply leave the air sitting in its sacs. It would secrete, or pump, the oxygen from this alveolar air directly into the bloodstream.

He had perfected measurements for the oxygen in the alveolar air. Now, since no direct method of drawing blood from the arteries existed, he developed and refined a complex method for measuring the oxygen in arterial blood. Oxygen could just passively diffuse from the alveoli into the blood if the balance of pressure was right. If, for any reason, that oxygen pressure in the alveoli was lower than in the arterial blood, it had to be actively pumped to pass from one to the other. The scientists' data showed this to be the case, to the extraordinary degree that the oxygen level at Pikes Peak was raised to be the same as that at sea level.

Another sequence of experiments utilized Henderson's recoil board. Lying flat, these boards magnified movements by sixty times. The distance through which the body recoiled afforded a fairly reliable index of the relative sizes of an individual's heartbeats. The test subject had to hold his breath, so that the heartbeat was measured rather than respiration. On 1 August Haldane's recoil test's curve of results 'dwindles strikingly', taken 'while he was feeling decidedly out of sorts soon after a carbonic oxide and low oxygen breathing experiment'.[12]

At sea level Haldane had been able to hold his breath for 40 seconds. After 48 hours on Pikes Peak this was down to 15 to 18 seconds. His stripped weight of 175 pounds on arrival was reduced by 8 pounds during his stay. In comparison with the others he was turning out to be a distinctly curious physiological specimen, likely due to the stringent ordeals he perpetually put himself through. Indeed the report notes that his having 'persistently 15,000 leucocytes per cubic millimetre' (leucocytes are blood cells that contain a nucleus) meant that Haldane 'could hardly be considered as normal'. Whilst the pulse rates of the other scientists rose on the summit, Haldane's started at 84 and gradually slowed to beating 15 or 20 times a minute less rapidly than before. Two minutes' rapid walking on the gradient of the track, however, saw this surge to 132 beats per minute. In terms of the daily haemoglobin count, the report asserts, 'the percentage of haemoglobin and the number of red corpuscles commenced to rise at once, this rise being especially rapid in the first two or three days in all of us except Haldane in whose case it was very gradual'.

It was time to descend to sea level, and run tests as to how long it took them all to re-acclimatize to the higher pressure. On 16 August the party left the mountain, choosing to walk down for the sheer delight of entering into a temperate zone once again. They spent some days running tests at Colorado College. On the summit they had noted how many of those climbing to the top did so 'inadequately clad and shod', taking between 10 and 12 hours. Five days after their descent a Texan couple, one a printer by profession taking a short break with his wife, dressed in their regular clothes and began their ascent of the mountain. Following the tracks, they encountered a snowstorm. They lay down beside the tracks half a mile short of the summit, where their snow-covered bodies were discovered the next day.

Douglas and Haldane accompanied Henderson back to the Yale laboratory at New Haven. Later Mabel FitzGerald came to New York, a city that Haldane found ruinously expensive, to wave the British scientists off on their boat. Hers had been a thrilling adventure on horse and mule back, railroad journeys and snowdrifts. Her measurements of respiration at different altitudes brought to light the fact that women breathe more, giving them lower carbon dioxide and haemoglobin levels than men. 'Your work has been much more adventurous than ours,' Haldane told her.

The scientists had written sections of their official paper together on the summit. Haldane continued work on it on board the RMS *Olympic*, which was 'the largest ship afloat, and is very gorgeous, besides being very fast'. Leaving on Saturday, they docked in Plymouth on Friday 15 September 1911. FitzGerald's paper had to be dragged and encouraged out of her, both hers and the team's to be published in 1913. The papers contained remarkable science achieved at exquisite cost. To a large extent their time on Pikes Peak was the high point of all the scientists' careers. Their mammoth paper was handed in to the Royal Society on 13 July 1912, and read on 5 December that year.

Academia was brewing up a storm of response.

13

PRELUDE TO WAR

Haldane read an abstract of the Pikes Peak Expedition's joint paper to the Royal Society in January 1912. Thirteen chief conclusions outlined the team's remarkable achievements, delineating their many new discoveries about the effects of acclimatization to altitude. Had the list stopped at eleven, the gathered scientists might well have indulged in a warm round of congratulation. Haldane's experimental methods were known to be innovative, exacting and exemplary, and Pikes Peak was set to be his crowning achievement. But surely, scientists reflected, this time he had let those confounded philosophical notions of his get in the way.

'Science is the application of abstract logical principles to a reality which they can never express fully,' Haldane would write in conclusion to his book *Mechanism, Life and Personality*, a collection of essays drawn from a course of lectures for senior students at London University delivered in May 1913. 'It is the business of philosophy to point out and define these abstractions. Philosophy directs us, also, to that spiritual reality which is the only reality; and from this point of view philosophy and religion are one.'

Haldane and Lorrain Smith had worked in Belfast 'at a purely physiological question – the cause of absorption and giving off of gases by the lungs'. Their paper showed results, he told his friend J. T. Wilson:

> in favour of 'active' absorption of oxygen, not to be explained as due to diffusion, but we must test the matter further, and see whether the vagus or any other nerve has any influence on absorption or giving off of gases, as has been shown to be the case in the secretion of gas by the walls of the swimming bladder in fishes. This question of 'active' secretion or absorption of gases is just one of the 'burning' ones in physiology just now, and men with vitalistic tendencies like Lorrain Smith and myself might be apt to be prejudiced. However, I don't think we were. When we began the experiment we on the whole expected to get a result in favour of diffusion, and thought at first that we had, especially as diffusion seems capable of doing all that is physiologically required in the matter, but the final results seemed dead against diffusion as the sole cause.[1]

Point Twelve in the abstract read out on 18 January 1912 suggested that the change in alveolar oxygen pressure 'appears to be due to a progressive increase in the activity of the alveolar epithelium in secreting oxygen inwards'. This prepared the audience for the climax. All the achievements garnered on Pikes Peak led up to Point Thirteen, which began: 'Acclimatization to high altitudes is due mainly to the increased secretory activity of the alveolar epithelium . . .'

Point proven. For Haldane, that point was active secretion

of oxygen in the lung. Just as his work on fish bladders had overturned established scientific wisdom, he was sure his Pikes Peak data established this new proof about the capacities of the human lung. For many of those attending, the point proven was a different one. There had always been something untrustworthy about Haldane. The man kept company with working folk, which was suspicious in itself. He was ever liable to pick up a good post-prandial conversation and run it off on some weird spiritual tangent. Still, the blighter spoke with authority and was hard to pin down. Now they had him. Haldane had finally let his philosophical lunacy overpower the balance of his scientific judgement.

Haldane's oxygen secretion theory was attacked in terms of science. The most spectacular among the attacks came from the Cambridge physiologist Joseph Barcroft, who closed himself in a glass tank for six days in 1920 with oxygen steadily reduced to 10 per cent, an equivalent of an altitude of 6,000 metres. His sole aim, in which he felt triumphant, was to refute the Pikes Peak finding. He used a direct method of abstracting blood from an artery, some scientists wondering whether Haldane's more indirect methods skewed his findings. Haldane dismissed the findings. Barcroft was both unacclimatized and ill at the time of the tests. Others have suggested that Haldane's 'mistake' came from an understanding that has since been corrected, that CO is a physiologically indifferent gas. However J. S. Milledge from seventy years later summed up the abiding prejudice of the time, suggesting 'possibilities of an unconscious bias in the rather subjective CO method'.[2]

Citing the full collaboration of J. G. Priestley in the second edition of Haldane's later classic text *Respiration*, his own experiences of the practical laboratory work of C. G. Douglas and Priestley, and a dinner with a high-spirited Haldane after *Respiration*'s publication, R. Passmore wrote: 'There is no evidence in *Respiration* that Haldane's philosophical views affected his judgment as a laboratory worker. Milledge's suggestion of "an unconscious bias in the rather subjective CO method" (?a euphemism for cooking results) seems a slur not only on Haldane but also on Douglas, who collaborated with him in all his later work with this method. Having known Douglas well, I find this inconceivable too.'[3]

Banners stretched across the soot-streaked villages of Yorkshire's West Riding. Men worked the honeycomb of mines deep underground, but many had fashioned themselves a day off. William Brown pushed through crowds waving their little Union Jacks. It was rare enough for a miner to be out in daylight, this July day being especially fine, but rarer still for him to catch a glimpse of royalty. King George V and Queen Mary were touring the area and Brown longed to see them. He heard distant cheers, he pushed and he jostled, but it was no use. It seemed that kings and queens were not for the likes of him.

With a babe in her arms, his wife had moved no further than her own front door. As she stood feeling the sun on her face and waiting for her husband, the King and Queen stepped up her garden path on a visit. 'Very comfortable and airy,' the Queen said after a tour of the bedrooms. The royal couple drove off in their large, glass-sided car. They were down the road and out of sight when William Brown returned home.

The King put in a spot of work down a mine, remaining in his clothes and borrowing a pick to work himself a little pile of coal, taking the pieces away as mementoes. The royal couple took tea at Conisbrough Castle, from where they could look down on the pithead of Cadeby Colliery.

At two o'clock that night, 9 July 1912, an explosion ripped through the tunnels below. Firedamp kept investigation parties away for some time. Finding 'tubs smashed to atoms, girders twisted in all shapes', and the first dead bodies, they called in the pit manager and rescue parties.

W. H. Pickering was the Chief Inspector of Mines for the District. Now aged fifty-three, a distinguished authority on mining, in 1910 he had been awarded the King Edward medal for extraordinary bravery in an earlier mining accident. He had also founded the Mining and Geological Institute of India, where the King of England was also the Emperor. George V recognized that Pickering was his perfect informant on the latest mining developments in this region of his visit. Since the King was in Pickering's neighbourhood, he sent a message to invite him to tea.

The message did not get through. Alongside another inspector, Mr Bury, Pickering was already underground masterminding the rescue attempts. A miner named Percy Murgatroyd was with him. 'Never shall I forget the horrible sight that met my eyes when I got to the point where the explosion had taken place,' Murgatroyd remembered. 'The bodies were shattered most awfully . . . I was the only man who wore a respirator. The air was very good, and there really seemed no need for one, but it was my business to penetrate into any of the workings that they might tell me to, so it was advisable that I should wear one.'

The rescue party stood to one side to let men go by carrying a stretcher. The stretcher was just a few paces further on. 'We were talking quite casually when all at once there was a trembling in the air. We had no time to seek a place of safety. The explosion was upon us. I remember a fearful roar, and then clouds of dust and smoke were surging all round.'

A second roar, even louder than the first, was the roof falling in. Murgatroyd could barely see the light from his electric lamp held right in front of his face. 'I staggered about in the thick darkness and tried to find my way out, but suddenly realized that I was lost. I came to a great fall and was so exhausted that I collapsed.'

He in fact fell over the bodies of his colleagues. 'I remember seeing Mr Pickering and Mr Bury lying on the ground as if asleep. I don't think they could have lived more than two minutes in that fearful atmosphere.' He lay down beside them for ten minutes before coming round enough to go in search of a telephone. 'I found one and rang up, and presently I heard footsteps approaching and two rescuers came upon me and brought me out.'[4]

The explosions stemmed from a gobfire, the 'gob' being rubbish piled in to shore up old workings in the pit. Dead men were brought to the surface that none could recognize, their features were so charred. Friends and family picked through their pockets to find items by which to identify them. On Sunday 18 August, almost six weeks after the accident, ten men were still working at bringing ventilation back to the sealed danger zone. As part of their work they came across more entombed bodies. Five of the men prepared to carry these bodies to the surface.

Everything once familiar in the tunnels had been twisted and smashed out of shape and out of place. Releasing and manoeuvring dead bodies was no simple matter. Charlie Burns, one of the men, knocked his breathing apparatus against a stretcher in the tight space. It jerked the mouthpiece from his mouth and his surprise gasp filled his lungs with the inert gas pumped in to stop the fire. Colleagues hurried to fix the mouthpiece back, but could not get it to stay in place. They held oxygen close to his face. It did little to revive him, and used up most of their own oxygen supply. One man, Bernard Hill, managed to get a message up to a rescue team waiting to relieve them. They rushed in to lead four men to safety. The body of Charles Burns was collected later. He was the eighty-eighth name added to the Cadeby death-toll.

Scores of rescuers were among the dead. Had all members of the rescue parties been supplied with breathing apparatus, they would very likely have survived. Had the breathing apparatus been more secure, Burns too would have lived. Haldane had laid down the principles of mine-rescue safety, yet inspectors who knew of his reports still took no canaries down the mines with them, and carried no breathing apparatus. Lessons must be learnt and applied from the Cadeby disaster. Surely they must.

Woodlands, the model mining village near Doncaster where the King and Queen had visited the cottage of Mrs William Brown, was the project of Sir Arthur Markham. A coal proprietor and MP, he built the village in the teeth of fierce opposition from his fellow directors. The sinking of Brodsworth pit had made an old mansion uninhabitable. Woodlands was laid out in the beauty of its park, each house with a bath as well as a garden. When managers then criticized social and educational initiatives he was putting into place, he wrote:

Why should you think it inevitable that colliers should live in a state of filth and piggery? If you try and make good clean homes and help social work, this tends to make better men. You have got to get out of your head that all this social work

is a pernicious fad. It is nothing of the kind. After all, the
theory that each man represents so much money or profit to
a company by the amount of coal that he gets and that the
obligation of the employer ceases when he has paid him his
wages is utterly wrong. This is a question you have never
really thought about. I want you to turn your mind for my
sake to the higher ideal.[5]

Markham's miners were used to meeting him as they worked
the coalface. Other coal proprietors had to puzzle over how
he managed not only to speak of 'the higher ideal' but to
turn a higher profit into the bargain.

As the Mining Act of 1912 was being debated, Markham
was vigilant about promoting stricter safety measures for the
men. A mine owner who spoke of implementing the higher
ideal, who fought for miners' safety, who took his concerns
for their welfare down the pit, had one obvious ally. In the
wake of the Cadeby disaster three pits joined together to
form the Doncaster Coal Owners' Mining Laboratory. Its
new director was Dr J. S. Haldane. Joining him as assistant
director was J. Ivon Graham, a young mining science gradu-
ate from Dublin via Cambridge University. Graham was soon
set to test various types of breathing apparatus, climbing up
and down ladders 'to the point of exhaustion'.

Industry in Britain, unlike in Germany, had yet to make
much demand on pure science. Haldane had forged a link
with the submarine engineers Siebe Gorman through his
investigations into diving and submarine safety, working
alongside their scientist Sir Robert Davis. Large breweries
were another exception, with laboratories that employed top
scientists. The Doncaster Mining Laboratory, representing
only three collieries, was for some years the mining industry's

only such scientific venture. In some ways they served as a canary, sniffing out the rank odour of government interference. Would the Doncaster canary cling to its perch when governmental forces drew near?

The flame that started the Cadeby explosion blew out from a gobfire and ignited the coal dust in one of the roads. Other small gobfires had occurred in these new Doncaster pits. The Doncaster Lab sought first of all to rule out any repetition of the Cadeby disaster.

Since explosions were clearly transmitted by coal dust, one strategy put into effect was stone-dusting, clearing away such inflammable dust where it was perceived to be dangerous. Experiments set about discovering why coal might spontaneously heat and ignite. Firemen (whose role was to handle explosives when necessary) were instructed as to how to detect gas, their findings backed by laboratory controls. In the meantime a special staff was trained to detect and deal with any signs of spontaneous heating from the coal.

The Bentley Colliery, where the Doncaster Lab was situated, was therefore a model of progressive management. While the official Cadeby report offered no suggestions as to how such a horror might be avoided in future, it consoled itself that the Coal Mines Act had not been breached. The safety measures implemented at the Bentley Colliery, on the other hand, were in severe breach of the Act. A visiting inspector smelt gas, and his safety lamp revealed the gas to constitute more than 2½ per cent of the air. His warning to the under-manager to remove the men was ignored, since the men were there not to work coal but to improve ventilation. They had recognized the danger and were dealing with it.

The Home Office brought a prosecution of Bentley Colliery. In November 1912 Haldane appeared for the defence at Doncaster Police Court, pointing out that the men were in the mine specifically to deal with the danger of gas. The defence lawyer, the MP Norman Craig, suggested that the Home Office would be far better employed following the men's example than prosecuting them for it. 'He attributed the summonses to the alarmist nature of the Home Office, who thought, owing to the unfortunate disaster in another pit, that unless they did something, right or wrong, public opinion would ask what had the Home Office been doing.'[6]

'The case was defended with energy and determination,' Haldane later recalled for mining students, 'and landed the Home Office in ridicule.' A fine of twenty shillings plus costs was imposed. 'But at least it opened my eyes to the effects of too much government control.' It also made other coal owners very wary about committing to their own mining reseach laboratories

As a special treat, Haldane once included his daughter Naomi in a trip down the Bentley pit. She wore a black dress left over from a time of family mourning, carried her own safety lamp, and experienced the weird effect of jumping as the pit cage plummeted. She seemed to be going up rather than down. Miners were 'nice', they teased her but held back from swearing. She came to see her father, 'the doctor', through their eyes. 'They respected him for their own virtues: courage and loyalty, hard work and expert knowledge of conditions.'

Down below Naomi was led to see, smell, touch and listen to everything, charmed by the sound of someone singing in a dark distance. The evening was rounded off by a visit to the music hall in Doncaster, where father, daughter and son Jack 'laughed and laughed. It was totally delightful, a raising of the level of excitement already set off underground among the darknesses and small lights and echoes.'[7]

Sure of some error in Haldane's Pikes Peak data on oxygen secretion, scientists long puzzled to work out what it was. It seemed impossible that human lungs, even in a situation of grave oxygen lack, should secrete, or pump, oxygen from the air sacs in the lungs directly into the arterial bloodstream, as Haldane believed he had proved. Haldane firmly rejected all evidence to the contrary and maintained his belief in oxygen secretion throughout his life. That life, however, was altered by the scientific opposition stirred in 1912. His team's paper, 'Physiological Observations made on Pikes Peak', having been read at the Royal Society in December, was published the following year. On 15 July 1913 Francis Gotch, Haldane's one-time colleague who had beaten him to the Waynflete Professorship, died. The Chair was once again available. Two candidates stood. One was Haldane, the other C. K. Sherrington.

The selection process was well under way when Haldane's *Mechanism, Life and Personality* was published in October. In October 1913 Haldane's mother wrote of her 'extreme gratification' for her copy which was 'clear, and above all full of truth, fearlessly expressed'.

Its timing made it something of a mission statement for the Waynflete Chair. Haldane was now affirming his position outside of both the vitalist and mechanist camps, a fine way of assuring that he had no supporters in either. 'The sphere of action of the "vital force" was a dim and misty sphere of unintelligibility – a purely negative sphere ... within the sphere of indefinite mist some mysterious factor was at work,' he wrote. The mechanists, however, have contended that the misty sphere is only the mist of our ignorance of the physical and chemical conditions, and that year by year this mist is being gradually dispelled by the advance of physiological investigation . . . this is a complete illusion. The advance of investigation has only served to make the misty sphere more evident; and not only does it exist, but there is not the remotest chance . . . that physical or chemical investigation will ever dispel the mist. The phenomena of life are of such a nature that no physical or chemical explanation of them is remotely conceivable.

The mechanistic theory 'breaks down completely in connection with the phenomena of life'. Yet 'the vitalistic theory, if one can call it a theory, is only a way of registering this failure, and does not help us to a real understanding'. Such, he maintained, was the cause for 'the helpless position in which biology finds herself'.[8]

Members of the Oxford selection committee, the establishment, carried some responsibility for biology's 'helpless position'. They read in the book's preface how 'the time is now more than ripe for bringing the great biological movement of the nineteenth century into definite relation with the main stream of human thought,' and wondered if such should be the stated mission of their next Professor.

The Danish scientist Arthur Krogh had worked under Christian Bohr, yet his and Marie Krogh's stance against the notion of oxygen secretion ran counter to Bohr and Haldane's. He wrote to Georges Dreyer, his fellow Dane and Professor of Pathology who was on the selection committee. Should Haldane be given the Chair? 'Even though I thoroughly disagree with Haldane on more than one point, as you know, I greatly respect his work and it would please me if he got it.'

On 18 October 1913 the Royal College of Physicians awarded Haldane the Baly gold medal, an award made every alternate year to the person deemed 'to have most distinguished himself in the science of physiology, especially during the two years immediately preceding the award'.[9] It wasn't enough to sway things. Sherrington was an acclaimed giant of neurophysiology, a future Nobel Prize winner. It was easy, even sensible, to make the safe choice. In November Sherrington was announced as the next Waynflete Professor of Physiology.

The announcement came through on 7 November. Haldane scarcely had time to resign his readership. His disappointment was acute but life must go on. That evening the Haldanes hosted a dance at Cherwell. The following day was a regular house and garden party. All was in honour of son Jack's twenty-first birthday.

The dance was 'very amusing', according to one of their guests, Aldous Huxley. 'The Haldanes always contrive to know and invite very good people to their functions.' Huxley went back for tea at 4.30 the following day, staying till 11.30. Forty folk including the children were shepherded into a room to kickstart the occasion, everyone getting a turn at dipping into a 'bran pie', a huge lucky dip from which they pulled out gifts. Instead of bran the Haldanes had filled the 'pie' with confetti. Once everyone had dipped in for their gift, they went back for handfuls of the confetti and chucked it at everyone else. 'After half an hour of this . . . one's hair, pockets, stomach and inmost clothing being completely filled with confetti . . . shyness, as such, almost completely ceases to exist. One then comes out into an ante-chamber, where seven highly trained, amateur officials remove as much of the confetti from one's hair and outer garments as is humanly possible.'[10] Fireworks followed, the children were shuttled off to bed, supper was accompanied by 'the most magnificent Nebuchadnezzars', each of these monumental wine bottles holding the contents of twenty regular ones, and the adults resorted to their own games. In blind man's buff a blindfolded person walked round a circle, prodded someone, asked them to make a noise such as 'the sound of rain falling on mud', and tried to recognize the person by the voice.

This party game was one of the last hurrahs for a naïve and innocent world.

In February 1912 Haldane had accompanied his brother Richard, then Secretary for War, on a clandestine peace mission to the Kaiser in Berlin. Haldane travelled as his brother's private secretary, essentially providing cover. On the face of it this was a trip on behalf of the Royal Commission on the University of London, which Richard chaired, to investigate technical education in Germany. In reality the Secretary for War had been deputed by the Cabinet to embark on a peace mission.

The two brothers arrived at Friedrichstrasse station on the morning of 8 February and headed for the Hotel Bristol, next to the British Embassy. By the afternoon Richard was already in conference with the Chancellor. The following day he met with the Kaiser. With Tirpitz as head of the German fleet in rambunctious attendance, much discussion centred on the sizes of the relative fleets. The British goal was to have Germany ease back on her naval preparations.

A series of intense negotiations was rounded off on 10 February. 'Johnnie has been splendidly helpful and sympathetic and the greatest comfort to me,' Richard wrote to his mother. 'We were besieged by reporters, whom I would not see and whom he kept off. So great was the excitement in Berlin that an interview with Johnnie, from which they thought we were not really negotiating, sent down the funds in the Bourse. This morning we left. A crowd had assembled to see us start, and cameras and cinematograph instruments recorded the scene. There was a crowd at the station, where we were treated like royalties. The Emperor gave me a little bronze statue for my writing table.'[11]

The statue was of Kaiser Wilhelm. While Lord Haldane was representing the whole Cabinet, seeking to trim the sails of the nations' naval race, Winston Churchill was making a speech in Glasgow. He branded Wilhelm's navy a 'luxury fleet'. Notions of Cabinet unity were smashed.

The speech was wilfully provocative. As such, it was effective. 'The agreement' – so ran Kaiser Wilhelm's telegram on 19 March 1912, obliterating all of Lord Haldane's work – 'is thereby broken by England – killed!'[12]

In May that year the two brothers went back to Germany, this time on a holiday. Having been misled once, Haldane's earlier peace mission labelled an educational survey, the press were not going to leave the Haldanes in peace this time around. They declared that J. S. Haldane was actually Prime Minister Asquith in disguise, and that the two men were in Germany to make a treaty.[13]

Haldane was, in truth, actively preparing for war. One question he was working on was the average ration for troops on active military service. A half-company of men volunteered for an experiment on Salisbury Plain. Kept for a fortnight on the existing rations, average campaigning conditions were adopted. The men's physical condition deteriorated rapidly. 'I well remember how alarmed I was at the appearance of the commanding officer as he marched in at the end of what was afterwards nick-named the "hunger march", Haldane recalled. 'Being a big man he had suffered more than the rest, and his face looked sunken and altered.' The experiment was repeated, the ration increased to near wartime levels. 'The effect was quite different; all the men were in better condition than when they started, and there was no loss of weight. The experiment was decisive, and its practical outcome meant a great deal during the war. When men can feed themselves in accordance with the dictates of nature there is but little trouble with food; but where, as in an army, the right quantities of food have to be arranged for beforehand, scientific control is necessary, and pays hand over hand.'[14]

As it became clear that Richard's negotiations with the Kaiser and Tirpitz about easing back on the naval race were coming to nothing, J. S. Haldane moved in to support the development of the British fleet. In October 1912 he was appointed to a committee under Rear-Admiral R. B. Farquhar to examine the effect of 'unsatisfactory ventilation on the inception and spread of disease in the Royal Navy'.[15]

The committee climbed aboard HMS *Vanguard* at Portland on 20 January. Over the next three days they sailed to Bantry and back, checking the condition of the atmosphere between decks throughout the day and night, both in harbour and at sea. The weather complied with the desired range of their investigations, whipping up a storm between fair passages. From November 1912 to April 1913 they visited twenty-seven ships, plus the submarine *E4* on 17 April, largely in the harbour. They interviewed various suppliers, and reviewed reports from the medical officers of another twelve ships, including HMS *Dreadnought*.

Launched in 1906, and powered by steam turbines, the

Dreadnought set the new standard for battleships. While the Royal Navy could be proud of having the supreme battleship of its day, it also put its historical supremacy over the seas in extreme jeopardy. The likes of Germany could never catch up in terms of numbers of vessels, but new technology meant that naval war was no longer a numbers game. U-boats could prowl offshore picking off a lot of proud shipping. The *Dreadnought* rendered older ships obsolete. Use superior technology to build your own new fleet and naval power could be yours.

Difficulties of ventilation came with the advent of ironclads. Electric lighting replaced tallow candles or lamps burning whale oil, affording improvement in the atmosphere between decks, but natural ventilation was virtually extinguished. Haldane's voice is apparent in the report's discussions of the men's living conditions.

> Ships nowadays take in coal on an average once a fortnight instead of once in six months; and this affects ventilation very materially for during the operation of coaling and the subsequent washing down the ship is practically battened down and all the ventilation is extinguished. Whereas formally all officers and men had their occupation on deck now the majority are employed below. And so life in a man-of-war has changed from one of the healthiest to one of the most trying occupations.

Investigations were exhaustive. The situation of the canteen was 'quite incompatible with the proper storage of butter, fish, eggs, meat' and with the maintenance of health of the canteen staff. 'Foul, hot or deleterious air' was noted in its travels at high pressure from latrines, sculleries and urinals into such distant places as the Sick Bay and War Room. The dry-bulb temperature of a wireless and telegraph office was 96 degrees. Its floor being over the boiler room, Haldane felt the heat through the thick soles of his boots. The fan had been stopped because of its noise, and to spare it choking on dust from the loading of coal. Haldane took his samples of the air: a high 20.7 parts of CO_2 per 10,000.

This was war work. Other scientists might prepare for war by maximizing means of destruction. Haldane, conversely, saw that war supplied new challenges to health. It placed man in radically different environments without appreciating their effects on the human organism. Industry was dangerous enough, but only a start. Experiences of coal-mine explosions were like a limbering up for a physiologist at war.

At Christmas 1913 Haldane was too busy building his private laboratory to attend the big family party at Cloan, where a German boy was teaching a Haldane sailor nephew to speak German. 'One looked at the young ones dancing,' Elizabeth wrote, 'German and English together, and never thought that in a few months they would, some of them, be fighting for their lives, trying to kill one another, and that all the matters that seemed so important to us would be as naught.'[16]

The Haldanes now had their own boathouse, roofed with local Stonesfield slates. Haldane kept his rowboat there, some good years of rowing on the Cherwell still inside him. On a summer afternoon in 1914 the boathouse punt was dragged from the river up the lawn, Aldous Huxley standing in it to guard the river Styx. This was for a performance of Aristophanes' *The Frogs* in the Cherwell garden. As Dionysos Lewis Gielgud wore a deep saffron robe and vineleaf wreath. Jack Haldane and Gervase Huxley led the men's chorus.

Naomi, her fair hair streaming round her white robes, led the women's.

The university year at Oxford ended. For many of the students and the younger staff, the next one would never begin. Though now in the role of Lord Chancellor rather than Secretary for War, Richard Haldane was dispatched to the War Office on 3 August. He had his orders from the Prime Minister. He mobilized the nation for war.

14

GAS ATTACK

A train rushed the Haldanes down to London in the wake of the declaration of war. In Richard's house at 28 Queen's Gate the white-faced Foreign Secretary, Sir Edward Grey, struck Naomi as 'desperately anxious and worried'.[1] He was oddly adrift from the fun and excitement. The male students from Oxford switched their summer clothes for khaki uniforms. The war would be over by Christmas, surely. They were desperate not to get there too late.

The sixteen-year-old Naomi took her first solo train ride down to Surrey to stay with the Mitchison family. Fresh from Oxford, her friend Dick Mitchison was now a second lieutenant with the Queen's Bays, where his war preparations included practising cavalry charges. He turned up at the family home in his new cavalry uniform. Naomi could not resist. The two got engaged. Marrying an officer was 'war work ... involvement in the great excitement'. Aldous Huxley resented the Haldanes 'marrying her off' so young, though the resentment was very likely personal pique. With

her own Haldane spirit of self-sacrifice, Naomi was a head-
strong type. Stop her at your peril.

For her part, Kathleen was laying her son Jack on the altar
of her imperial beliefs. That, at least, was Naomi's take on
her brother's war service. Giving up one's sons was the 'war
work' of the mothers. Naomi and her parents took two train
rides up the Highland Line to Nigg in Perthshire, where the
Third Battalion of the Black Watch had their base. Staying in
a small farmhouse, they saw what they could of the enlisted
Jack. In the autumn the family travelled down to South-
ampton. Faces held firm, they waved the young man on his
way to France.

In 1911 Haldane had travelled to Göttingen to visit Pat
Haldane, the son of his brother William. Pat met him at the
station, unrecognizable at first because 'he had grown and
looks much more of a young man,' Haldane told his mother.
'I am sure his sojourn here has done him good and he speaks
German quite freely and seems to have lost a good deal of his
shyness. He is enjoying his life here too and does not seem at
all anxious to come home too soon.'[2] Haldane was accompanying Pat's sister, Edith. They found Göttingen to be 'a
beautiful town and a delightful place to live in', and went
driving through the Harz mountains together.

Pat now wore khaki, while his young German friends
from those days were dressed in field grey. Pat's war was a
short one. His father William wrote to 'My dear J' on 18
January 1915:

Many, many thanks for your letter . . . I had not realized what
Pat and I have been to each other. I certainly hope you will
be spared this. Even as regards Pat I know you were fond of

him and he of you. It was a shell . . . The back of his head
badly fractured and his legs. He was never conscious and died
at midnight.[3]

Two figures could be found in the spacious drawing room
at Cherwell, John and Kathleen Haldane numb with grief for
a while as news came in of the deaths of family, students,
friends and colleagues. 'I am now too old to join the army
myself, but . . .' Haldane summoned his fighting spirit to
write to the Secretary of State at the Home Office in
November 1914. The Board of Mining Examiners had
refused permission for Geoffrey Phillips to sit the exam.
Haldane knew the man from working alongside him in the
Doncaster pits, testing rescue apparatus. Phillips wanted to
take the exam then join the army. If he wasn't allowed to do
so, Haldane would resign and open the Board to public
humiliation. 'I am not too old to take my share in preventing
official misunderstanding and wrong-headedness from placing
unnecessary obstacles in the way of men who are anxious to
join.'[4]

'We may all do something, but you have done more than
any of us,' Mary Haldane wrote to her son on 15 February
1915. She was put in mind of Abraham's preparedness to sacrifice his son Isaac. 'That I feel very strongly, in so far as you
have not withheld Jack from fulfilling the career he has
chosen in following the path of duty.'

That path was a particularly wild and dangerous one. On
4 February Jack wrote to his father:

I am enjoying life here very much. I have got a most ripping
job as a bomb officer, teaching bomb throwing to a number
of men . . . The best people at it seem to be the reckless kind,

who are always breaking rules and things in peacetime, or else
NCOs who are sufficiently educated to have faith in the uni-
formity of Nature. The average man certainly does not like it.
However, the really interesting thing is the trench mortar . . .
the kind of weapon *you* would like. Please send me a small (3
or 4 figure) table of sines, cosines and tangents. It may be of
use for calculating ranges etc.

With shellfire exploding around him for the very first
time, Jack thought of his father. How much he would be
enjoying this! His father's example had given him the
courage he needed. 'Courage is perhaps not a virtue in
itself,' he reflected later, 'but the form taken by other virtues
in extreme cases. You do not know how just a man is until
he has risked his life rather than do an unjust act. In my
father's case the combination of scientific curiosity and the
desire to help his fellows evoked courage; and once evoked,
it was contagious.'[5]

On 20 February Jack wrote to Naomi: 'Bomb-throwing
is the next most exciting thing to being under fire, but I am
getting into it now.' Something in the young man had
always been inclined towards the extremes of war. Aged six
he had torn up a sapling and swung fruitless swipes at a boy
who was bullying him. 'I wish I could kill,' he shouted as
the bell called him back to the classroom. 'I wish I could
KILL!'[6]

In early March, Naomi was told: 'The chief effect on one
of rifle fire, apart from a pointless desire to duck when you
hear the shot, which is too late, is annoyance that so comic a
sound (for of course it is only as a sound like whiwww . . .
that one is aware of a bullet) may have so tragic an effect.'

'My pet bombs for ordinary work weigh about a pound

& are thrown by hand (not by a stick or string) after lighting a fuse by a lighter,' he told his mother in March. Throwing bombs from one section of the trenches provided a focus for the enemy's retaliatory strikes. In April Jack wrote: 'I am popular with the men (who call me the Rajah of the Bomb) and the general and most of the colonels, and fairly loathed by the company commanders whom I get shelled.'[7]

Kathleen brought the spirit of her son's war service to the defence of the family's honour. Throughout their marriage Kathleen was liable to pick up a pen and dash off correspondence in her wild and expansive handwriting, either at her husband's suggestion to help during an overload of work or behind his back, drawing in testimonials or keeping undue influences at bay. In April 1915 Sir Henry Cunyngham was doing his best to inveigle Haldane into accepting a knighthood, claiming it would add to his powers of persuasion on wartime commissions. Kathleen 'detested' the whole idea. 'Frankly,' she wrote in a quite magnificent letter to Sir Henry,

> I do not know anything which Jack would consider such an insult to his father as that the same title should be bestowed on him as was given some years before to the uncle for whom he has as much good natured contempt as he has admiration for his father. I think you will agree with me that under present circumstances, this is a view to which some consideration is *due*.
>
> When John's brother William – known by the nickname of 'Wheedle' – was knighted for his political services (chiefly in cash), or for his relationship to the Lord Chancellor, the amusement which the event caused in Scotland was enormous.

I have seldom come across so much derisive enjoyment. Several people however agreed with me that it was a stroke of luck for us. I can remember four or five occasions when I was told 'not even *this* government could knight John after doing the same thing for William. You may consider yourself safe.' – or 'They are bound in decency not to give John the same thing. It would be too absurd.'

If some honour was obligatory, making John a Privy Counsellor, a role of official adviser to the King, would do the job. Otherwise:

I think the least a grateful country could do would be to make him a Bart. [Baronet, with the title of 'Sir'.] He surely deserves this quite as much as his old Uncle Sir J. Burdon Sanderson did! (I think *this* would please his *mother*, and for her sake he would not dislike it so much. The knighthood would emphatically *displease* her. She is an extremely shrewd woman, & knows very well the comparative value of her sons.)[8]

The sense of natural dignity of a Haldane is on rampant display in Kathleen's 'outrage' at this potential knighthood. Such an offer is a snub and a diminishment, the government having no right of patronage over her husband. It was as absurd and obscene as a servant offering her master some reward for good behaviour. Kathleen's letter joined a storm of dramatic events to sweep the whole debate over Haldane's ennoblement out of the door.

Haldane was at Cloan for the weekend of 22 March, accompanying his sister Elizabeth to receive a convoy of 100 wounded men at Perth. Otherwise he stayed busy at his private laboratory at Cherwell, which had been mobilized for war work. From 12 April Mary thanked her son for his 'affectionate good wishes' on her ninetieth birthday.

> They have been very happy years, notwithstanding that some have been attended by anxious cares and sorrow . . . I constantly think with joy and thankfulness at the happiness my children have brought me, and not the least of this has come through the channel of yourself. I am greatly interested in what you have written to me of your special work. The saving of life and power of working is, after all, the boon you can give and you have been able to do so much in this direction – not regarding the risks you have run of your own life and health.

'The chemist keeps his sword sheathed,' Bismarck once said, 'but his inventions will decide peace and war.' Haldane's 'special work' involved equipping man with the knowledge and techniques for survival in hostile environments. The exact nature of that hostile environment was only just emerging from the mind of a German scientist.

On 2 July 1909, Fritz Haber invited the technical heads of the German chemical company BASF to his laboratory. They witnessed the process, akin to that used in creating water-gas, through which he synthesized ammonia at 70 drops a minute. Chilean guano was Germany's previous source of ammonia for both fertilizers and explosives, which Britain intercepted in wartime. As BASF improved on the Haber process, by 1915 Germany was able to manufacture all the ammonia it needed.

Like Haldane, Haber had once been a student at the

university of Jena. When Haldane made his 'educational' visit
to Berlin in 1912, Haber was the founding director of the
city's new Kaiser Wilhelm Institute for Physical Chemistry.
With the onset of war, Haber dedicated his institute to the
development of new techniques in chemical warfare. Bald,
with round spectacles pinching his nose, he donned the uniform of a reservist officer and drew fellow scientists into a
new frontline troop, Pionierkommando 36. Haber would
win the Nobel Prize for Chemistry in 1918. Four other
future Nobel laureates worked alongside him: Otto Hahn,
James Franck, Gustav Hertz, and Richard Willstätter, whose
Nobel Prize for Chemistry was awarded in 1915. Erwin
Madelung and Wilhelm Westphal were equally prominent
scientists on the team, and were joined by Professor Carl
Duisberg, director of the chemical industrial giant IG Farben.
Duisberg was a passionate advocate, and wealthy backer, of
research into chemical warfare. Science and industry marched
hand in hand towards the conflict. As Albert Einstein would
remark in 1917, 'Our entire much-praised technological
progress, and civilization generally, could be compared to an
axe in the hand of a pathological criminal.'[9]

At its brazen simplest, initiating chemical warfare required
resolving three problems.

The first involved getting the science right. With a nose
for future Nobel laureates, let's simply accept that Haber was
the right man for the job.

The next problem was one of ethics. Simplest was to abide
by the rules of the Hague Convention, whose signatories
agreed 'to abstain from the use of projectiles the object of
which is the diffusion of asphyxiating or deleterious gases'.
An addendum from 1907 prohibited the use of 'poison or
poisoned weapons'.

America uniquely refused to stifle 'the inventive genius of its citizens in providing the weapons of war', and would not sign. Such a policy would later let it harbour refugee German scientists and develop the world's first successful atomic weapons programme. The same moral logic which applied to atomic weapons, that their devastating effect would bring war to a halt and so save lives, was applied by Haber to the release of poisonous gases. As a signatory to the Hague agreements, however, some ethical wordplay was needed. Kaiser Wilhelm need not fear, Haber assured him. No munitions would be used.

In fact the weapons were already stored in the warehouses of Germany's chemical companies. The nation had a vast dominance over the world's trade in dyes. In 1913 the world produced 160,000 tons of dye; 140,000 tons of that came from Germany. Chlorine was a necessary part of the process. Fitting release valves and angled pipes to chlorine cylinders barely counted as weapons manufacture.

The ethical question still required finding a front-line company commander prepared to allow the release of poisonous gases from among his troops. Inclined towards old-guard morality, many German commanders were disgusted by the prospect. Haber, cigar clenched in his mouth, puffed up and down the front line. He was a zealot. One commander, Duke Albrecht of Württemberg, accepted Haber's persuasion and allowed his 'Stink pioneers' (as the German troops labelled the newcomers) to join his Fourth Army. The operation was labelled 'Disinfection'.

From ancient history the Spartans offered a pioneering example of chemical warfare. They burnt wood soaked in pitch and sulphur to hold back the Athenians. It took two attempts, since their airborne poison relied on a favourable wind. In addition to their moral repugnance, German commanders feared that the introduction of poison gas into warfare would eventually work against them. Their troops faced prevailing winds from the west.

This was the third problem, one which accorded with Haldane's philosophy that nothing could be seen as separate from its environment. Scientists could release the most expertly primed chemical weapon, but in so doing they surrendered control to the forces of nature. Attempts at gas warfare in January 1915 through the explosion of T-shells carrying teargas had seen the gas vaporized by the cold air on the Eastern Front. In April the weather was pleasant in France, but meteorology is one of the more wayward of sciences. Winds have a habit of being unpredictable, and in the low-lying fields of Flanders dips and troughs can send them skirling in fresh directions. Wind speed also affected the delivery of chlorine gas, but since a killer concentration for chlorine was as low as 1 in 1,000, allowance could be made.

One hundred and sixty-eight metric tons of chlorine were aligned in almost 6,000 steel cylinders along 4 miles on the south-eastern side of the Ypres Salient, manned by 1,000 gas soldiers from Pioneer Regiments 35 and 36. For five weeks they waited, as pleasant breezes blew in their faces.

Reports from captured soldiers and Belgian spies alerted the Allied troops to the possible release of poison gas. British chemists were alerted, but their task was somewhat akin to preparing for a Mars landing. Lethal gases had never been thrown into the air before. They had to guess at the gas mixture, the quantities, the release methods, the effects of its mixing with air and winds, the levels at which the mixture might hang and the distance it might carry, and how it might affect the organs and tissues and eyes of the men who came into contact with it. They could make informed guesses, but the variables seemed infinite.

British troops tunnelled beneath Hill 60 and fired an underground mine on the evening of 17 April. In such a flat land the few meagre hills afforded commanding views of the whole crowded terrain of battle and would be fought over throughout the war. Hill 60 was in fact formed from the diggings of a nineteenth-century railway, offering a view over the Belgian city of Ypres. When the British took possession of it, German gas cylinders were in place on its flanks. The Germans presumed they had been discovered. Their counter-attack on Hill 60 of 20 April included teargas shells.[10] They were hardly keeping the usage of gas warfare a secret any more. Wait much longer, and any element of surprise would be lost.

Rats swarmed like a dark river across the narrow stretch of no man's land just south of Hulluch Road. They were abandoning the German trenches. A British sentry on duty for the 16th Division reported the sight. The rats' retreat was attributed to a leaky gas cylinder in the German front line, confirming suspicions of an imminent attack.[11]

Tired of waiting for a south-easterly wind, the Germans dug in more cylinders to the north-east. The weather was pleasant on the afternoon of Thursday 22 April. A light breeze blew from the north-east, in the direction of the Algerian 45th Division and the French 87th Territorial Division. The clock turned 1700 hours and red signal lights dropped from a balloon. Seventeen hundred hours was regularly marked by fresh bombardment from the German lines. The shells that fell in this new offensive held lead tubes containing about 600 cc of a bromine compound, teargas.

Dressed in what was effectively mining rescue apparatus, gas pioneers meanwhile released the valves of almost 6,000 cylinders. Approximately 2.5 times as heavy as air, chlorine turns to liquid under a pressure of 4 atmospheres. Close on 150 tons of chlorine now rose into the air, squirted upwards under its own pressure over an 8-minute period. The cloud mixed with the moist air to appear white at first, turning a greenish yellow as it gathered volume. The ground was warm, prompting the cloud to rise to heights of from 10 to 30 metres. This made it less lethal, but immensely more alarming. Every second it moved half a metre closer to the Allied troops. The rival front lines were close, at some points only 50 metres apart. Closest were the Algerians.

Some fell, suffocating, their bodies in spasm. Others ran with shouts of 'asphyxier, asphyxier'. The Germans spoke of them fleeing like hares, darting from side to side in sudden blindness and panic. Their eyeballs showed white, one soldier remembered. 'They literally were coughing their lungs out; glue was coming out of their mouths.'[12]

The gas reached the French lines of territorial soldiers in shallow trenches, and then drifted on to the Canadian. The poison cloud blew in pace with the running men. It sank into trenches and hollows where men took protection.

Pockets of gas lingered, pausing the advance of the German forces, who were also dumbfounded by the effectiveness of their device. They attained one of those rare heights in the area, Pilkem Ridge with its 15-metre elevation, then dug in and waited for the counterattack.

And waited. No one was left.

The gas attack served two main purposes for the Germans. It masked the redeployment of German troops from the

Western to the Eastern Front, and it served as an experiment. German scientists were as uncertain as their Allied counterparts how poisonous gases would react on release into the atmosphere. The 22nd of April was a massive field-test. 'A breakthrough was not intended. The attack only served for the improvement of the position and trial of gas.'[13]

Sir John French, leading the British Expeditionary Force, telegraphed a message to Lord Kitchener. 'Apparently these gases were either chlorine or bromine. Will send further details later but meanwhile strongly urge that immediate steps be taken to supply similar means of a most effective kind for use by our troops. Also essential that troops should be immediately provided with means of counteracting effects of enemy gases which should be suitable for use when on the move.'[14]

Kitchener in turn sent a telegraph to Haldane in Oxford, who travelled down to the War Office in London the following morning. Anecdotal evidence made it apparent that the gas used was chlorine, but in scientific terms the evidence for this and for the means of its delivery was inadequate. Haldane volunteered to cross the Channel to France that very afternoon to learn all he could. He should not go alone, however. 'This is a job for a chemist,' he advised Kitchener, suggesting Professor H. Brereton Baker of Imperial College, London.

While Kitchener and Haldane were making these arrangements, Winston Churchill swept into the room. He was First Lord of the Admiralty. Told of the gas attacks, he came up not only with a solution but with a media campaign.

'Oh, what you want is what we have in the Navy,' he assured them. 'Smoke helmets or smoke pads, and you make them out of cotton wool or something. You'd better get the *Daily Mail* to organize the making of a million of them.'[15]

Haldane sought more detail. An example was sent for, brought over by the Director General of Medical Services. The gas mask or 'smoke helmet' was nothing but a piece of lint tied over the mouth by a string. The lint served no barrier to any poison gas, and even if it did, the nose received no protection. Man tends to breathe through his nose, not his mouth. Haldane pointed out as much.

The inflated reputation of this 'gas mask' stemmed from its discovery on the *Emden*, a German cruiser captured in the Indian Ocean. A sailor had possibly made it himself. It might have been some use against smoke. It was useless against gas. 'In the then state of mentality, fostered by ignorant newspapers,' Haldane later recalled, 'it was supposed that being a German contrivance it must be very efficient.'[16] Believing the matter settled, and the naval respirator consigned to history, Haldane phoned the Doncaster Mining Laboratory. Just one chemist had not gone to war, a T. F. Winmill. The chemist accepted the task of experimenting on a respirator that would remove chlorine and bromine from the inspired air, and Haldane prepared for France.

In the absence of anyone else to battle with, Haldane was quite capable of being at odds with himself. Ten minutes late at Charing Cross station for his appointment with Brereton Baker, he was distressed over the loss of 18 shillings. They had been in a paper bag when he started out. Now all was lost.

The paper bag was long gone. However after a pause for self-collection, and some patting down, the silver coins turned up in his pocket. The two men boarded the train for Dover. After a meal of cold meats at the Lord Warden Inn, they caught the last regular steamer of the war to ply the route between there and Dunkirk. The crossing was set to be rough. What a grand opportunity for self-experimentation. Baker agreed to take a prophylactic against seasickness and Haldane not to. Neither was sick, which made that particular experiment amount to nothing, though plenty of opportunities for sickness lay ahead.

The boat took a long time to manoeuvre its way out of Dover harbour, negotiating the booms laid to trap German submarines that had been very active in the area. A makeshift wooden pier received them at Dunkirk, where a grand car with sliding windows awaited to ferry them towards General Headquarters.[17]

The car was better than the driver's navigation. Destined for GHQ but heading who knew where, they passed mile after mile of transport vehicles guarded by sentries, some looking spectral, their coats of white sheepskin luminous in the moonlight. Half a mile before each of the sleeping towns a sentry stood in the middle of the road and swung a lantern. Another sentry stepped up while the papers of those in the car were examined. Town by town, they approached Cassel, whose hill let them step out and look down on the town of Ypres.

The city's magnificent Cloth Tower still stood, a Gothic silhouette. Its days of rubble would soon arrive, but all was quiet in the bombardment for that moment. In the fields below them that day, the Indian Lahore Division had thought their attack on Mauser Ridge was supported by French troops. The French troops were late, the Indians alone. Already battered by conventional arms, the Indian forces fled in front of a fresh chlorine cloud released from the German cylinders. The division lost 2,000 casualties that day.

GHQ was based in the town of St Omer. After half an hour's briefing the men were taken to the Hôtel de

Commerce, Haldane giving Baker an exhibition of 'snoring choking noises' through the brief run of the night. In the morning Sir Wilmot Herringham, of Bart's Hospital and the Vice-Chancellor of London University, had his brother-in-law drive Haldane and himself to the town of Bailleul.

Gas attacks reached the edge of Bailleul, felling cattle and browning the grass, withering the buds on the trees, but since the town rides on one of the few substantial hills in the region the poison stretched no further. As a physiologist, Haldane needed to see the effects of gas on human bodies. He had plenty to choose from.

No sooner is chlorine in the bronchial tubes than it starts to strip their linings. Gasped further in on the next breath, it attacks the lungs. As tissue turns fluid, a mess of mucus blocks the windpipe and soon fills and swells the air sacs in the lungs. Men turn blue as they writhe and gasp for air. Those that run pant with the exertion, breathe more, and fall with their legs still kicking in flight, grasping at their throats.

Some soldiers died quite rapidly in the trenches, from spasm of the glottis. Others died later, as liquid filled the lungs and asphyxiated them. As their blood was starved of oxygen, victims turned blue and started panting. Those that faced recovery probably had to pass through a stage of bronchial pneumonia.

At 0410 hours on 24 April 1915, near St Julien, Canadian soldiers of the 8th and 15th Battalions found dawn approaching them in the shape of a 15-foot green cloud. High school science lessons, the simple fact that ammonia in urine helps to crystallize chlorine, led officers to shout out a curious order. Piss on a handkerchief, on any available rag, and hold it over your mouth. Water was in short supply at the front.

Some men were too parched to urinate, or too frightened or shy. They fell. Others survived. The Germans had the experience of their previous attack behind them. They expected the lines to break, and were bolder in advance. Even as they coughed, as their eyes streamed, the Canadians managed to let loose a barrage of fire to stall the offensive.

A 4 foot 6 inch Canadian chemist, Lieutenant Colonel George Naismith, ran a mobile laboratory that tested the quality of drinking water. On 23 April he gave the first formal diagnosis that the gas used was chlorine, which Haldane was able to confirm. The Canadian doctors were more confounded. One examined the throat of a major and stuck long steel pins up his nose. What else was he to do? The doctors were adept at amputating limbs. Faced with gas poisoning, rest and fresh air was the best they could prescribe.

Haldane would soon provide doctors with direction for treatments of individual poisonous gases. Luckily they had already hit on his primary point for treatment of gas victims. Rest was the very first factor to be considered, victims to stay quiet rather than shout orders, to be carried from the trenches where possible. Those seriously affected should be separated to leave the more moderately affected in a place of calm and order. Next in importance to rest came judicious supplies of high-strength oxygen, in short and frequent bursts. Protection from cold, special stimulants or drugs, venesection (or bleeding) and methods to clear the lungs of fluids were other factors on the list of doctors' priorities.

Haldane was familiar with chlorine poisoning, studied in connection with fatalities on submarines and what he termed 'an alarming personal experience in a sewer connected with bleaching works'. It soon became clear that the gas used was 'chlorine in a concentration of about 1 in 10,000, used with great skill in a good breeze, so that an enormous volume of cooled and poisonous air was carried over our troops and very large numbers of men were disabled and fatally injured'.[18]

The most severe cases saw panting, wheezing sounds fill the men's chests. Their lips were plum-coloured, their veins distended, and they were more or less stupefied. On Haldane's arrival at Number 2 Casualty Clearing Station he spoke with a Canadian officer. The man was blue in the face, suffering from severe bronchitis, and plainly exhausted. He spoke to Haldane in broken words. 'It might be better,' he said, 'if I can get a little sleep.'

Haldane took a blood sample from the man, to see if his blueness had any cause other than want of oxygen. It didn't. He returned to the man's bedside with the result. The man was dead.

Accurate knowledge of the exact cause of death was vital. Dr McNee, a pathologist from Glasgow University, performed an immediate post-mortem. Albuminous liquid, tissues turned to an egg-like consistency, was squeezed out of the man's swollen lungs. Haldane wrapped up a lung to take with him for microscopic examination in Oxford.

Back at the BEF HQ in St Omer, Haldane wrote a letter to Lord Kitchener. It was released to *The Times* for publication on 29 April, the first official report of the unleashing of chemical warfare on the modern world:

The symptoms and the other facts so far ascertained point to the use by the German troops of chlorine or bromine for purposes of asphyxiation. There are also facts pointing to the use in German shells of other irritant substances, though in some cases at least these agents are not of the same brutally barbarous character as the gas used in the attack on the Canadians. The effects are not those of any of the ordinary products of combustion of explosives. On this point the symptoms described left not the slightest doubt in my mind.

In the Hôtel de Commerce that night, Haldane used his edition of Herbert Spencer's *Moral Philosophy* to put himself to sleep. The following day he was back in London, marching with rage into the War Office.

On disembarking at Dover on 28 April, Haldane bought a copy of *The Times*. 'RESPIRATORS WANTED: Appeal for Home-made Appliances' ran a headline on page 10. 'As a protection against asphyxiating gases used as a weapon of warfare by the Germans' two basic patterns for gas masks were offered. One was for a pad of bleached absorbent cotton wool, the other a piece of 'double stockinette', to be sent in packages of not fewer than a hundred. The War Office was asking households to provide the model of respirator advocated by Churchill, and denigrated by Haldane as absolutely useless.

The following day's *Times* announced that women had 'besieged' the Royal Army Clothing department in Pimlico. Off the record was Haldane's own siege of the War Office. He reported his indignation to Kitchener, and won an assurance from Surgeon General Sir Alfred Keogh, Director General Army Medical Services, that these respirators would be kept in London. None would be sent to France. The call for households to make them was a propaganda exercise for the home front, so that women could feel useful rather than despair for their menfolk

Back in Oxford Naomi was dispatched on her bicycle to

warn the neighbours against wasting their time and resources on these sham artefacts. Meanwhile Haldane with his colleague Dr A. Mavrogodarto, affectionately called Mavro, set forth on experiments designed to devise the real thing.

The scene was set for one of the most distinctive households Oxford must ever have known. Anything that could be stripped or hacked into respiratory material was made use of, be it stockings, shawls, woolly vests, underwear, or Aldous Huxley's scarf. In the laboratory at the back of Cherwell Haldane and Mavro took turns at sealing themselves in the air-tight chambers and piping in quantities of deadly gas. Huxley leant forward to stare up close at the paper as he typed up the notes, while Haldane would break from the experiments to run to the wind-up telephone in the passage at the back of the dining room, reporting his findings, demanding action, ordering supplies, spinning into a fury when he was denied. 'Damn you!' he yelled at one point, determined to get beyond whoever was blocking the line at the other end, 'I'm the Lord Chancellor!'

Then back to work. The stink of chlorine permeated the whole house, and the sounds of Haldane and his gathering team coughing, and vomiting. The war was on, and these private chambers in Oxford were a new front line. For every day that troops were deployed in a zone of gas attacks without adequate protection, thousands might die.

This was 1915, with millions of men deployed in desperate conditions. It was no time for immaculate science. Delivering a state-of-the-art gas mask in a month or two would be too late. Before such a thing got into mass production, there might be nobody left to use it. The men themselves were the best resource available. Urine-soaked handkerchiefs were one thing, but surely science could do better. Grabbing what was to hand, how could a front-line soldier construct the most effective respirator?

'We tried various arrangements of cotton-wool with car-bonate, bi-carbonate and hypo-sulphate of soda,' Haldane mentioned in his report of 3 May 1915. 'None of these were very effective except against very small percentages of chlo-rine.'[19]

This translates, of course, to a process of trial and error. Haldane and Mavro experimented on themselves, with dif-ferent concentrations of chlorine, to mostly dire physical effect. The laboratory notes are reminiscent of those with carbon monoxide some twenty years earlier:

0.001% – strong smell, little discomfort
0.002% – irritation though the air could be tolerated
0.01% – excessive irritation, pain and sense of constriction of the chest. Irritation of the eyes.
0.1% – practically impossible to take in a breath and irritation of the eyes excessive.

That penultimate figure of 0.01 per cent amounts to a ratio of 1 to 10,000, which his report from the Clearing Station had already stated to be a potentially lethal dose. As with the miners, Haldane was now able to relate the soldiers' reported experiences against his own to reach a diagnosis: 'Judging from the symptoms described by officers and men, they had probably been exposed to 0.02% for 20 to 30 minutes.'[20]

Haldane's conversation with Kitchener en route for Oxford had not been to Kitchener's liking. The sight of the dead and wounded in France had shocked Haldane deeply. His report to the officers in HQ had been as emotional as it was clinical. Scientists had been forewarned about the dangers of gas attacks. They had time to suggest basic precautions. Yet the men in the front line had been wholly unprotected. He found no need to be less confrontational with Kitchener. The Secretary for War asked decent questions, but had one main concern. He wanted reprisals.

'The great K was very genial, not the hard stern man I had been led to expect,' Brereton Baker recalled of his later meeting with Kitchener. 'He listened to my account, which I made as concise as possible, but he wasn't in a hurry. He then went on to talk of reprisals. He said that he had had a talk with Haldane, but that he was too philosophical. He said "I think you are the man I want." I made some suggestions and he told me to go away and do my damndest.' Baker proceeded to ask Sir Frederick Donaldson[21] for a shell in which he could pack chemicals. Horrified at the suggestion, Donaldson 'began to argue about the impropriety of anything of the kind, and I told him that I did not like it, but I was there to obey orders. That fetched him up sharp and he said he was the same.'[22]

Haldane was called for by Kitchener and asked to visit Baker at Imperial College. If he would not work on weapons, at least he could work on respirators.

One model for a possible respirator came back from France with Baker. Based on a German respirator obtained at the front, it was made of cotton waste moistened with a solution of hyposulphate of soda (hypo) and carbonate of soda. After rough tests, Baker thought it satisfactory. Baker's wife Muriel, herself a trained chemist, travelled with the men towards the War Office. As the men talked of respirators, she offered an idea. Why not split open a lady's stocking to hold cotton waste? The party stopped off at a shop near Harrods. Stockings, black gauze and cotton waste to hand, the men met at the War Office with Sir Alfred Keogh. The new respirator was decided between them, moistening the waste with a solution of hypo, washing soda and glycerine that Baker had come up with in St Omer. The waste was held in a fold of black gauze that was wide enough to cover the eyes.

Haldane alerted Keogh to the fact that this respirator could only be a stop-gap measure. Better respirators of a box type would be needed. This was agreed to, though in the normal manner of Haldane's dealings with the army, agreement stalled before implementation. Military objections to breathing through a tube were so strong that the provisional box respirator had to be discarded and was not universally adopted for another year.

As the pattern for this new mask was sent for manufacture, Haldane took a prototype back to his laboratory. It needed more tests.

The cotton waste respirators turned out to be effective against very dilute chlorine. Increased concentrations, however, meant that the gas seeped through. The situation was made worse with larger pads, since the exhaled carbon dioxide was caught in the pad and breathed in again and again. This was not so much trial and error as trial and refinement. If something worked once, would it work against increased levels of poison? How might it work better? What could be substituted? The experimenters had a subjective way of measuring success each time. They asked themselves a question: 'To what degree has my body just been poisoned?'

Soldiers were based in trenches. One material readily available to them was earth. Haldane went out into his Oxford garden for some raw material. Slightly moist earth turned out to be a highly efficient substitute for cotton waste. Chlorine is absorbed when it reacts to carbonates or other substances in the soil. Fill a pad with earth though, and the same problem of re-breathing carbon dioxide presents itself.

Empty beer bottles were also available at the front. Haldane heated one, and lowered it into cold water so that its bottom dropped off. Putting cotton wool or cloth scraps in the neck and base, filling the rest with loose earth, breathing in through the bottle's neck and out through his nose, a soldier had an efficient respirator. Till official ones came the soldiers' way, such would do. As would wetting and wringing out any woollen object and holding it over the nose and mouth, or tying an earth-filled handkerchief so as to breathe through it. The measures became an official advice pamphlet.

This was not mere scientific theory, waiting to be tested out on soldiers. Haldane had thought his way into the soldiers' environment, their predicament, and their capabilities. What he was devising was wilfully makeshift. It could be made by individual men in their millions. He offered them nothing that he had not tested on himself, entering his gas-filled room.

Besides the dangers of cloud poisoning, the troops also faced attack by T-shells filled with teargas. T. F. Winmill, the chemist from the Doncaster Mining Laboratory, took a sample of benzyl iodide and held it out to officers and men who had suffered from teargas attacks. It smelt the same as their memories of the gas. However when an actual substance was obtained from a German shell, it turned out to be a bromine compound.[23] Reports of human experience were vital, but this showed how such reports needed testing with scientific rigour in laboratory conditions.

Handwritten lab notes tell of Haldane and Mavro's series

of experiments with xilyl bromide. A product of coal tar, which is of no value for making explosives, its use by the Germans as an eye irritant was quite probable. Of all the likely variants of vision disabling gases, it was also the easiest to make. The notes for the test concluded:

With 0.4cc sprayed (about 1 in 150,000), air was extremely irritating to nose and throat, causing coughing and great discomfort: no anaesthetic action or nausea noticed. Eyes badly affected at once, and couldn't be opened. With respirator there was no discomfort in breathing, though some came through, and nearly all the stuff seemed to be absorbed. With three layers of gauze and respirator, Mavro stayed in ¼ hour without having to close eyes, and with only slight smarting (whereas I had to come out within about ½ a minute and began coughing and choking when respirator not breathed through). With respirator and one layer of gauze I went in later. No discomfort in breathing and not much smarting of eyes. The respirator gave practical protection. With three layers gauze the protection was a good deal more. On taking off gauze and respirator after 15 minutes, Mavro had some coughing and eyes got bad, but by that time the air wasn't nearly so bad, as judged by the effect on me, coming in again.

So much for xilyl bromide. What about benzyl bromide, with its smell in low concentrations of mustard and cress, again a product of a process involving coal tar?

With .10cc effect on nose and throat marked, but not excessive: on eyes very great ... H. [Haldane] went in with woollen fabric dry over eyes. Eyes moderately affected. On taking it off, effect very bad. Then went in with oiled (olive) woollen fabric. Protection to eyes was now very effective. Same with one layer of oiled gauze. Could feel pungent effect in nose, with no effect in eyes.

The gauze stopped air blowing against the eyes, black gauze affording better vision than light-coloured. A smearing of oil absorbed the vapours, olive or linseed oil best of all as a good absorbent of chlorine. Even with three layers of oil, vision remained fairly clear. Haldane doubled the gas concentration.

.5cc sprayed into chamber, about 1 in 130,000. H. went in with helmet charged with solution and dried. Air very virulent to nose and throat causing coughing, and eyes very bad – couldn't well be kept open. Air much worse, however, with helmet off.[24]

Haldane had his information in place. His 'Memorandum on Asphyxiating Gases' was sent off to GHQ in France on 3 December. Haldane followed.

At his home in Berlin on 1 May, Fritz Haber hosted a party. His wife Clara was not in party mood. A scientist in her own right, one of the first women in Germany to receive a Ph.D., marriage to Haber should have empowered her career. Instead Haber preferred to domesticate her. She was disgusted by his perversion of science to the cause of chemical poisoning. James Franck remembered her as 'a good human being that wanted to reform the world'.[25] Paul Krassa, a friend of both Habers, recalled how a few days earlier Clara 'was in despair over the horrible consequences of gas warfare, for which she'd seen the preparations, along with the tests on animals'.[26] The party celebrated the success of Germany's first gas offensives. Clara stepped away from it and into the garden, Haber's service revolver in hand. Her first shot was into the air, alerting the world to her action. The second was into herself. She died two hours later, in the arms of her young son. The following morning Haber set out to oversee gas attacks on the Eastern Front.

On 1 May German troops launched an offensive against the British troops of the 1st Dorsets on Hill 60. They opened the valves on sixty cylinders already in place, setting loose the chlorine cloud.

The 1st Dorsets improvised, wetting rags to hold over their faces, remembering to breathe in through the mouth and out through the nose. Winds turned, so the German troops were affected with the same clouds of poison that they had released. The Dorsets rallied and managed to hold on to their trenches. Yet they suffered. A register of just one of the companies showed that of 170 who started the evening, only 38 remained.

On 2 May the 2nd Lancashire Fusiliers met with a chlorine cloud released from a 3-mile line in front of Ypres. The men, however, were prepared. Many had thrown away their temporary protection of cloths moistened with carbonate of soda. Instead they relied on Churchill's respirators. Despite assurances given to Haldane that these models were for domestic propaganda purposes only and would never leave London, 90,000 of them had been dispatched to France. That meant that 90,000 men faced possible gas attacks with no effective protection whatsoever. As the cloud passed, their medical officer reported 30 per cent in a state of collapse.

Three days later an official tally reported: 'Lanc. Fusiliers have ceased to exist for military purposes not fifty men available for duty as result of German gases.'[27]

On Haldane's arrival back in France, victims of the clouds of gas filled the hospitals. British troops reported 2,314 casualties on 1 May, 227 of them fatal. On the night of 5 and 6 May, when a German gas offensive retook Hill 60, men used the cotton wool respirators. Another 22 men died among 557 gas casualties.

A large school in St Omer had been converted into a hospital, with a room set aside as Haldane's experimental laboratory. A small glass-fronted cabinet, like a miniature greenhouse, was his latest gas chamber. The gas of choice was chlorine. Faced with the urgency of the work, the War Office called back from active duty colleagues who had experienced the extremes of Haldane's experimental regimen. C. G. Douglas was swiftly on the scene, Jack Haldane was pulled back from his bomb squad to come to his father's aid, and J. Ivon Graham formerly of the Doncaster Mining Laboratory set down his stretcher. As a Quaker, Graham worked in a non-combatant role with the Friends' Ambulance Service, running rescue missions through places of great hazard. 'Certain gassing now, but maybe live to tell the tale,' was part of the deal in working with Haldane. The sons Graham would father after the war put their existence down to his answering Haldane's call.

The investigators' role was to compare the effects on themselves of various quantities of chlorine, both with a respirator, and without. Haldane had trained Jack 'in the practice of courage', reading Sir Walter Scott's *Tales of a Grandfather* to him as a boy, inspiring him with those 'legends of the war-like exploits of the Scottish nobility'. The historical bonds between fathers and sons found material for a whole new and perverse chapter as Dr Haldane settled Jack inside the glass chamber, turned on the gas valve, and studied the effects of gas poisoning on the young man.

Put a regular soldier in charge of a machine gun, Jack reckoned, and he was in his element. He might well stick to his task in the face of a gas attack, and restrain himself from coughing, gasping and flailing. In a laboratory experiment, however, nothing would focus his mind away from his feelings. Chlorine stung the eyes and provoked an urge to gasp and cough. A trained physiologist could enter the gas chamber and be in his element like the soldier with the gun. Haldane's select team members brought the appropriate element of self-control along with them.

The masks of course had to be used for fighting. They had to be effective in full action and not just when sitting down. A wheel was constructed inside the gas chamber for the investigators to turn, and once outside they would keep on their masks or helmets and run 50-yard dashes.

'As each of us got sufficiently affected by gas to render his lungs duly irritable, another would take his place,' Jack later recalled. 'None of us was much the worse for the gas, or in any real danger, as we knew where to stop, but some had to go to bed for a few days, and I was very short of breath and incapable of running for a few months or so.'

His account of the tale included sardonic comment on the lack of regard giving to Britain's pioneering gas scientists. 'This work, which was mainly done by civilians, was rewarded by the grant of the Military Cross to the brilliant young officer who used to open the door of the motor-car of the medical general who occasionally visited the experiments.' For medals, those in uniform who did take part in the tests made do with buttons. 'The soldiers who took part in them could, however, for some time be distinguished by the peculiar green colour of their brass buttons due to the action of the gas.'[28]

The 8th of May saw Jack Haldane ordered to the front, in anticipation of an enemy gas attack. On the same day the Black Watch was due to take part in an Anglo-French attack to become known as the Battle of Aubers Ridge. Bad weather delayed the attack by a day. The 9th of May saw Jack making slow progress in their direction – if his platoon was going to fight, he wanted to be there as their commander. Chlorine poisoning still affected him, so that his fastest run was 'a moderate trot worthy of an old gentleman with chronic bronchitis'.

He was yet to reach the reserve line when the Allied bombardment began, and he was not much further forward when the counter-battery kicked in. A blast felled him, leaving wounds in his right arm and left side. He continued, rallying his troops before he was felled by a second blast. Aldous Huxley, then staying with the Haldanes, notes curiously that 'Jack appears to have been hit in right arm and left side by portions of J. Johnson.'[29]

He was dazed on coming round. A Black Watch officer flagged down a passing car and asked that Jack Haldane be taken to the nearest dressing station.

'Oh, it's you,' the driver said. It was the Prince of Wales. He and Jack had last been together in Oxford the year before.

Naomi believed that the period working with her father had saved her brother's life. Had he been on the scene earlier, he would most likely have been killed alongside most of his fellow officers. The wounds he did receive ruled out Haldane's recommendation that his son be named Chemical

Adviser to Douglas Haig's First Army, a role that carried with it the title and pay of a general.

Haldane meanwhile returned to London, arriving on Sunday 9 May. Despite repeated requests, the official respirators had failed to arrive. He went to the War Office to seek the reason. Two or three thousand had been made, he was told, but with great difficulty. The design was simple. Something must have gone wrong with the manufacture. Haldane drove on to see Lord Kitchener at St James's Palace, and got the necessary authority to investigate and deal with the matter.

On the Monday morning he drove down to the factory of 'John Bell, Hills and Lucas' in South London. The managing director was in despair. About two hundred women were struggling on at the work, but their rubber gloves were in tatters and their fingers burnt. Try as he might, the manager could locate no more gloves in all of London.

Masks to be put over the mouth and nose of soldiers clearly shouldn't be burning through rubber gloves. The main chemical ingredient of the masks, used to soak the cotton waste content, was to be sodium carbonate, commonly known as washing powder. Haldane checked the recipe in use in the factory. Instead of carbonate of soda, they were using caustic soda.

The adjustment was made, all other jobs were cleared from the factory, and hundreds of women set to work on night and day shifts. They were soon producing 70,000 respirators a day.

Several pockets of scientists on both sides of the war were now engaged in gas research, looking at the physiological effects of different gases, and their possibilities both for offence and defence. Haldane brought with him a lifetime's experience of dealing with hazardous gas conditions, and an acute awareness of official incompetence and delay in putting effective measures into operation. On 14 October 1913, the twentieth century's worst pit disaster had occurred at Senghennydd in Wales. The explosion was heard in Cardiff 11 miles away. Four hundred and forty men and boys were killed, rescue operations mounted over several days to recover scattered survivors. Haldane examined photographs of the rescue apparatus involved, and wired a warning straight back to the chief inspector of mines in the area. This was the same dangerous kind of apparatus as was used by the London Fire Brigade that spring. The warning went unheeded, and the consequences could have been tragic. Nine men using the apparatus were overcome at one time. Fortunately men without apparatus were at hand, and able to go to their rescue. Haldane knew that bad rescue apparatus was more dangerous than no apparatus.

A central laboratory was set up at a school in St Omer. When Major MacPherson of the Newfoundland Medical Corps devised a 'helmet' consisting of a chemically treated flannel bag with mica window, Haldane insisted on further tests. He feared that men who wore it would be exposed to breathing their own exhaled carbon dioxide. Two of its main developers donned the helmet and ran at the double around the cloisters to no obvious ill effect.

Back in London, Haldane's doubts about this 'hypo' helmet continued. He met with Brereton Baker at the Army Medical College on 21 May. Giving the helmet one sniff, he claimed that anyone would choke on wearing it, and backed continued use of the original respirator. To test the claim, he and Baker climbed to a room at the top of the building. With chlorine gas filling the room to the high concentration of one part in 1,000 of air, Baker put on the helmet and Haldane the respirator.

'He retired in 4 minutes and had not stopped coughing when I came out 20 minutes later,' Baker wrote in his diary. 'The helmet was a bit stuffy, but no CL_2 came through. Haldane was intent on crabbing it, said no one could move in it, so I ran up & down the passage with it on.' Baker had proved his point, though Haldane's sense of the inadequacy of the helmet also had merit, as the next line in Baker's journal admits. 'I must confess I was a bit pumped, but I made as light of it as possible.'

The Haldane name was becoming rampant in the press. Richard Haldane was at heart a philosopher. His friend the philosopher Andrew Seth Pringle-Pattison observed that he 'philosophized to satisfy a religious need, and the philosophical conclusions on which he rested were held by him with all the intensity which religious convictions possess for the ordinary man.' Referring to those such as Kant and Hegel who had given most direction to his philosophical life, Richard once spoke of Germany as his 'spiritual home'. The phrase went on record, to be ripped from its context and used to justify absurd allegations. In May 1915 the current Lord Chancellor, who as Secretary for War had been most responsible for Britain's war preparations, suddenly found newspapers casting him as a pro-German agitator infiltrated into the heart of British government.

'The newspaper attacks on Richard will only, I think, recoil on the heads of those who make them,' Haldane wrote to his mother. 'They are very discreditable.'[30]

The attacks were also highly effective. Lord Haldane's resignation from office was the one Unionist Party requirement before entering a wartime coalition government, and

took effect on 25 May. By now the Haldane name had
become a poisonous one in public opinion, led through the
media by the *Daily Express* and by Leo Maxse as editor of
The National Review, while rumours spread around high society slandered the whole family. The Duke of Argyle sent
Maxse information from his solicitor regarding financial
irregularities of William Haldane. '"They dare to say I was
the illegitimate daughter of the German Emperor,"' Mary
Haldane told her friend Violet Markham, 'in a voice full of
indignation; and then humour overcame indignation and we
both laughed.'[31]

Lady Mansfield Clarke assured the Duchess of Wellington
that John Scott Haldane was experimenting with bombs to
blow up the kingdom, the Duchess in turn rushing the news
on to Maxse.[32] At least this rumour had some source in an
actual incident, even if the pursuant logic was hideously per-
verted. As part of mining experiments in Doncaster, a series
of experimental explosions had taken place to disabuse
mining engineers of the notion that while colliery explosions
were propagated by coal dust they were always started by
methane. Coal dust was spread on shelves at Alltofts Colliery,
where a long gallery of old boilers was constructed. A small
charge of gunpowder stirred up the dust, and a larger one
ignited it. J. B. S. Haldane was there when a larger than usual
trial began: 'After a run of about thirty metres, if I remember,
the explosion changed its character to a detonation. The last
two boilers were torn to pieces, and a large portion of one of
them flew over our heads 300 metres or so away. The
Coalowners' Association had sufficient influence to keep the
Press quiet, but an explosion was reported at Pontefract, some
six miles away.'[33] Haldane wrote of a subsequent experiment
under the Explosions in Mines Committee appointed by the

Home Secretary, recalling 'an explosion in my presence which blew the large steel tube in which the experiments were conducted into fragments which were scattered over the surrounding fields'.[34]

As a committee was formed around chemical defence against gases, 'entire newspapers were in full swing in the disgraceful agitation against my brother,' Haldane wrote. Much to his astonishment, his name was omitted from the committee's roster. The problem was that the names had to be published. 'So far as I could gather it was considered under the circumstances wiser to leave me out, though this was certainly never wished by any responsible soldiers.'[35]

Haldane's influence reached the committee through his protégés, particularly C. G. Douglas. Eventually the army would come to see the need for the box respirator he had first advised to Kitchener, but he was effectively removed from the further developments of gas masks that would happen during the war. By early June that year, he was satisfied that the War Office had finally ensured supply of the Baker/Haldane form of respirator to the troops. That summer the Institution of Mining Engineers announced the award to Haldane of its gold medal for 1914–15, for work that 'had been of direct humanitarian value to mining communities in every part of the world'.[36] On 6 June Haldane joined the 'Experiments Committee' at GHQ 'for the purpose of receiving, investigating and reporting upon investigations of all kinds which may tend to assist the operations of the troops'.[37] On 24 June he became a member of the Royal Society's 'Sectional War Committee for Physiology'.

Meanwhile an earlier innovation saw Haldane's work assume some primary importance beneath the battlefield. Seventeen-year-old Private David Hood of the Argyll and

Sutherland Highlanders later recalled how miners working the tunnels 'decided they'd do the same as they did when mining at home. I was ordered down a mine listening post with a canary in a cage. I had been there for about four hours. All of a sudden the canary toppled over. At the same time I felt very drowsy.'

The early warning nature of the canary's fall hadn't been instilled in him. A colleague was sent down to keep him company, listening for sounds of German movements in their rival tunnels. 'Well this is a bit daft,' he said to himself, after some moments with the sleeping Hood and the fallen canary. 'What about this canary?' The colleague went out to fetch a rescue party. The next thing Hood knew was 'they'd dragged me out and got me onto a stretcher. Halfway down the trenches – I was one of those pig-headed people I suppose – I wasn't going to be carried down on any stretcher and I got up and got violently sick. I suppose that was the only thing that saved me.'[38]

Haldane's safety measures sometimes went awry as instructions failed to reach the lowest ranks. Soldiers strapped respirators to their chests because that's where they felt the pain. The 'mistakes and delays at home over respirators' shook Haldane's faith in the ability of the authorities to deliver the appropriate education. 'A man who fails or fumbles' over tying on his respirator 'may easily lose his life or be disabled for the time. With proper instructions to the men there should be no trouble in defying the gas.'[39]

On a visit to a submarine a young officer saw Haldane glance at their cage of canaries and explained: 'Oh, not just pets, sir! I am told they give valuable information. When the atmosphere gets dangerously polluted they begin to sing very loudly and flap their wings.'[40]

Major H. J. Humphreys had keener experience, having joined a tunnelling company after years as an inspector of mines. He thought he was immune to CO poisoning before his arrival in France. Canaries, he advised, 'ought, of course, to be placed near the mouth of the person they are intended to protect. Sometimes they are some distance away.'[41]

Carbon monoxide poisoning was a mounting threat to the tunnellers – in one six-week period, one company suffered 150 casualties, 16 of them fatal. From early in the war colonies of mice were kept at tunnelling headquarters, men later given the choice of canaries or mice as 'the tunnellers' friends'. Most came to opt for canaries, their brief lunging flight to the bottom of the cage being far more obvious than a mouse's foetal curling. The canaries' claws were trimmed, for otherwise dead birds might remain on their perches. Those that survived several missions achieved pet status in tunnellers' camps safe behind the lines. As the demands of war outstripped bird supply, an army aviary was set up in Calais where Haldane's canaries were bred.

Jack came home on leave, an operation failing to remove the shrapnel from his arm. By the early weeks of June his temperature was dropping. It was hoped he could continue his convalescence at Cloan.

Joining him at Cherwell was Captain Unwin, a casualty of the gassing of Hill 60 who lay unconscious for two days at Bailleul Clearing Station. Several of the most severe casualties of the gas attacks were sent to the hospital in Oxford, so Haldane could observe their symptoms and direct their recovery. Meanwhile his gas research continued. What were the effects of breathing nitrous oxide from explosive charges? What protection could be offered to the troops from attacks by new gases of warfare such as mustard gas and phosgene? Haldane stayed in constant communication with his colleagues at the front, particularly C. G. Douglas, attuning his work to meet their needs. Douglas found refuge at Cherwell during his times of leave, and was annoyed when his reports sent to the Physiological War Committee failed to reach the Senior Partner. 'As usual what you write is full of suggestion,' he wrote from France to Haldane, 'which is more than can be said of the other reports I receive from home. I wish you were holding the hands of the people researching, they have so limited an outlook.'[42]

Mary Haldane, who was in correspondence with Sir John French among others, wrote to her son that word 'coming from headquarters is very good and telling. It was not the only time that you have risked your life when it stood in the atmosphere of black damp.'[43]

On a more philosophical level, on 15 November 1915 Mary wrote to her family: 'To us all, this war has been the means of impressing the reality of a future life. In fact we may say a *fuller* life. This life is but a shadow compared with what is to come. Our noble fathers and brothers and sons have given us examples of self abnegation and devotion to righteousness and truth that we little dreamt of witnessing.'[44]

With three more years to run, the war was still to accumulate horrors on all sides. Gas would claim half a million Russian casualties on the Eastern Front. For the British, J. K. Dick-Cunyngham was at the front after an early gas attack and would never forget 'the awful expression of fear and alarm on the faces of the dead and dying'. Some months later he was responsible for placing cylinders of gas in position for release against the German lines. 'I well remember how keen the men of the 16th Division were to handle the beastly things,' he recorded, 'stroking them as if they were pet toys, and right well did they work to get them in position.'[45]

The horrors of war multiply themselves. It takes some doing to turn the tide, to begin the long process of healing from the very middle of conflict. Haldane was set to do exactly that.

15

DEEP OXYGEN

'I belong to an older and more risky occupation than that of coal mining,' Haldane told mining students in 1919, 'to an occupation which includes women as well as men, and can trace its history and honourable traditions back more than 2,000 years. It is a history I have good reason to be proud of.'[1]

He was speaking as a doctor of medicine. Tracing back across millennia, Hippocrates was his model. 'Hippocrates,' he told a different audience that same year, 'taught that it is beyond the wit of man to cure disease by direct means. He was not a quack. He pointed out, however, that the body is no mere machine, but a living organism, and that it is of the "nature" of a living organism to cure itself; also that by persistently studying the working of the "nature", we can learn how to help it towards cure – how to tide it over emergency and give it what it requires to effect the cure – how, in short, to be a "physician".'[2]

Haldane's war work had taken a new turn in 1916. Sir John Cadman, known to Haldane through their joint work with the mining industry, asked him to design oxygen apparatus to help munitions workers affected by accidental gas poisoning. Such apparatus was already available in many forms. Sooner than adapt the apparatus of others, Haldane took his brief as an invitation to reconsider the whole nature of breathing. What is oxygen's role in the healing process, and how is it best directed?

Haldane had not stopped poisoning himself in order to find a remedy. 'I am downstairs, today,' he wrote to his mother on 19 March 1916, 'but still very stiff, & not fit for very much. No doubt K told you that I got knocked up, with a high temperature and various other symptoms during a long experiment in the respiration chamber last week. I wasn't very well when the experiment began, on the 8th, and perhaps I went on too long.'

War now served up a steady supply of victims. As Joseph Lister found when German field doctors took up his methods of antiseptic surgery in the French–German war of 1870, a flood of casualties can provoke unexpected advances in medical science. 'Like many others,' Haldane admitted, 'I did not at first realize the practical difficulties of oxygen treatment.'[3]

Work began with poison-gas victims in the Ashhurst Military Hospital near Oxford, patients directed there from the trenches in France so as to be near Haldane. In early 1917 he was handed a letter from his Oxford colleague Sir William Osler, sent from Osler's compatriot Colonel Jonathan Meakins of the Royal Canadian Army Medical Corps.

After two weeks leave back in England from the warfare in France in 1916, Meakins had been deployed to a small War Office hospital just off Hampstead Heath in London, working on a condition known as 'soldiers' heart' or DAH (diffuse alveolar haemorrhage), first observed in soldiers of the

American Civil War. Thousands of men were now being invalided out of France with similar severe chest pains, shortness of breath, and racing heartbeats. Investigating this illness, Meakins was alerted to patterns of disturbed breathing. He brought in a Haldane gas analysis apparatus to teach himself something of respiratory physiology, but was singularly frustrated by the results he could achieve. On being redeployed to a hospital in Brighton he wrote his letter to Osler, seeking help in learning to master the Haldane apparatus.

When Osler showed him the letter Haldane wrote to Meakins at once, with the time of his train's arrival at Brighton station. He kept an eye out for a Canadian military uniform so as to recognize Meakins on the platform. 'He had two large Gladstone bags,' Meakins recalled. 'I offered to take one but he resisted, but I insisted. I wondered why he had so many clothes but I soon found out. When I lifted one of the bags it seemed to weigh at least one hundred pounds and turned out to be full of small oxygen cylinders and some metal valves, etc. The other contained some Douglas bags, a small gasometer and tubing, along with a few clothes; a truly Haldanian assortment as I was soon to become well acquainted with.

'To describe Dr. Haldane would be beyond my powers,' Meakins continued, and in trying for such a description included the best top-level medical diagnosis we have of Haldane's physical condition. 'His quiet humour, his twinkling eye, the large unruly moustache, the bent back which I am sure was due to advanced spinal osteo-arthritis, his brilliant mind and patience with the neophyte. I soon learned of two absent-minded habits he had – never leave a pencil or a box of matches near his reach as they would invariably find a resting place in his pockets!'[4]

Meakins wife Dorothy, known for her beauty and sharp wit, had travelled to Britain to be with her husband. The young couple (Meakins was then thirty-four years old) hosted Haldane in their home for the evening. They shared dinner and a brief conversation before having an early night, presuming Haldane was tired after his roundabout journey with the two heavy bags. They did not yet know Haldane's reputation as a night hawk.

Kathleen had always hated those Gladstone bags of Haldane's, but his habit of using them persisted to the end. Leaving the clothing behind, they hauled the bags off to the Brighton hospital the following morning. 'He put me straight as to the gas analysis,' Meakins remembered of the day:

> was most interested in the patients who I put through some exercises by climbing stairs; went into periods of deep thought sucking on his wheezy pipe and asking some questions. We collected some samples of expired air and alveolar air which he examined and measured the patients' minute respiratory volume. All this was really honestly mysterious to me but it soon became my daily intellectual diet.
>
> He left the next afternoon, leaving his equipment behind for me by taking his bags and clothing. His parting remark was 'I wish you were at Taplow!!!' In a short time my orders came. I have often wondered what Bill Osler and John Haldane had to do with them as Taplow was on the main line from Oxford to London. I never asked so I never knew but one should never be inquisitive in the army!

The 15th Canadian Field Hospital in Taplow, also known as the Duchess of Connaught Red Cross Hospital, was the war contribution of the Astor family. Formed from a single-storey sequence of interconnected huts built around a large building formerly used for winter games, it was sited near the lodge of their Cliveden estate in Buckinghamshire. On its opening it was declared 'the finest military war hospital in the world. There is nothing to beat it as a temporary hospital anywhere.'[5] The hospital started with 125 beds, with plans to increase it to 1,000.

In early 1917 Meakins had between 600 and 700 patients in his care, drawn from all Allied nationalities with the addition of a few prisoners of war. Rather than using the huts, his large ward was placed in a former indoor tennis court. Eight beds were transferred across from a neighbouring badminton court, which with its running water and electricity was freed for conversion into a laboratory.

Tall and imposing yet with a real love for the men in his care, Meakins was perfect for instilling the necessary sense of ordered calm so important to the recovery of gas victims. With the patient base and the infrastructure now in place, all that was needed for the project to proceed from palliative care to forging true breakthroughs in medical science was a fully trained physiologist as part of the staff. Haldane knew none better than Captain J. Gillies Priestley, with whom he would eventually write the classic second edition of his seminal work *Respiration*. Priestley had just been invalided home from the Near East and was on extended sick leave. Haldane drew on his extensive War Office connections to have Priestley deployed to Taplow, then worked to raise substantial funds for the project from the Medical Research Committee. All was in place.

Dorothy Meakins lived as close to Taplow as she could, though with the wartime cost of living so high their homes became ever more humble till eventually they were taking in lodgers. Their favourite home was just half an hour's walk away from the hospital, so Meakins was able to make time from his work for favourite activities of punting and family riverside picnics, just as Haldane loved to do at Cherwell. Their young son was soon joined by baby daughter Diana, to whom Nancy Astor became godmother.

The Taplow project had two of the highest-level consultants imaginable. Sir William Osler visited for a few hours on one day a week, and Haldane spent a full day a week there. He brought in equipment from the company Siebe Gorman, and managed to magic up from London any parts needed as the team devised new apparatus in their hospital laboratory.

Soldiers who had apparently made a full recovery from gas poisoning, with sound lung and heart function, still became breathless on exertion. Haldane suspected that the lining to the air sacs in their lungs remained damaged, and put this theory to the test. Strapping the soldiers into the type of light rescue apparatus used in mines, he had them walk up and down stairs and take exercise. The oxygen mixture felt like a new lease of life. However while a normal healthy man breathes more deeply on exercising, he does not breathe any more often. These men were panting, their breaths were still shallow, the addition of oxygen made little difference, and their pulses ran wildly.

This observation led to a new puzzle. How does shallow breathing produce anoxaemia, the lack of oxygen in arterial blood? In 1908 Arthur Keith, a professor at the Royal College of Surgeons, had shown that the different parts of the lung open out in succession, like the different parts of a Japanese fan. With shallow breathing, only parts of the lung open properly. These parts overventilate as a result, while the unopened parts underventilate. Haldane recognized that this uneven distribution of air to the lung was the cause of the anoxaemia, which troubled poison-gas victims but also those with bronchitis, asthma, pneumonia, emphysema and all such conditions that cause shallow breathing.

Sooner than help damaged lungs, pure oxygen adds its own irritation. Haldane calculated the necessary percentages of oxygen that had to be added to air to relieve certain conditions, and geared his oxygen apparatus to administer such exact amounts. A reducing valve and tap regulated the supply, while a gauge showed how long the oxygen would last. The oxygen flow paused when the patient was exhaling. As production and delivery of the equipment were severely limited in time of war, this reduction of oxygen usage by 90 per cent allowed for extensive provision to the troops. The company Siebe Gorman supplied Haldane's oxygen apparatus in their many hundreds to British and American forces in France. 'The same results can be got by simpler methods, using two or three times as much oxygen,' Haldane wrote near the end of the war, as his lightweight version for use with stretcher cases was being added to production. 'My apparatus prevents waste of oxygen.'[6]

Though his patients were victims of wartime gas attacks, Haldane still had his personal bank of self-inflicted experience on which to draw. 'The immediate effects of suddenly giving an abundance of oxygen to a cyanosed person may sometimes be unpleasant, as well I know from experiments on myself and others,' he wrote in 1917.[7] 'The heart may become tumultuous in its action, and the breathing irregular for the time, or the patient may wake up to the realization of pain or discomfort. His respiratory centre may also wake up to reaction against accumulated CO_2.'

Meakins's letters home from near the end of the war told how proud he was of the war work 'the McGill team and its colleagues did during the war at Taplow and other hospitals, as the intensity of the situation and exposure to the quantity and variety of problems led to imaginative therapies that would have taken many years longer to emerge in normal life. The application of science to clinical medicine and the development of the two hand-in-hand was radical at the time.'[8] At the close of war the 36-year-old Meakins was appointed the first Professor of Therapeutics at Edinburgh. He went on to become a founding figure at McGill Medical Faculty in Montreal, caring for veterans in a nearby hospital till his death in 1959. The extent to which he followed other young men into the particular spell of proximity to Haldane was shown in 1920, when he joined Joseph Barcroft's expedition to the Peruvian Andes to investigate Haldane's Pikes Peak findings.

Haldane would become known as 'the father of oxygen therapy'[9] for his development and advocacy of the use of high levels of oxygen as treatment, his work moving out beyond its military application. Oxygen therapy could also work, he noted, for '"shock" after wounds or operations or anaesthetics',[10] while 'in the sudden accesses of dyspnoea which sometimes occur in (or after) influenza oxygen seems usually to produce relief at once, & need only be given for about a minute.'[11] How soon his methods would take effect outside of army medical practice remained a bone of postwar contention. 'The most futile methods – I can use no other expression – of oxygen administration,' he maintained, 'are still commonly employed.'[12]

The first step of good practice, Haldane directed, should be to know what the oxygen is aiming at, where it is going, and in what quantities. Beyond that, the physician was left in Hippocratic territory, the body proving itself to be a self-regulating organism interacting with its environment. 'The aim should be cure, and not mere temporary palliation of symptoms. We can cure the patient if we can tide him over the bad stage of anoxaemia. Nature will do the rest.'[13]

Nature was having a spirited last fling with the walnut trees at Cherwell. The house had been positioned around three magnificent specimens, each around 250 years old. In the summer of 1918 the trees developed a phenomenal crop. Patients at Somerville military hospital had a standing invitation to walk in to Cherwell and rest a while in its surroundings. Bowls filled with walnuts, salt and crackers awaited them on the hall table.

As a walnut's roots touch the water level, the tree starts to die. The water level in Oxford is not deep. That 1918 crop was a final gift of bounty. The postwar nut crop was miserably small. Within a few years the rotted trees were cut down and carted away. Haldane helped with the summer chore of bringing in the hay, but the garden was truly Kathleen's domain. She believed in vegetables rather than flowers, and kept a bountiful supply of caged rabbits for the pot. Aldous Huxley posed a riddle: 'Problem: if five men can dig a garden in a fortnight, how long would it take two women, one of whom was Mrs Haldane, to accomplish the same piece of work. Answer: two days.'[14]

Floods brought mud to fertilize the water meadows. Known as the North and South Meads, the meadows were relics of a medieval farming system, fertilized by mud washed in with regular floods. Traditional management meant cutting the hay at the end of June and grazing what was known as the 'aftermath' between 1 August (Lammas Day) and the last day of November. The Haldanes gathered in two hay crops a year, the aftermath grazing done by Kathleen's herd of Jersey cows. Large-uddered creatures, their teats had to be stretched and then milked by hand. Kathleen conscripted Naomi to help her in this lengthy milking schedule, milk for the household poured into white enamel setting pans and set on slate shelves in a north-facing dairy.

Attached to the traditions of minor Tory landed aristocracy, Kathleen took the chance to extend Cherwell and its meadows through the acquisition of almost 10 acres between their home and the Marston Ferry road. With what amounted to a small farm now under her control, she started to sell her Jersey milk from what became the first grade A tuberculin-tested herd in the south of England.

Aldous Huxley's 45-year-old mother had died of cancer in 1908, leaving the fourteen-year-old Aldous a note: 'Judge not too much and love more.' Aldous stayed on at Eton until a fresh disaster struck. He was sixteen, a painter, the keenest of readers, an avid explorer of the natural world, when his eyes suddenly began to inflame. An attack of the eye infection keratitis left him almost totally blind. In this state he was first brought to stay with the Haldanes for a while.

The Huxley boys were treated so much as kin that Naomi was allowed to walk out with them without a chaperone. She took many a long walk with Aldous's older brother Trevenen. By September 1913 Aldous's sight was improving somewhat. With the aid of a strong magnifying glass he peered into an entrance examination paper and entered Balliol College to study English Literature. Trevenen completed a postgraduate career while Aldous was an undergraduate, but was prone to great depression. During the first days of war in August 1914 he wandered away from a sanatorium and hanged himself from a woodland tree.

In the wake of this fresh tragedy, Aldous came to stay with the Haldanes again. With Balliol emptying as its students entered the war, Cherwell was a much more companionable place. His very poor vision occasioned his own war wound. Walking the downstairs corridor of Cherwell he bumped into a basin of nitric acid left outside Haldane's lab by an assistant, which splashed on to his knee. Huxley stayed with the Haldanes through October 1915, when Naomi was brought back to Cherwell in an ambulance from her own wartime service as a nurse in St Thomas's Hospital. She had contracted scarlet fever. Cherwell became a plague zone for a while.

Jack soldiered on well enough after his first war wound to re-engage with his father's work. 'Jack and I are just starting for Birmingham in connection with gas experiments,' Haldane wrote to his mother on 4 December 1915. 'He has got his leave a little extended, to enable him to visit bombing schools in London and Hull.'

Jack's main engagement through the autumn of 1916 was running the bombing school back in Nigg. From there he managed to return to the front, this time joining the Black Watch in Mesopotamia, chasing war action in what would become known as Iraq. In early 1917 a leg wound from a British bomb put an end to his fighting. After a month of leave in Bombay Jack was removed to the regimental depot in Bangalore.

News of war casualties kept dropping on Oxford like stun grenades. The normal student population of the city was around 3,000. By war's end, 2,700 of Oxford's men had been killed, lecturers and students alongside workers from the city. In August 1917 Sir William Osler heard of the death of his beloved son Edward Revere Osler (the great-great-grandson on his mother's side of the American patriot Paul Revere). Friends saw the life fade from William Osler, who died himself some two years later.

Haldane absorbed news of each casualty, and returned to the trenches of France to instruct the troops in the proper administration of his oxygen apparatus. In one subsequent demonstration run by Colonel Barley, General Allenby marched to the front of the room. Known as 'The Bloody Bull', Allenby was the commander of the Third Army. He would go on to head the Egyptian Expeditionary Force, where T. E. Lawrence remembered him as 'physically large and confident, and morally so great that the comprehension of our littleness came slow to him'. Allenby seized the gas equipment from the servant acting as the demonstrator, 'put the slobbery rubber mouthpiece to his own mouth, and saw all was well'.[15]

War was fought at the bedsides of the wounded and in the laboratory as well as at the front. From Germany Fritz Haber studied the speed and effectiveness of Allied measures to protect troops against the gas attacks he devised. Russian resistance was hopeless, the French were tolerably effective, but his real admiration went out to the British. For Haber, the introduction of poison gas turned war into a game of chess. You devised your own strategies and guessed at your enemy's. Your attacks could be nullified by effective defence, and opened you to reprisals. It was a thrilling game, and the British were excellent players. While Haber set his institutions to work in Berlin, developing new approaches to gas warfare, Haldane worked his committee meetings in London, his hospital team at Taplow, the resources of his Oxford laboratory and the mining laboratory at Doncaster. 'Poisonous gases,' he wrote, 'have been used in warfare with the intention of putting men out of action, hampering artillery, preventing supports from advancing and inspiring general terror.'[16]

Terror is evoked when threat is felt to be ever-present, dreadful in its impact, and unknown. Haldane urged medical officers to be aware of different smells that might be gas. 'This may be musty, pungent, aromatic, like lilac, garlic, mustard and grass, bitter almonds and so on.'[17] Men might feel secure with their anti-gas protections. Haber's job was to release gases that worked their way around and through such protection. Haldane's main goal was to extend that protection, in terms both of prevention and cure. Haber and his future Nobel prize-winners kept Haldane and an array of top scientists constantly busy.

Phosgene had the smell of mouldering hay. Substituted for chlorine at the end of 1915 it billowed towards the Allied lines as cloud gas, which would break up on touching a moist surface and release hydrochloric acid. Chlorine created spasm. Phosgene slid more smoothly down, penetrating the innermost recesses of the lung. No soldier died on first contact. 'A man may feel able to carry on with work for an hour or two with only trivial symptoms: then he rapidly becomes worse and passes into a state of greyish white collapse with progressive oedema of the lungs that may soon be fatal.'[18]

Haber mixed phosgene with chlorine to achieve a combination of effects, but new mixtures were not the only game. 'I have been kept busy lately,' Haldane wrote on 25 August 1917, 'by the new gas the Germans are using.'[19]

These new gas shells fell without much of a bang, first dropping on Ypres and its neighbourhood between ten and one on the night of 12/13 July 1917. Men sneezed, their throats itched, but their chests felt clear and their eyes did not water. The smell was 'unpleasant', some said, 'oily', 'like garlic', 'like mustard'. Some men vomited but the effects did not seem so bad. An officer put in the mouthpiece of his respirator and clipped his nose but did not bother with the mask, leaving it to hang down so that his eyes were unprotected. Men who had been away at the time of the attack returned to the dug-out, noticed no unusual smell, and went to sleep. 'From two to five hours later they were awakened with pain in the eyes which rapidly became intolerable, often feeling as though they had sand or grit in the eyes. The eyes and nose were running, as if they had a violent cold in the head . . . Nausea became marked and repeated vomiting occurred and persisted for some hours.'[20] By the following day the eyelids of some had swollen, eyes and noses were running pus, while blisters were appearing on the lower part of the face, chin and sometimes the neck. Morphine helped men bear the pain.

The chemical adviser of the Fifth Army reached through the shell holes to retrieve fragments for analysis. The shells were marked with a green cross on the base and a yellow cross on the sides. The adviser tucked one particularly large piece under his arm and carried it away. Beneath his uniform the patch of red skin corresponded to where the shell had been held, and the wrists and backs of the man's hands swelled and blistered.

Mustard gas, also known as Yperite (for where it landed) and Yellow Cross gas (for those marks on the shells), had been introduced. Chlorine is judged to have killed 1,976 soldiers of the British Expeditionary Forces by the end of the war. Mustard gas killed 4,086. It was a gas for Fritz Haber to be proud of. On announcing its availability to the German General Ludendorff, however, Haber added a proviso. Do not release it till the war can be won within the year. Given a year, the Allied forces will have mustard gas of their own. Soldiers struck by the gas needed to change their clothes for new ones. This might be possible for Britain, but the resources of Germany were so stretched that no extra outfits were available.

Haber was right. The British released mustard gas against German forces a year after first suffering it themselves. At the beginning, though, they were working with a great unknown. The slightness of the gas's smell led C. G. Douglas to wonder 'whether the sense of smell was abolished by the action of the gas (sulphuretted hydrogen for instance, though having a characteristic odour when very dilute, is practically odourless in strong concentrations)'.

On 14 August 1917 Haldane was homing in on the constituents of mustard gas, using dichlorethylsulphide in experiments. This was war. Animals did not come out so lucky as in most of his experiments. 'Two drops of the liquid from a yellow cross shell were injected subcutaneously into a rat, taking care that none of the liquid got into the external skin. In about one hour the rat began to secrete liquid from the nose and rub it in,' Haldane began his report. Cats joined in the sacrifice, dying from exposure to just two drops of the shell contents. Things were looking better by 16 August. The latest cat's eyes were bandaged with cotton wool soaked in Vaseline. Joining the cat inside a large box was a sheet of blotting paper containing two drops from the yellow cross shells. 'This cat showed no salivation and very little nose irritation. Its skin appeared itchy and its ears red. The tongue also looked rather red. It was quite lively when the bandage was taken off.'[21]

Humphry Davy, famed for his miner's lamp, was the first chemist to synthesize nitrous oxide. Amused by its effects, he called it 'laughing gas' and arranged parties around it. The poets Coleridge and Southey came to play, along with the founder of the Wedgwood pottery empire, Josiah Wedgwood, and Peter Roget, who would go on to compose *Roget's Thesaurus* but as a young doctor wrote about laughing gas. It was very different to nitric oxide and, as Davy was to discover, highly dangerous. Haldane was first alerted to its possible wartime consequences by a late nineteenth-century report on a Mysore gold-mine disaster. A candle set a box of dynamite on fire. Workers encountered fumes on trying to put the fire out. 'Most of them seemed alright when they came out, but one after another they developed symptoms of acute bronchopneumonia and oedema of the lungs in the course of the next 24 hours, and about 20 died.' The London Fire Brigade had lost several lives in recent years, breathing nitrous fumes from acid, just as 'Davy nearly killed himself by attempting to breathe nitric acid.'[22]

Haldane alerted medical officers to the dangers such poisoning posed for gun crews at the front. It was also proving fatal at sea. HMS *Russell* struck a mine just off the coast of Malta in April 1916, but floated for twenty minutes before capsizing. Caught in the aftermath of the explosions, sailors on board were poisoned by nitrous fumes. Haldane worked to discover the reasons for the poison's delayed reaction. 'Perhaps it depends on the fact that nitrites are true tissue poisons (apart from their actions on haemoglobin),' he speculated, 'and that the lungs bear the brunt of this action, just as they bear the brunt of poisoning by oxygen when an animal is kept in an atmosphere of pure oxygen at atmospheric pressure.'[23]

Another wartime experiment focused on the possible effects of oxygen reduction in a crowded submarine. Haldane had himself locked in an airtight room, the carbon dioxide of his outbreaths absorbed by the same purifier as at work in those submarines. The oxygen rate in his sealed unit was made to fall at the same rate it would in a crowded submarine. After a few hours a light would no longer burn in the chamber. A few hours after that and a particularly unpleasant phenomenon happened for the tobacco-loving Haldane. His pipe was handed to him through an airlock, but suck all he might he could not conjure it into fire.

The objective was to last 48 hours, to see if sailors could last that long without the addition of extra oxygen. Haldane soldiered past that limit and into his third day of confinement. At 56 hours the oxygen in the chamber's air was down to 10 per cent. The purifier failed at this point and Haldane emerged. His lips were red, he showed no signs of mountain sickness or anoxaemia, his health was fine. Hopefully the submarine's sailors would be as acclimatized to such conditions as Haldane was. An unacclimatized laboratory assistant joined Haldane inside the chamber for a subsequent test. He turned blue, collapsed, and was dragged out to safety.

Another shipboard danger was arsenic poisoning. Haldane conducted a series of tests on the action of fumes from arsenic trifluoride, which concluded that 'this substance has no use as an offensive agent in warfare'.[24] In June 1916 Haldane reported 'there had been trouble through several crews of submarines feeling ill with some sort of poison'. He travelled to Harwich and 'found that the symptoms were of a gas containing arsenic'. The source was some impure acid used for electrical power.

'They were extraordinarily prompt in taking action as soon

as I told them what was wrong,' Haldane wrote to his mother. 'It is always satisfying to have anything to do for the Navy, as they act at once, and understand at once. One only wishes that the Army was the same!'[25]

'You have had a very interesting time,' Mary Haldane responded to his earlier experiments, 'though not unattended by concern and anxiety. Arsenic is a most penetrating poison and I *can* imagine most difficult to grapple with.'[26]

U-boat action was a more regular danger at sea. On an August Friday afternoon in 1913 Richard Haldane arrived in New York on a lightning trip to address the American Bar Association, accompanied by his sister Elizabeth. They took the same steamer, the *Lusitania*, home on the Monday. That same year the *Lusitania* entered dry dock in Liverpool and was fitted with gun mounts. She was still ostensibly plying the Atlantic as a luxury liner on 7 May 1915, carrying the wealthy Andrew Vanderbilt and the playwright and impresario Charles Frohman as well as munitions for the British forces. Near the coast of Ireland U-boat *U20* had the ship in its sights and fired. Its torpedo hit the ship's starboard side. The ship took 18 minutes to sink, with the loss of 1,198 lives. The press adopted U-boats as a sign of war dropping to malign depths, as previously evidenced by poison gas.

The year the *Lusitania* was sunk, Haldane was invited to Yale to deliver the Silliman lectures. Postponing the trip by just a year, in October 1916 he set sail for New York. U-boats had agreed not to fire on civilian shipping without warning, but then they had issued exactly such a promise before the *Lusitania* was attacked. A crossing was far from safe.

★

In 1916 Haldane was awarded the prestigious Royal Society medal, with particular regard for his findings on the chemical changes in respiration. The invitation to deliver the Silliman lectures was a similar honour. The lectures were supposed to confirm 'the presence and wisdom of God as manifested in the Natural and Moral World', without recourse to 'Polemical and Dogmatical Theology'. Delivered during an eight-day stay, to an enthusiastic audience including ex-President Taft,[27] the lecture series formed the basis for Haldane's classic work *Respiration*. Yale University published them verbatim, the proofs in Haldane's hands by the end of his three-week visit to the country.

Why did Haldane put himself through so much personal suffering? In the middle of a war, why sail across U-boat-ridden seas? Reflecting on why people should take up any profession, he later said: 'It is the desire to be useful, or to reach such a degree of efficiency that they can in future be useful, which in the main moves them. The desire to be wanted in our world is part of our nature.'[28]

Accepting the spiritual nod from the remit of the Silliman lectures, Haldane extended this idea of a man surrendering his own sense of identity to accord with something bigger, and told his audience: 'In losing our individual lives we find our true life, and in no part of human activity is this losing of the individual self more clearly realised than in scientific work. When, but only when, we see that the natural world appears to us as it does through the devoted scientific work which has fashioned its present appearance, we have found God in the natural world. The life of such a man as Charles Darwin is in truth a standing proof of the existence of God.'[29]

Haldane's subsequent tour, starting with a speech at the Harvey Society in New York, saw him lecture at the Harvard

Medical School and the universities of Philadelphia and Johns Hopkins, and dining with Murray Butler, the president of Columbia University, who would go on to win the Nobel Peace Prize in 1931. Conversation focused on the war. 'Among all the people I met in America the sympathy with us in the war was extremely strong,' Haldane wrote home to his mother. 'The universities, at any rate, seemed to be quite solid. I think America would very soon come in if things began to go against us.'[30]

Haldane took the chance to see his recommendations for mining and industrial safety being put into effect. A 400-mile train trip took him to Pittsburgh to the laboratories and experimental stations of the US Bureau of Mines, with its £200,000 research grant. 'I was given quite a royal reception, as everyone seemed to know all about my mining work, and I found my own analysis apparatus etc in use in all the laboratories. I was motored all around, and out to the experimental mine a few miles away, and then visited one of the Carnegie steel mills.'

A run of grand dinners in his honour included one at the Tavern Club in Boston, chaired by Major Henry Higginson, the businessman and founder of the Boston Symphony Orchestra. The President of the Museum of Health and Safety hosted a grand lunch in Haldane's honour in the historic Delmonico's restaurant on 44th Street, New York. After the speeches, the party moved off to inspect the tunnels being driven under the East River, from Midtown to Queens. 'I had another enthusiastic reception by the engineers, as they were using the method I introduced for getting the men out safely.'

Haldane's strongest impression from his American trip was the high standard of both teaching and research in the best universities.

In place of the pompous ignorance of physiology and pathology which one meets with so often among medical teachers in Europe, there was everywhere considerable knowledge of, and enthusiastic belief in, scientific methods. Clinical laboratories, and keen young men to work in them, were appearing in all directions. Side by side with this clinical scientific activity there was an equally marked development in the pure scientific laboratories and their research work, and in the broadness of view which goes with originality.[31]

The trip back to Britain was in USMS *New York*, Haldane transferring from a Cunard ship whose passage was cancelled because of war duties. The *New York* was 'a fairly slow boat', built on the Clyde some thirty years previously. After 'a pretty strenuous time' Haldane was 'glad of the rest'. On 5 November the ship ran through a heavy gale up the Irish Channel to Liverpool.

'Your letter I value extremely,' Mary Haldane wrote in response to her son's American news, 'and have read it again with great interest already. You certainly have had a magnificent reception. I wish America politically would follow in the footsteps of the America of Science. It is almost impossible to understand its policy.'[32]

America entered the war six months after Haldane's visit, in 1917. Those days of rest on board during his Atlantic crossing provided a rare quiet spell in Haldane's war. In March 1918 he wrote from Oxford to his brother Richard: 'I've been trying to arrange to get down to Cloan, and to Edinburgh, where I'm much wanted for experiments there. But I simply can't manage it just now, as I'm so busy with the work at Taplow, & also at the Hospital here, and with arrears of other work.'

With less than a fortnight to run before the Armistice of 11 November 1918, Haldane was in Paris for an Allied conference on gas warfare, and pushing his latest models of oxygen apparatus through production. His pamphlet on oxygen administration had just been issued by the Chemical Warfare Medical Committee. At war's end he was fifty-eight.

This was no moment for rest, however. Peace brought his son Jack home to Cherwell, and to a period of years working alongside his father. Lock themselves in Haldane's private gas chambers for a further series of Herculean self-experiments, and father and son could reach undreamt-of heights of discomfort and achievement.

NEXT STOP, EVEREST

'Remember, Jack had been killing people for several years, apart from the breaks which followed their attempts to kill him,' his sister Naomi noted for any biographers of the future. 'This does something to shift one's personality on its base as happens with a knock on the head or a bad trip with some powerful drug. Return is slow. Nothing any more looks innocent.'[1]

By December 1918, Jack was demobbed and living at Cherwell, helping his father treat gas victims at Ashhurst Hospital. Jack was soon offered a lectureship at New College. Naomi now lived in London with her baby and husband, but came back to Oxford at weekends whenever she could. The family punted along the river and sat together on its banks.

'This must have been the happiest part of his life for my father,' Naomi recalled. 'He had someone of his very own to share with, to take pride in, someone who marvellously had escaped from the flames of death which we all felt still behind us. And Jack? Inevitably they talked philosophy, at that time still tied up with science; at least with physics and biology, the science of life, death and what was life.'

He had gone off to war a virgin. Sex was now part of his healing process. Haldane opened a letter addressed to his son – those initials they shared, J. S. and J. B. S., were always so ripe for confusing. 'Bred to hard-won chastity', Naomi recalled how he was 'deeply shocked' by the expressions used by this surprise lady correspondent. She took the letter from her father, and explained it away in her 'first major lie'. Lie or not, her parents chose to buy into it. Breakfast continued calmly.

Haldane's philosophical ideas provided some of Jack's healing.

> He was in touch with his father's thinking in which there was a cautious approach to what could be called 'God' for want of a more expressive word . . . much more like some small pattern of living matter: what made it happen and survive, how the environment on the whole held us in sheltering arms and induced us, again on the whole, to love one another which was in fact our only chance of survival. Wars and hatred tore at this living pattern. People working together freely in amity and good purpose helped it. In a sense this was a religious pattern, perhaps a basic religious pattern without the trimmings of priesthood or the desire for secular power.

The white damask tablecloth was spread, silver shone in the candlelight, and Haldane dined less and less in College. Naomi noted his 'increasing estrangement from the Oxford scientific and indeed intellectual Establishment'. Much better was to be at home, conversing brilliantly with his son over informal suppers. He was 'very much his old self, slightly eccentric but warm and kindly to everyone'.

Some of the most cheerful moments of the First World War took place high above the Earth. In 1911 Parmalee and Turpin had strained their aircraft but could not even fly around Pikes Peak. Aviation raced ahead from those days while physiology struggled to keep up. Aeroplanes soared to 20,000 feet. Without supplemental oxygen pilots were quite literally on a high from oxygen starvation. How wonderful to be young, an aviator, and riding free above the clouds of war-stricken Europe. How great to share that feeling with your fellow man. Pilots of opposing forces let go all thought of engaging in combat. Instead they grinned and waved at each other. What fun it all was.[2]

Oxygen lack can lead to euphoria, and recklessness. For aviators choosing not to shoot each other out of the skies, recklessness might be a blessing in disguise. For researchers confining themselves to pressurized chambers, it presents a real danger. They are breaking the bounds of the known, and relying on their own expert judgement to keep them safe. Even the judgement of Haldane was liable to be challenged under such circumstances.

Where some men flew, others aimed to walk. Two of the primary goals for explorers were reached in the first years of the century: the North and South Poles. The third great challenge remained: the ascent of Mount Everest. Chief among pioneers of such an ascent was Dr Alexander Kellas. Born in Aberdeen in 1868, this fellow Scot shared Haldane's history of walking as a youngster through the Grampians. At seventeen he made a three-day trek across peaks of the Cairngorms, sleeping nights under a shelter stone. Regular breaks from his post as a lecturer in Chemistry at Middlesex Hospital Medical School started in the summer of 1907, with mountaineering trips to Sikkim. While Haldane was testing the limits of man and altitude on Pikes Peak in 1911, Kellas was making the first ascents of Sikkim's Chomiomo (22,404 feet/6,829 m) and Pauhunri (23,375 feet/7,125 m). His were the first expeditions to the Himalayan region to appreciate the worth of employing Sherpas.

By 1919, nobody had climbed Himalayan heights of over 20,000 feet more times. Kellas was the perfect acclimatized colleague for Haldane's sequence of high-altitude experiments, a man he called his 'close friend'. From inside a sealed chamber in London they could explore new realms together. As Yandell Henderson, who had shared the Pikes Peak tests with Haldane, commented on such tests: 'The scientific treatment of the physiological effects of low oxygen, mountain sickness, and acclimatization should retain something of the zest of a noble sport. In this field an investigator is himself the subject observed, and in his own person suffers discomfort and overcomes hardship as great as any explorer of a new country. Yet it is also in this field that physiology has most emulated the precision of physics and chemistry.'[3]

Two sets of preliminary experiments took place in the small steel pressure chamber of Siebe Gorman on Westminster Bridge Road in London over four days in 1919. The pressure was dropped to simulate periods spent at 11,600, 16,000, 21,000 and 26,000 feet. Tests for acclimatization took place in the larger pressure chamber at the Lister Institute, where goats and two divers had once tested Haldane's early calculations for the diving tables.

To look at him, Kellas was not an obvious man for such an experimental task. He had recently become prone to auditory hallucinations in which voices threatened his death, though in retrospect this was possibly a case of precognition. The Everest explorer George Mallory said of him in 1921: 'Kellas I love already. He is beyond description Scotch and uncouth in his speech – altogether uncouth . . . His appearance would form an admirable model to the stage for farcical representation of an alchemist. He is very slight in build, short, thin, stooping, and narrow-chested; his head . . . made grotesque by veritable gig-lamps of spectacles and a long-pointed moustache. He is an absolutely devoted and disinterested person.'[4]

Haldane and Kellas entered the chamber together and the door was bolted shut behind them. The air in the chamber was not pulled out by the pump, but rather pushed out by the air still inside. That meant the air was hard at work. The only energy source it had for such work was heat. As the heat was spent, the atmosphere in the chamber grew cold and foggy.

In one early experiment Haldane and Kellas's intentions were quite clear; they would 'remain for an hour at about the lowest pressure possible without very serious impairment of our faculties for observation'. At a pressure of 445 mm (millimetres of mercury, the barometric reading, equivalent to an altitude of about 15,000 feet, 4,570 m) Haldane's breathing rate had already increased from 16 to 24 breaths per minute, and his pulse was up from 85 to 112. At 320 mm Haldane had great difficulty in making observations or even counting his pulse. Especially difficult was calculating the pulse from a 20-seconds observation, or remembering at what point on the seconds hand the observation had begun. He made one last note, scrawling the description of his condition as 'very wobbly', then passed the notebook on to Kellas.

Haldane stayed sitting with his head hanging low, but his

answers remained sensible. 'Keep it at 320,' he answered, whenever Kellas checked about changing the pressure. The observers outside pressed notes up against the window. Surely something was wrong? Kellas was blue, Haldane motionless. Kellas smiled back. He had his instructions. 'Keep it at 320,' Haldane kept insisting, and so they would. The pressure dropped to 300 mm, and then briefly to 295 mm (26,500 feet, 8,080 m). 'Keep it at 320,' Haldane persisted, 'still determined' after 75 minutes, after which he consented to a slight rise.

At 350 mm Haldane picked up a mirror to check the colour of his lips. Cyanosis due to anoxaemia would have turned the lips blue. He stared and stared for some time, without coming to any obvious conclusion. Kellas was in fact the bluer of the two men, just as inhabitants of the high Andes are blue till taken to lower altitudes, yet he like them kept more of his wits about him. He kept the notes, read the barometer, and managed the regulating tap. Kellas had a greater history of acclimatization to low pressures than Haldane. In staring at the mirror, Haldane had been looking at the back of it and not the front.

The pressure was slowly raised to 450 mm. Haldane's mind cleared. Feeling and power returned to his legs and arms. His memory drew a blank, however, when it came to the time spent at low pressure. He could recall no details. Clearly both men's actions were irrational. Stubbornness made them extend an experiment that should have been brought to an immediate halt.

Jack Haldane was one of a second pair of observers in these initial experiments. The pressure in his chamber took 10 minutes to come down to 330 mm. His companion soon dashed down the note 'like last-stages of drunk. J. B. S. H.

respirations 45. Pulse can't take.' Both men had turned blue and shaky, and were clearly finding it hard to stand. Jack managed one barely legible note of indignation before his senses started to return: 'some bastard has turned tap'.

A miner who puts his head into a cavity filled with methane falls as though a man has punched him to the ground. When he comes round, after breathing pure air for a few seconds, he looks for revenge. Haldane knew a miner who had revived twice from such a methane attack, and promptly knocked a bystander to the ground. He noted how his own behaviour on coming out of the steel chamber was 'distinctly abnormal', and told how 'a well-known inspector of mines, on returning to the surface after he had been affected by CO from an underground fire, first shook hands very cordially with all the bystanders. A doctor who was present then offered him an arm; but this the inspector regarded as an insult, with the result that he took off his jacket and challenged the doctor to a fight.' Of himself, Haldane noted: 'When unable even to stand, owing to experimental CO poisoning or to anoxaemia produced by low pressures in a steel chamber, Haldane has always been quite confident of his own sanity, and it was only afterwards that he realized that he could not have been in a rational state of mind.'[5]

Subsequent experiments at the Lister Institute did show some acclimatization setting in. On the last day of the experimental series the pressure was reduced to 315 mm. At a pressure equivalent to a height of 26,000 feet (7,920 m) Haldane mounted the ergometer and cycled up a remarkable 3,300 foot-pounds of work, stopping after 4 minutes because 'he was exhausted and vision was becoming blurred'.

Haldane turned distinctly blue, but kept on doing gas analyses and other operations throughout the stay, moving about as usual with no loss of memory afterwards. So he could recall every detail of the latest sacrifice of his son.

Jack entered the Lister chamber 'as an unacclimatized control'. After 2 hours at 366 mm, the equivalent of an altitude of 21,000 feet (6,400 m), 'his breathing had become increasingly rapid and shallow, and he had gradually sunk into a partially stupefied state'. The quick breaths made it hard to achieve, but he was inspired with the notion of bursting into song. The emergency of his situation was recognized, the experiment was stopped, and Jack was ejected. He recovered, but his memory didn't. The final hour of the experiment remained a blank.

In 1921 Kellas became part of the first Everest expedition. Suffering from dysentery, he was stretchered even on the early stages before the mountain was in sight. 'It appears that febrile infections at high altitudes are extremely dangerous,' Haldane noted. Kellas died from 'unsuspected loss of acclimatization'.[6] He was buried on a hillside looking out over those three peaks which he alone had climbed: Pauhunri, Kangchenjhau and Chomiomo. 'It was an extraordinarily affecting little ceremony,' Mallory noted, 'burying Kellas on a stony hillside – a place on the edge of a great plain and looking across it to the three great snow peaks of his conquest. I shan't easily forget the four boys, his own trained mountain men, children of nature, seated in wonder on a great stone near the grave.'[7]

Haldane and Kellas's work gave confidence to subsequent expeditions, including George Mallory's of 1924. Brigadier-General C. G. Bruce, a member of the 1922 Everest expedition, 'said that the Expedition's great encouragement, from the physiological point of view, came from Dr Haldane, who was the only man who told them what he believed to be a perfect possibility – that the highest points of the world could be reached without the help of oxygen, provided they had the right men and the right weather'.[8]

Perhaps George Mallory was the right man, the first to climb the peak, and only lacked the right weather. No one can know. He disappeared into mists on his final push for the summit. His frozen body was found in 1999, at 26,800 feet (8,170 m).

By the 1930s the ascent of Everest, in the view of Joseph Barcroft, had become 'merely an engineer's problem'. Design oxygen apparatus that was portable and efficient enough, and climbers would be powered to the summit. Haldane countered the view of this Cambridge physiologist,[9] maintaining that if they acclimatized to the rarefied air, and started the final ascent from above 26,000 feet (7,920 m), mountaineers could manage the ascent without oxygen.[10]

Yandell Henderson, the Yale physiologist who co-led the Pikes Peak expedition, declared that Haldane and Barcroft did not so much think differently as breathe differently. Men such as Barcroft, who suffered acutely from mountain sickness, had 'what Prof. Henderson calls "sea-level respiratory centers." For them, oxygen is the breath of life. They are the ones who should fly direct and wholly unacclimatized to the North Col of Mt. Everest, don an improved oxygen apparatus, make the ascent, and get back below 15,000 feet while the supply of oxygen holds out. For them the ascent is an engineering problem.'[11]

Others would adjust during the slow ascent through Tibet. For such men, while still hazardous, an ascent without oxygen was the best option.

For Haldane, part of the glamour of such an ascent was the

extreme to which it tested the ability of human physiology to adapt to its environment. Another test would come when man took the opportunity to pass beyond the stratosphere. Just as the Pikes Peak findings paved the way for the aero-nautical achievements of the First World War, Haldane now set in place the physiological expertise that could support technological innovations of the future. He designed his legacy for the space age.

In 1921 the first edition of his *Respiration* included discus-sion for a prototype spacesuit. This adaptation of a diving suit was pushed into design by students at Harvard Medical School under Professor Philip Drinker, the inventor of the iron lung. In 1933 Haldane received a letter from a young American, Mark Ridge. Ridge proposed soaring 13 miles into the stratosphere in an open-basket balloon. Drinker, along with many other prominent scientists,[12] offered his sup-port. Drinker's own interest was in equipment used to overcome barometric pressure; his 'study of respiration had to do with high pressures in connection with his "lung" and what he did not know of low pressures would fill a book'.[13] Dr Timothy Leary, Medical Examiner of Boston, advised Ridge that the 'only person in the world who could speak with authority' on the subject was Haldane.

The one place in the USA where Ridge might have tested his suit belonged to the US Navy's Experimental Diving Unit. With his felony on record as the first man to break the Massachusetts' statute forbidding parachute jumps except in emergency, the navy would have nothing to do with Ridge. Haldane, however, had access to the pressure chambers of the Siebe Gorman company.

In 1932 the Swiss physicist Auguste Piccard attached a sealed gondola to a balloon and ascended to 53,152 feet

(16,200 m). It allowed him to collect data on the upper atmosphere and investigate cosmic rays, without encountering atmospheric pressure. A man in a suitable spacesuit would be in much more intimate contact with his environment, and the vast reduction in oxygen supplies that he would need would save huge weight. Piccard's gondola required a vast balloon to carry it. With a man in an open basket, a smaller balloon could go much higher.

Ridge outlined for Haldane the basis of his design. 'From abdomen to neck suit shall be inflated to 1/3 atmospheric pressure; a rubber casket shall prevent any leakage from suit itself to helmet; lining interior of helmet shall be 4lbs of soda lime and 4lbs of silica gel, to absorb CO_2. Would the administration of ammonium chloride be of any benefit to me?'

Sir Robert Davis of Siebe Gorman undertook to make the 'dress, which was only a modification of the self-contained diving-dress previously introduced by his firm'.[14] Modifications had to withstand extra-severe pressures. At heights above 63,000 feet (19,200 m) low pressure sees the boiling point of water drop to 98 °F. Human blood would explode.

Ridge travelled to England, staying with Haldane at Cherwell in between the experiments in London. 'Lindbergh was thought to be a nut before he flew to Paris,' *Time* reported. 'This boy is air-minded, conscientious and daring. He comes from a good family. His education is average. He is willing to try for an altitude record if it will mean scientific progress.'[15] Ridge put on the new suit, and was closed into the steel chamber. Oxygen was supplied at 1 litre a minute measured at atmospheric pressure, Ridge breathing pure oxygen for half an hour before reaching the lowest pressure of each day. Once the lowest pressure was reached he was kept there for some considerable time, so Haldane could check for any symptoms of bubbles in the tissues.

On 16 November 1933 the suited Ridge endured a low atmosphere the equivalent of 50,000 feet (15,240 m). 'History has been made,' the 27-year-old declared on emerging. He sent a telegram back home to his father: 'Success, 50,000 feet, going 60,000 Monday, everything fine, staying weekend with Dr. Haldane.'[16] The tests continued, the pressure being reduced on successive days until two weeks later it was down to 17 mm, the equivalent of 90,000 feet (27,430 m). This was the lowest the chamber could go.

Plans continued to test the suit in a high-altitude balloon flight. The Royal Air Force noted the success of the experiments on this 'stratospheric suit' and took a strong interest in the design. As Haldane noted in 1935, such a suit 'could be used for aeroplane ascents without any limit to the height attainable with safety'.[17] Since the suit and not the cabin would be pressurized, it also meant that any shot breaking the cabin's window would not mean instant death for the crew.

Such a design needed protection. Ridge was blocked from his dream balloon ascent for fear that his balloon could be blown into the hands of rival governments. A development of his design helped Royal Air Force Lieutenant M. J. Adam fly a Pilot Swain's Bristol 138 to a world aviation record of 53,937 feet (16,440 m) in 1937.

In 1942, aged just thirty-six, Ridge's dream of a balloon ascent finally burst. He was committed to a Boston mental institution. The high-altitude flights made possible by the Haldane-Davis suit he pioneered were already having their impact on the war. 'Little Boy', the nuclear bomb to be dropped on Hiroshima, would be armed at a height of 31,000 feet (9,450 m).

Beyond its usage in such military aircraft as the U2 spy plane, which flew so high that it could not be attacked, Haldane's stratospheric suit was the early model for the spacesuits worn by astronauts on Extra Vehicular Activity. These astronauts employed the same decompression techniques Haldane administered to Ridge, their bodies kept at one-third or more of sea-level pressure, the astronauts breathing pure oxygen both before and during their space walks.[18]

As above so below. Haldane never lost his enthusiasm for improving the safety, efficiency and working conditions in the mines. At 8.30 in the morning he would pull on his boots, jump on his bike, and hare off to Oxford station. Used to his last-minute arrival, porters would grab his bike from him on the platform and see him safely into his first-class seat on the train. Train journeys were never idle for Haldane; he used them to write up his papers. In 1914 the Haldanes had acquired a Daimler, but they donated it to the war effort and never bothered to replace it with another. Taxis eventually replaced the bike, though Haldane invariably appeared with his boots unlaced at the very last minute. The boots were made by the local cobbler Mr Bennet, working from home. A last of Haldane's foot was kept for the purpose, to which a model of any corn that Haldane grew was added to ensure the snuggest fit. Boots laced up, off he would go for his day's work in Birmingham.

Sir Arthur Markham, the founder and chief supporter of the Doncaster Mining Laboratory, died in 1916. His death 'was a shock to me,' Haldane told his mother. 'I scarcely know now what will become of the Doncaster Laboratory.'[19]

'How difficult it is to see light through these dark clouds,' his mother counselled. 'But it does come eventually. The work of great workers and organizers is not lost but reappears where it is not expected. When things look darkest the light breaks out.'[20]

Sir John Cadman was the giver of light in this instance, eventually arranging for the laboratory's transfer to Birmingham University in 1921. Before his death in 1916 Sir Arthur Markham had agreed with Cadman that such a move made sense. It opened the laboratory's work up to the greater facilities of a university, and to the staff and students of Birmingham's mining department. The university location also made it more accessible to other collieries. Historically, it brought the mining research within reach of the North and South Staffordshire collieries where Haldane had done his earliest mining research. Coal-owners in Warwickshire, Staffordshire, Doncaster and Scotland offered finance, along with the Mining Research Board. The university itself provided no money, though Haldane at last acquired the title of Professor.[21]

In the mines of America Haldane admired the use of electric cap lamps. Fitted to the head, these brought light 2 feet closer to the working surface than a hand lamp could manage, and so gave three times the illumination. The safety lamps in use in Britain were dim, the black coal absorbing 90 per cent of what light they did throw off. Having nowhere to focus, miners' eyes were prone to rapid left–right eye movements, a condition known as nystagmus. Many were not aware of this nervous affliction, but the associated headaches, sleeplessness and depression forced others from work. Haldane focused his laboratory on improving the illumination of safety lamps, and counselling proper treatment.

He continued to respond to news of colliery disasters, dashing to the scene. When the Doncaster colliery car was unavailable, he gamely squeezed his rheumatic figure into a motorcycle sidecar for transport from one colliery to another. J. Ivon Graham applauded his 'imperturbability', instanced on one occasion when Haldane was being driven along a road near Selby in the Doncaster Rescue Station's first rescue van. As a back wheel came away, he was dumped from the rear to the front seat, the van lying on its side on the grass verge. He hated being fussed over. Well into his seventies he raised strong objections, when at the bottom of a Scottish mine, to being transported across a particularly awkward length of road in a tub.[22]

Haldane's work on the prevention of silicosis also continued, to the extent that he could predict 'there seems no obstacle to the entire prevention of silicosis in coal mining work'.[23] Enforced compensation for miners with silicosis, brought in under the Workmen's Compensation Act, brought a surge of claims. It became necessary to differentiate what diseases were in fact due to the breathing of free silica. Haldane introduced methods to measure the amounts of silica used in underground stone dusting, the belief being that 'free silica' (fine dust insufficiently diluted in air) did no damage so long as it was mixed with other dust.

'The lungs of town-dwellers, for instance, are more or less blackened by smoke particles,' he noted, 'but remain perfectly healthy; and the same applies to the lungs of coal miners.'[24] Haldane believed human physiology had a way of protecting itself against soft dust. 'The well-known "black spit" of a collier,' he wrote in 1935, 'which continues for long periods when he is not working underground, is a healthy sign showing that dust particles are being removed from the lung.'[25]

From his mining research laboratory he did recommend the use of respirators against other dusts. 'A great excess of

dust of any kind is apt to cause some fibrosis, and is in any case very unpleasant and irritating to the respiratory passages.'[26] However subsequent medical advances in the understanding of pneumoconiosis suggested that black lungs were a greater danger to health than Haldane anticipated.

He worked the bridge between coal-owners and miners all his life. 'As regards nationalization,' he told an inquiry in 1919, 'I share the general British distrust of too much bureaucratic control, and I think that, so far as public health and safety are concerned, it would hardly be possible to nationalize coalmining without legally stifling initiative and the sense of individual responsibility.'[27]

His response to a later inquiry drew laughter from his audience, when he was asked if his work had been largely done under government control. 'If I took orders from the Government I should have done nothing whatever in this world.'[28]

Just as workers might roll up their sleeves, the 65-year-old Haldane rolled up his sleeve on their behalf. He covered the bared arm with burns, testing the curative effects of tannic acid. His recommendations on mine safety saved the lives of untold thousands worldwide, and continue to do so wherever they are applied. His suggestion of tannic acid as treatment for burns in underground fires kept many alive who would have died.

In Cardiff on 16 June 1925, members of the Institution of Mining Engineers settled down to a talk by Haldane. 'In the present very depressed state of the coal industry we have need of all the cheer we can get and all the knowledge by means of which we can extend the use of coal by adding to its value,' he told them. Championing the role of coal, his lecture unfolded a tale of how the steam engine's performance could be vastly improved. 'In every case where either fuel economy or size of engine is of predominating importance,' he concluded, 'the steam-engine and coal will in future replace the internal combustion engine and oil.'[29]

Believing that 'engineers have been prevented from seeing clearly what the maximum efficiency of a heat-engine is,' Haldane had therefore proposed his own solution. As one member of the Cardiff audience commented on his 'heat-engine' views, 'It is just like him to enter on a subject like this and attack all that is thought to be orthodox.'[30]

Unorthodox views did not steal up unnoticed on Haldane. His book *Gases and Liquids* saw him leap out of his regular areas of expertise and into the ring with physicists. The book 'throws to the winds,' he told his friend Wentworth Thompson, 'not merely van t'Hoff's theory of osmotic pressure, but also the thermodynamics of Kelvin and Clausius, which Clerk Maxwell also accepted. I am thinking of going off to New Zealand when it comes out!'[31]

The book was supposedly simple, though Haldane's friends found it far from easy. 'Anyhow,' he consoled himself, 'there's no d[amne]d relativity or quantum theory in it.'[32]

Fire ripped through the post office tunnel beneath Holborn in London in 1929. Following an initial gas blast, broken gas pipes and connections caused explosions throughout the system and set a building on fire.

J. S. Haldane had been appointed Gas Referee to the whole country in 1924, appointing two men to assist him 'in the office and testing work, of which there will be a good deal, I fear'.[33] He donned the hat belonging to this other strand of his working life, and duly appeared at the scene of devastation in Holborn. One essential recommendation was that tunnels, like sewers, should be ventilated. Nobody need fear bad smells coming out. 'I can honestly say,' he told the inquiry, 'that I have passed many interesting days in sewers, and always come out with a keen appetite.'

Unusually for such a public inquiry, the newspaper reported laughter.[34]

Gas refereeing was a constant source of work and income for Haldane over more than three decades. In 1921, as the Doncaster Mining Laboratory was relocating to Birmingham along with J. Ivon Graham and his mother, Haldane was drawn to London for several days a week. 'There is a great deal of correspondence with County Councils, gas companies etc all over the kingdom about the new arrangements for testing gas and the instruments for the purpose. We have several assistants and clerks, but so many new questions are cropping up that we must give very close attention to the work.'[35] He hoped for some gas disagreements that he could referee in Scotland, so as to make a visit to Cloan, but sadly none came up.

Gas refereeing has vanished as a profession. Some sense of the role can come from seeing Haldane in the aftermath of one typical incident, a gas explosion at a house in Acton, London, in February 1927.

'About 3 a.m. Mr and Mrs Waterworth were awakened by a smell which was described as being similar to that of burning rubber or tar,' Haldane's report narrated.[36] The husband checked the house, found nothing, and returned to bed. 'About three quarters of an hour later the whole family were awakened by an irritating vapour which was described as choking and which was visible as a blue haze.'

The ground floor contained a shop. The family heard a rumbling noise beneath the shop door as they prepared to run for safety. 'Unfortunately, Mr and Mrs Waterworth went into the kitchen before leaving the house, and while they were there an explosion occurred which blew out the walls and completely wrecked the house, burying them in the ruins.'

A two-day public inquiry saw Haldane and his colleague interview many witnesses and conduct a thorough investigation of the scene. A Short's leakage detector showed no sign of coal gas. Other possible factors were discounted as Haldane homed in on his original suspicion. 'The peculiar smell and irritant action of the fumes noticed in the house, and the fact that these fumes were visible as a blue haze, seemed to indicate that the gas had originated from bitumen or other material round an electric main.'

Such was, indeed, the ultimate discovery. An engineer at the nearby electrical substation had heard a screech from the rotary, discovered a bad short circuit on one of the feeders, but had no authority to turn off the supply. The cables to the exploded house were among the few still laid in bitumen. The cables had burnt to a heat of at least 1,000 °C. The consequent distillation of the bitumen into a gas mixed with air was enough to destroy the whole flimsy house once it ignited.

Had the attendant been allowed to turn the power off at the substation, the explosion would not have happened. He should be granted such authority in the future. With these and other recommendations for improved public safety duly registered, Haldane the Gas Referee waited for his next call to arms.

Though stationed closer to the margins of academia than before, the laboratory at Cherwell remained a magnet for both emerging and illustrious scientists.[37]

'Your name is a power in our country,' Richard Haldane wrote to Albert Einstein in 1921. Richard had paved the way for Einstein's visit to Britain. 'There is no doubt that your visit has had more tangible results in improving here the relations between our two countries than any other single event.'[38]

The Oxford leg of the visit brought Einstein to Cherwell, Naomi's son Denny careering into him on a small tricycle before the two great scientists settled in the study for a talk. Haldane later instructed Naomi in the essence of Einstein's theory of relativity, but the two scientists' conversation was likely to have been a lively philosophical one. 'Nature just mocks us,' Haldane later told a distinguished audience, 'when we attempt to divorce her from conscious perception; and she still mocks at Einstein. There is no such thing as a physical world existing apart from consciousness; no such thing as absolute space or time or space-time, or absolute mass, motion, or energy.'[39]

Einstein wrote to Mary Haldane about their conversation. 'I am also *proud* very proud in hearing from your own testimony the satisfaction you have had in your intercourse with my son,' she responded. 'My brother Professor Burdon Sanderson, of Oxford, used often to lament that we were so far behind Germany in scientific research and I am much pleased with what I have been told of your impression of our country.'[40]

'We were such good friends that my husband took a great deal of trouble to ensure that the professor should have an appreciative audience,' Kathleen remembered of Einstein's visit.[41] Haldane made his calls, pulled in his favours, and the Milner Hall of the new Rhodes House filled up for the beginning of the inaugural lecture. Gaps started appearing some minutes in. The audience had seen the iconic figure. Most were going to get little else out of the occasion. Lone figures creeping from the audience became a general drift.

'I don't blame them,' Haldane said. 'If their maths are good enough to follow him, their German certainly is not.'

At the end of his lecture Einstein blinked out at the small pockets of his remaining audience. 'Next time,' he promised, 'the discourse should be in English delivered.'

'*Gott bewahre!*' said Haldane, under his breath.

PHILOSOPHY AT A CANTER

Hippocrates, the founding father of medicine, prescribed powder from the barks and leaves of a willow tree to ease pains and fevers. Modern medicine caught up in the nineteenth century, isolating salicin as the magic compound in willow bark. In 1897 Felix Hoffman, a chemist at the German company Bayer, synthesized a salicin compound to ease his father's arthritis pains. The first tablet forms of this powder, now known as aspirin, went on the market in 1915 – well timed for Haldane to pop a couple now and again. His wartime experiments savaged his lungs beyond the point of real repair.

The Treaty of Versailles, mopping up the First World War with a tough dose of retribution, required Bayer to give up their aspirin trademark. By the 1920s the drug was in regular use to treat lumbago, rheumatism and neuralgia. All perfect for Haldane with his bag of such symptoms. Ten aspirin a day now kept him going. Naomi had been used to her father outpacing her on their long walks together. On postwar walks she found herself taking the lead.

Bent by the lumbago, his clothes were especially tailored to fit the new curves and angles of his body. As with Lord Edward Tantamount in Aldous Huxley's novel *Point Counter Point*, he 'turned uneasily this way and that, pivoting his bent body from the loins'.

Tantamount, a man of great wealth with a passion for science, which he conducted in his private laboratory, was Huxley's version of J. S. Haldane.[1] Tantamount was known as 'the Old Man' rather than 'the Senior Partner'. He displays a trenchant and prescient view of the need for 'sustainable living'.

'Progress! You politicians are always talking about it, as if it is going to last,' Tantamount complains, and embarks on a sustained critique of 'intensive agriculture'. Mineral deposits are finite. 'Only two hundred years and they'll be finished. You think we're being progressive because we're living on our capital. Phosphates, coal, petroleum, nitre – squander them all. That's your policy.'[2]

This voice from 1928 was fuelled by a twenty-first-century notion of the whole planet as a self-regulating organism. Haldane of course did not just prefigure the Gaia Hypothesis. He went way beyond such a planetary limitation. 'Nature' rather than 'Gaia' was the term he used, and its scope was universal. 'I wish to emphasize as strongly as I can,' he pointed out

that the belief in a merely physical world surrounding us has no basis. Our environment is not something indifferent to our lives, but belongs to them. Surrounding Nature is not an influence outside our lives, but within them. From the standpoint of biology, Nature is not merely a healing and beneficent influence within the living body, as Hippocrates first clearly pointed out and every educated doctor takes as axiomatic, but is a healing and beneficent influence in the whole of our environment to the farthest depths of space.

While Nature led the inquirer to the far reaches of space to admire its workings, focus could also chase evolution back in time through diminutions of the smallest size. 'He believed thoroughly in evolution,' the *Scotsman* reported of him. 'He believed that we should trace back life further and further, and that some day we should trace it back into what is now called the inorganic world, and when we had traced back life as far as that, the inorganic world would be no longer inorganic; it would be an organic world.'[4]

Such philosophy was developed at a canter through debates with his son Jack. J. B. S. Haldane would develop his theories along Marxist lines. Haldane's belief in God, his friendship with the likes of such virtuous capitalists as Andrew Carnegie, Sir Robert Davis and Sir Arthur Markham, and very likely the sheer dehumanizing aspect of centring life on economic principles whatever their political flavour, kept Haldane shy of any overt socialist commitment himself. He explained his own position:

The mere physical and economic conception of reality seems to leave us with a conscious life made up of grim drab experience, variegated by passing sensations and thrills such as those of inferior cinemas, sensational literature and newspapers, and windy oratory, forgotten next day. Such a conscious life is nothing but that of a degenerate. The more earnest-minded men who accept the supposed realism, but rightly despise the world it represents, are, it seems to me, the real moving spirits in labour unrest; and they are striving after what seem to us to be Utopias. Where they really fail, however, is in not seeing to what an extent there is already a spiritual world around them, realized in the comradeship of daily life.[5]

A man who has spent a great deal of his working life with miners needs no instruction on comradeship. Haldane was delighted with Jack's investigations of loss through sweat in miners at Pendleton Colliery. 'Important results,' he wrote to his mother, 'which may also have a practical bearing on mitigating the effects of heat & making the work easier.'[6]

The idyll of having his son at home included the onerous task of deputizing for him, tutoring his physiology students in 1920 while Jack was on leave at Edinburgh. In 1921 the idyll came to an end. 'Jack has been offered a very good appointment at Cambridge as Reader in Biochemistry,' Haldane told his mother. 'It is to make and direct researches there in his own subjects with very little teaching. The offer is such a very good one that it seemed hardly possible to refuse it . . . His leaving here will of course make rather a blank for us.'

Future meetings would include one in a courtroom, where the father appeared as a character witness when the son was named as co-respondent in a divorce trial. The weaning of Jack took a decade or two more than normal, and their relationship in Haldane's latter years became one of sustained and belated adolescent rebellion. When the son is forging his own identity, his adolescent behaviour is often reflected in the father. Kathleen, once called 'big-shield' by Mary Haldane, set her pen flying across the Cherwell notepaper to protect her husband once again. This time her letter was a plea to Julian Huxley in the wake of Jack's novella *Daedalus*, the book first delivered as a speculative lecture on science, postulating the

notion of test-tube babies born outside of the body, an idea
that would spur Aldous Huxley's *Brave New World*. It also triggered a great deal of fun and comment around Oxford. J. S.
Haldane was 'frightfully upset' about it. 'Will you abstain altogether from poking fun at him on account of it? . . . I knew
he'd object, but had no idea till today how really unhappy he
is – odd people these Liberals and no accounting for them!
But an' you love me, keep people off him, or he'll hate you
all! (which is not only sad for him but extremely inconvenient
for me.)'[7]

The children's nurse, Betsey Ferguson, had passed away in
1898. Richard, John, Elizabeth and William held the cords
that lowered her coffin into its grave. 'We have much reason
to hold her in grateful and affectionate remembrance,'
Richard caused to be inscribed on the tomb.

The grace that some manifest near their death, Mary
Haldane displayed through many years of ripening old age. 'I
can't feel old,' she declared. 'It has been the happiest part of
my life.'

'Some bodily powers, I suppose, are going,' she admitted
to the Archbishop of York when permanently in her bed in
her nineties, 'but I begin to feel moving within me in a way
which I sometimes cannot understand the power of the
world to come.'

Just before her hundredth birthday, Haldane sent her a
letter about his visit to Newcastle. The lady's birthday had
been toasted at a grand dinner in which her association with
the city was recalled. Haldane told the guests:

She lived at what was now Jesmond Towers, and could recall
her father wearing pit clothes in which he used to go under-

ground. In those days, owners were also managers, inspectors, and everything else.

My family records go even further back than that. My Christian names 'John Scott' came from the Newcastle district. John Scott was a hostman of Newcastle in the eighteenth century, and the hostman of Newcastle had the duty of entertaining the foreign buyers who came to the district. That was their original duty, but they assumed the duty of regulating the price of coal. Those, of course, were the happy days when Newcastle could regulate the price of coal.[8]

The following day the Lord Mayor showed Haldane around the portraits of his ancestors hanging in the Council Chamber. From there he paid a return visit to his mother's childhood home of Jesmond. 'I had no idea before how beautiful the situation is,' he told his mother. 'Many of the rooms, and the staircase, are almost unaltered. I can just dimly remember them, and the stable buildings.'[9]

The stretch of his mother's memory was part of the expanse of Haldane's life. 'It seems only a short time since your advent into this world,' she wrote to him in 1920, 'when your birth gave such extreme pleasure to your father. It is now sixty years ago, but seems like yesterday in my recollection. In fact, almost more vividly remembered as I am able to forget about what happens day to day. I suppose it is the effect of old age.'[10]

In early 1917 she declared her spiritual companionship with her son John. 'At present we seem almost in touch with spiritual things, and they scarcely need to be brought before us by any human reminder.'[11]

Old age brought memories of death as well as birth. Two years before she died her memories went back to the death of her teenage son Geordie: 'The agony of 1875 has been present with me, and I seem to have been living it over again.'[12]

A wireless installed at Cloan kept Mary Haldane up to speed with the news, and she made a good stab at reading the first edition of *Respiration*. 'In my memory Cloan consists of you,' *Peter Pan*'s creator J. M. Barrie wrote to her after one rapturous visit to the 99–year-old lady's bedside. 'I see you vividly knitting that shawl (to which my compliments) and looking the dearest person I have seen for years and years. You really do make the intruder into that serene room feel more hopeful about the world. Some of the loveliest lines in English poetry are very like you. It would not be bad to call you an ode to immortality. Of course I am using strong language, but this is frankly a love letter.'[13]

Mary Haldane's memory reached forward through the new generation and back through the old. Her mother was born on the old London Bridge, in the office of her grandfather Sir James Sanderson, the Lord Mayor of London. She passed on to Mary her memories of visiting Newgate prison as a child, in the company of the prison reformer Elizabeth Fry, seeing the prisoners lying in chains.

From her own memory bank Mary could draw on the days of the man-trap and the gibbet, watching the first balloon ascent and seeing Stephenson's first locomotive chug along the rails. In the cholera epidemic of 1832 a glass of port was added to her and her sister's regular dinner-time ale, 'to strengthen their systems'.[14]

The 9th of April 1925 brought hosts of greetings to the centenarian. Fond messages came in from the King and Queen, John Haldane brought a cushion cover as his own present to his mother, while deputations from Auchterarder lined up to present gifts to her through Richard. In honour of the day, the Haldanes presented the town with a refurbished library and Institute. Inmates of the town's poorhouse joined Girl Guides in a celebration tea, sharing a huge cake ablaze with one hundred candles.

In reaching her centenary year, Mary Haldane had done enough. 'She just slept away,' Haldane reported of his mother's death, 'and until she lost consciousness her mind was as clear as ever, and her memory just as good, though she had not been out of bed for years.'[15]

'Her life,' reflected her friend the Archbishop of York, 'was like the course of a river which becomes ever deeper, broader, fuller, in its flow as it draws near the sea. No wonder, then, that her son could write; "My mother passed away in the fullness of spiritual splendour."'[16]

J. Ivon Graham, Haldane's assistant at the Mining Research Laboratory, to whom Haldane was now as close as a father, sent a posy of violets and a letter. In thanking him, Elizabeth added a final comment: 'We feel very lonely.'

Richard had corresponded with his mother every day. His life now seemed devoid of its ultimate meaning. Two years earlier, on 4 January 1923 the new Labour Prime Minister had stopped by at Cloan. He won Richard's agreement to return to the Cabinet, this time as the first Labour Lord Chancellor. Richard took the move to please his mother as much as anything. It removed the indignity forced on him when he was required to leave the woolsack in 1915. He left office in 1924 but remained the Labour leader in the House of Lords. Out for a Saturday morning drive through London on 2 July 1925, shortly after Mary Haldane's death, Sir Robert Perks 'nearly ran over a bent, contemplative figure crossing Birdcage Walk and, on looking up . . . saw it was the Labour Lord Chancellor'.[17]

Richard died on 19 August 1928, succumbing to diabetes as his father had done before him. Pipers from the Black Watch droned a lament as Richard was buried in the church-yard of the family chapel at Gleneagles.

For those who shun peerages and knighthoods, one alter-native can be a pleasure to accept. Haldane was made a Companion of Honour in 1928, 'for his scientific work in connection with industrial disease'. The honour is in the gift of the reigning sovereign, and includes up to sixty-five mem-bers at a time, just forty-five from Britain.

The Royal Society awarded Haldane its Copley medal in 1934. The medal is the Society's supreme accolade for science. John Scott Haldane received it in tribute to 'his dis-coveries in human physiology and of their application to medicine, mining, diving and engineering'. Presented annu-ally since 1731, the award placed J. S. Haldane on a very singular roster alongside the likes of Max Planck, Albert Einstein, Louis Pasteur, Joseph Lister, Charles Darwin, George Ohm, Michael Faraday, Humphry Davy, Joseph Priestley and Stephen Hales. Haldane was also joined to the history of the future, when such as his young friend Niels Bohr would receive the Copley medal. Haldane saw Bohr's quantum theory of atomic structure as an incursion of bio-logical ideas into the realm of physics, a promising foretaste of some future mergence of the natural sciences.

Haldane's respect for scientists of old was so strong that he selected a fresh new career for himself. He became the biog-rapher of his fellow Scot, John James Waterston. The Royal Society might have learned to hold Haldane in high regard, but he had lessons to teach them about their treatment of others. 'I think I'll have a shot at the Royal Society system of selecting papers & excluding "speculative" ones,' he wrote to his friend D'Arcy Thompson. 'It makes the meetings, Proceedings and Transactions as dull as ditch water,[18] and quite unrepresentative of the progress of British Science.'[19]

Waterston's paper of 1845 was a pioneering and careful explication of the kinetic theory of gases. It was also one of those 'speculative' papers the Royal Society had set itself against. One of the paper's referees declared it was 'nothing but nonsense, unfit even for reading before the Society'. Waterston had submitted the paper from India, without keeping a copy. Once a paper had been dismissed, the Society retained it and effectively blocked publication elsewhere. 'It is probable that in the long and honourable history of the Royal Society,' Haldane stated in his biography, 'no mistake more disastrous in its actual consequences for the progress of science and the reputation of British science than the rejection of Waterston's papers was ever made.'[20]

Waterston's career never recovered from the blow. Sunstroke in India left him prone to giddiness and collapse, and stopped him writing up his ideas as a book. Still, he managed to remain genial. Back in Scotland he took an active interest in the lives of his nephews and nieces. On the morning of 18 June 1883 Waterston read newspaper reports of a fire in Sunderland in which many children were suffocated. Borrowing some pennies from his Edinburgh landlady, he took a tram out to Leith to walk along the breakwater being built there. High tide was in. His distress at those Sunderland children's deaths, Haldane speculated, led Waterston to faint. Faint or jump, his body was presumed snatched by the sea.

Eight years later, the distinguished chemist Lord Rayleigh discovered a rejected Waterston paper in the archives of the

Royal Society. It was duly published, 'containing a full statement of the afterwards accepted kinetic theory of gases and of temperature'.[21] Rayleigh looked no further after making this one find.

A conversation with D'Arcy Thompson led Haldane to meet with Waterston's surviving relatives. The man's niece was especially helpful, handing over his papers. 'I saw very soon that he was one of the greatest physicists of last century,'[22] Haldane declared, the biographer's passion now ablaze within him. 'The whole story is to my mind amazing. Physical chemistry and thermodynamics would have developed quite differently if Waterston's papers had been published and heeded.'[23] He rooted about in the Society's Archives and Library, discovering a further fundamental paper rejected by the Society in 1852, including what Haldane termed Waterston's Law 'as to the relation of the density of saturated vapours to absolute temperature'.[24] Haldane's biography of Waterston was written as a preface to his edition of Waterston's collected papers.

Haldane recognized that this book, as with so many aspects of his life, would be controversial. 'I know that many people will be jarred by my criticisms of Kelvin, Carnot, Clerk Maxwell, van't Hoff, & van der Waals,' he wrote to Thompson, reeling off the names of great physicists he felt to be less than Waterston, 'and by my estimate of Waterston's contributions. Still, I can't help it. When, also, I think of Faraday as a deacon at the Sandemanian meeting-house, & Kelvin as an elder of the Kirk, I can't help thinking that they had more intellectual limitations than Waterston had.'[25]

'It is quite impossible to express, adequately, our gratefulness to you for your interest and kindness in preserving, for all time, the name of one who might otherwise have sunk into oblivion,' Waterston's great-nephew assured Haldane, in appreciation of the work he had done in bringing Waterston's life and work to public knowledge. The next line showed that Haldane had even mastered the biographer's art of conjuring a life at his own financial cost. 'This has appealed to us even more than the personal generosity which has made the publication possible.'[26]

A highly individual honour came Haldane's way in 1924. 'The Council of the Institution of Mining Engineers wish me to become President,' he wrote to his mother, 'and I can hardly refuse if they can't agree on someone else, but I have only given a provisional acceptance, as I rather think they ought to have a mining engineer, and I also feel that I have quite enough on my hands.'[27]

As a non-engineer Haldane was unique enough in simply being a member of the Institution. To elect someone from outside of their profession as their primary representative must be the rarest thing in any industry. Haldane responded with a characteristically individual opening address. He told his audience of mining engineers:

> It is not with scientific abstractions called 'Labour' and 'Capital' that British mining engineers have to work, but with their fellow-countrymen, their own flesh and blood. These fellow-countrymen will give loyal and efficient service, will face any danger, will forgive imagined or real mistakes, and will take the rough with the smooth, the bad times with the good; but what they will not tolerate is being treated as if they were mere tools, to be cast aside without compunction. Neither high wages, high dividends, nor welfare schemes will satisfy them in this respect, but only

discerning and sympathetic treatment, the treatment of comradeship in a common enterprise – such comradeship as
existed in and between ranks during the war, or such comradeship as is taught in the Gospels . . . In fighting the
difficulties and dangers of mining work; in fighting for the
economic stability of mining undertakings, including the
interests of shareholders; and in fighting for the highest welfare of those employed and their families, a mining engineer
finds that spiritual reality in his comradeship in those around
him.[28]

Having turned a lecture on mining engineering into a
spiritual address, Haldane was unlikely to be shy of an offer
extended to him for 1927–8. A bequest by Lord Gifford to
the universities of Glasgow, St Andrews, Aberdeen and
Edinburgh saw the bi-annual series of Gifford lectures begin
in 1883. The intention was to 'promote and diffuse the study
of Natural Theology in the widest sense of the term – in
other words, the knowledge of God'.

Attracting pre-eminent thinkers in their fields, it is intriguing to see how many of the lecturers were intimates
of Haldane. Following William James's seminal talk 'The
Varieties of Religious Experience' in 1902 came Haldane's
brother Richard. During the war Haldane's philosophy friend
from Oxford, the Australian Samuel Alexander, gave his
series of lectures entitled 'Space, Time and Deity'. His university colleague from student days in Edinburgh, Andrew
Seth Pringle-Pattison, delivered several series of the lectures.
Niels Bohr would lecture in the future.

Haldane took 'The Sciences and Philosophy' as the theme
for his twenty lectures, to be delivered at Glasgow University.
D'Arcy Thompson, the childhood friend who shared

Haldane's birthday, visited Cloan and left us a moving account of observing these lectures in preparation:

> John is an extraordinary man. He has a knack of approaching every subject in the spirit of the consulting physician, that whatever the other fellow thinks or says may be presumed to be wrong. This has grown on him, till nowadays he seems to have convinced himself that neither physicists nor physiologists know anything about their subject: – and who am I that I should think otherwise. But what interests me most is his extraordinary working power. He is more than half-crippled with rheumatism; he is always more or less in bodily pain; but he works by night and by day. When he is at home in Oxford, he travels once a week to Birmingham, and at least twice a week to London. He has three books on hand at the moment, including a set of Gifford lectures. These last he writes sitting in an armchair with a pad on his knee, – one page after another. I would have to surround myself with books; and after a long morning's work I should have written one paragraph, which I should probably tear up in the afternoon. But John's sister comes in to ask how many pages he has done; neither of them ever dreaming for a moment that these pages, once written, need cause any more thought or trouble. But whatever faults or eccentricities he may have, John is a very good fellow indeed, who wouldn't do an ill turn to anybody; on the contrary, he is almost quixotically anxious to do good to all mankind, – and to teach them all a thing or two.[29]

Haldane's Gifford lectures provoked a flurry of heated correspondence in the *Scotsman*. A balanced viewpoint was struck by the *New York Times*. Its review of the lectures in book form concluded that 'so evident is the sincerity throughout and so active the search for a biological basis on which contemporary science, philosophy, and a religion free from theological trappings may be reconciled, that the peculiar virtues of *The Sciences and Philosophy* must be given adequate if qualified recognition. It is in many ways an unusual and fascinating book.'[30]

Haldane became an Honorary Fellow of the Royal Society of Medicine, and collected honorary doctorates from Oxford, Cambridge, Dublin, Edinburgh, Birmingham and Leeds. Now he and D'Arcy Thompson were set to share the platform to receive the honorary degree of Doctor of Science from the university of Witwatersrand in Johannesburg. The trip out to South Africa in the summer of 1929 was for a meeting of the British Association for the Advancement of Science. The occasion saw Haldane at his Machiavellian best, seeking to bring the ideas of his Gifford lectures into the scientific mainstream.

One element common to scientists who are able to trumpet their own glory is the skill to wrap up their findings in a snappy new word or phrase. Haldane was pretty wanting in this regard. One abject low in such an attempt, labelling his own beliefs as against those of the vitalists or mechanists, was his coining of the term 'neo–Hippocratism'.[31]

The South African politician Jan Smuts was much better at the game. He coined the terms 'holism' and 'holistic', and in 1926 Haldane chose these to fit his own views. In correspondence with Smuts before the British Association meeting in South Africa, Haldane set him up as the lead speaker in a debate to be called 'The Nature of Life'. To lead the opposition, Smuts found the very person Haldane was calling for, 'an ultra-mechanistic [theorist] . . . to speak after you'.[32] A local professor, Laurence Hogben, was chosen as their stooge. He was so vehemently, unabashedly leftist in his views that Smuts's holism would shine out in contrast as the moderate standpoint.

Haldane travelled out to South Africa on the RMS *Windsor Castle*. A stop at Madeira allowed for a brief reprisal of the Pikes Peak experience, with a ride on a cog railway up a 3,000-foot peak and then a toboggan journey back down again. Haldane made frequent visits to the Sultan of Zanzibar in the adjoining cabin, a 'bright and entertaining' man whose presence on board required their ship to receive a fifteen-gun salute into Cape Town. Along with Sir Charles Parsons, Haldane also spent a morning down in the engine room and the stoke holds. Parsons, the inventor of a multi-stage steam turbine that transformed shipping, was the perfect companion for such a venture. Set to use the South African meeting to get his message across, Haldane took the chance of a little on-board practice in having his way. 'The captain seems a very nice man,' he told his sister, 'and I've arranged with him to try the effects of salt on the stokers when it gets hot!'[33]

Haldane met many times with Jan Smuts and his wife Isie, getting along famously. When Smuts visited Oxford later that year for a series of sell-out lectures at the Sheldonian, Haldane gave him guidance as to how to handle English audiences. Such was Smuts's charm that he managed to bring Kathleen into his and Haldane's holistic way of thinking. She was even able to ignore the fact that Smuts was a Boer.

Jan Smuts was a farm boy till the age of twelve, finding his essential teachings from nature. He read law at Cambridge and took top prizes at London's Inns of Court, but his most compelling teachings came from the poetry of Walt Whitman. Ten years younger than Haldane, Smuts shared

Haldane's Calvinist upbringing. Discovering Whitman's conception of 'natural man' was like a Damascene conversion, releasing him from the Calvinist sense of sin.

Smuts led guerrilla units against the British forces during the Boer War, and then was brought in to help draw up the terms of peace. Lloyd George brought him into his War Cabinet in 1917, making him Minister for Air and so responsible for forming the Royal Air Force. In the discussions leading up to the Treaty of Versailles Smuts was foremost among those seeking to establish moderate peace terms for Germany, and subsequently played a significant role in setting up the League of Nations. He had recently concluded his first spell as Prime Minister of South Africa when he and Haldane met. During that time he had made sure to resist all movement of the country towards a system of apartheid. These constant shifts towards peace and harmony can be read as holism in action, the sense that people belong to one interactive whole, and that you can never separate yourself from the consequences of your actions.

'The Nature of Life' debate was run jointly by the physiology, botany and zoology sections of the Association, D'Arcy Thompson joining Haldane among the principal speakers. Smuts opened the discussion 'with a brilliant restatement of his holistic faith as against the mechanistic interpretation'.[34] Hogben retaliated as planned, shoving the argument towards the left. In a clever twist, he adapted J. B. S. Haldane's recently published mathematical theory about the mechanics of natural selection to his cause, setting the son's views against the holism being espoused by his father. It was not good enough.

'Our debate seems to have been the most popular item,' Haldane wrote to his sister. 'We had the largest hall in the

University, but hundreds of people couldn't get in.' He had 'two longish talks' with Princess Alice, born in 1843 as the third child of Queen Victoria. 'Extremely popular' in South Africa, she came to the debate, 'stayed to the very end, & said she was convinced by my arguments!'[35]

'A lot of people in S. Africa,' he later told his daughter, 'are more or less converted! What interests me most, however, is the way in which physiologists at home are coming over. There may soon be no more mechanists left among them.'[36]

On disembarking back in Britain from his South African voyage, Haldane went straight to work. The Mersey Tunnel connecting Liverpool with Birkenhead was under construction, rock beneath the river bed allowing it to become the largest tunnel of its kind so far built. Haldane was on hand for a smoke test, examining the effects of any petrol tank blaze caused by a possible car collision. He was brought in to the project for his expertise on ventilation: three ventilation stations on each bank of the Mersey were designed to keep the percentage of carbon monoxide from car exhaust fumes down to below 0.02.

The man who had switched from his penny farthing to the new-fangled invention of the bicycle was now engineering mass transport by automobile. He had been among the very first to experience submarine travel. Next would come Haldane's chance to see what his altitude work had helped inspire by way of air travel.

THE GREATEST PHYSIOLOGICAL
SELF-EXPERIMENT OF ALL

Long lives tend to ebb towards their close. Haldane's was different. New projects kept him powering forward day after day. He was like a vast stooped wave that crashes with a roar on the shore, its water whispering down through the pebbles, and then is gone.

His body became Mount Grampus for his grandchildren. They climbed across the crags of his knees, over the mound of his stomach, and reached for the 'chocolate tree' in his waistcoat pocket, a gold box attached to a gold chain containing a chocolate as the child's reward. The adventure formed a loving memory for the grandchildren. It was remarkable, and somehow typical, that a man crippled by rheumatic pains would lead the children on in such a way. Ignore the pain, and live life as a game while you can.

Over in Germany he was saddened to see the universities he admired so much going so wrong. Haldane's name led a petition to the German government, protesting at the pressure put on universities to evict Jews from their posts. The teachings of his professor at Jena, Ernst Haeckel, were now being used to support the eugenicist policies of the Nazi party. Haldane took walks out into the natural world to clear his mind of such aberrations. His grandchildren joined him in new field experiments, plunging thermometers inside hayricks to test for fermentation.

Another demonstration for the grandchildren sought to share what most intrigued him of late, the question of vision and after-vision. He had them stare at a bright red light, then switched it off for them to find themselves staring at a green one. A lecture for the children was illustrated by a paper card with holes cut into it, to generate both image and after-image.

In a more adult format, a lecture called 'Vision of Brightness and Colour' formed the inaugural address to the Edinburgh Royal Medical Society.[1] Haldane's active interest in the subject stemmed from his work on miners' nystagmus. Something of a Prospero for his audience, he switched light and darkness, candles and lanterns, to lead them on a tour of vision and illusion. Instead of Prospero's staff he handed around blackened tubes together with mounted strips of white, blue and black paper. The white paper would turn yellow, the blue white, and the black a very distinct shade of yellow.

'You will find a blackened tube a most instructive piece of apparatus,' he told his audience, 'if you look through it with the eye, not merely of a sceptic or physicist, but of a physiologist. Through the tube a patch of clear blue sky fades rapidly into pure white.' He explained the whys and wherefores, and quite typically reached back through history, bringing back an unacclaimed scientific predecessor as one of his models. An excellent description of coloured shadows, and the disappearance of those colours when viewed through a blackened tube, was part of a Royal Society paper of 1794 by Count Rumford, now 'practically disregarded and forgotten'.

His friend and colleague from Yale, Yandell Henderson, reported the true nature of this latest interest of Haldane's. 'When asked why he had in the eighth decade of his life devoted so much interest to this topic, he replied that 'it affords an experimental basis for Berkeleyan idealism'.[2] The Irish philosopher George Berkeley had been integral to Haldane's metaphysics since his student days. In 1709 Berkeley published his *An Essay towards a New Theory of Vision*, which Haldane nodded towards near the conclusion of his Edinburgh address: 'Nature only mocks at us,' he told his audience, 'when we try to demonstrate a physical universe independent of experience of it. We are thus, as Berkeley pointed out, driven back on sense-experiences for a criterion of reality, so that a physical world out of relation to them is only an abstraction.'

These last years were subsumed by Haldane's philosophical drive, culminating in 1935 with the compendium of his philosophical ideas and their sources, his book *The Philosophy of a Biologist*. He admitted that science more usually fought shy of any religious reference and feared 'that it might perhaps appear as if I were throwing doubt on the existence of a real and orderly universe. This is far from my intention. We find what is both real and ordinary in our universe; but it seems to me that we can only realise this ultimately when we realise that it is a spiritual universe. Only then does it appear as real, and not, like the universe which is merely interpreted physically, a universe of artificial abstractions from their underlying reality.'[3]

The journalist Betty Ross visited Haldane's study – 'a veritable city of books' – to discuss the nature of life. His 'silky white hair, flowing moustache, a soft Scottish accent, coupled with his gentleness and charm' were aided by blue eyes that twinkled as he quoted Walter de la Mare to her:

> '"It is a very odd thing
> As odd as can be:
> That whatever Miss T. eats
> Turns into Miss T."[4] . . . That really hits the nail on the head, and shows the impossibility of explaining the phenomena of life in physical and chemical terms.'
>
> Asked what the world most needed, his reply was swift and succinct. 'Religion!'
>
> And the reason?
>
> 'Because science is not enough! Since from its very nature it does not deal with the values which are supreme, it cannot guide us by itself. Reason in its highest form is religion. And real religion, extending to every part of our lives, is what we need most today.'

The need as he saw it in the 1930s can still be seen as current in our new millennium.

> 'Many people are at a loose end. The old theology, with its miraculous revelations, no longer convinces them, and at the same time they are very confused and oppressed by science. Spiritual reality is the only reality. If we lose sight of this spiritual world we are not realising ourselves – because we have lost sight of what alone is ultimately real in ourselves.'[5]

Yandell Henderson decided the late summer of 1935 was high time to play academic politics on Haldane's behalf. 'He is the founder & master of the School of which you and I are disciples,' he wrote to C. G. Douglas while en route back to America from a congress in Russia. 'He is the greatest physiologist – bar none – since Karl Ludwig.'[6] It was high time Oxford addressed the want of any outstanding recognition of his services to them and to science, and elected him Professor Emeritus. 'Such election would be welcomed among physiologists everywhere and among scientists the world over.'[7]

Henderson's curious usage of the term 'disciples' for adherents to a school of physiology is set in context by remarks of Violet Markham, a family friend and the sister of the Sir Arthur Markham who founded the Doncaster Mining Laboratory: 'Apart from his high standing in the scientific world, [John Haldane] was one of the most simple and delightful men I have ever known. If he had not been a great scientist he might have been a great saint, for he had something of the quality of a great saint which drew people to him like a magnet.' As Violet Markham's guest one summer at Bradenham, Disraeli's old home, Haldane's fellow guests were largely ex-soldiers and younger men. They

had heard of him as the scientist who had done much to minimize the danger of gas attacks during the 1914 war. Far from being alarmed by his reputation, their hearts were all won by the simple, friendly ways of 'the Professor', as they called him. They gathered round John Haldane, plying him with questions: 'Now, Professor, tell us . . .', 'Do you think . . .?', 'Can a gas attack . . .?' etc. I have rarely known a guest excite so much admiration and affection in so brief a weekend, and he in turn delighted in their youth and eagerness to hear and to learn.[8]

Haldane's own eagerness to learn and contribute saw him embark on one more mammoth quest on behalf of industrial hygiene. His friend Sir John Cadman invited him to investigate the conditions of extreme heat endured by workers in the oilfields of what are now Iran and Iraq.

It was never bad for him to escape the tail-end of an English winter. In February 1926 he had written to Naomi from the Egyptian Nile: 'It is difficult to realise the cold in England, though as I look at the hills here in the moonlight they are all white, just as if they were covered with snow & not sand, in spite of the north star being quite low down, & strange stars like Canopus and the southern cross appearing.'

His letters matched their audience, and so to Naomi he wrote of literature – and the benign effects of such a climate on his health. 'I am feeling much better & clearer in my head, & have drafted half the Gifford Lectures for next year, & read several novels – Adam Bede, Sense & Sensibility, two of Stevenson, & part of a very trashy American book, George Arrowsmith by Sinclair Lewis. I am quite clear that if he came up to be judged by Osiris his soul would be sent away in a pig in accordance with the picture in the Book of the Dead!'[9]

In Egypt he had 'climbed over the roof of the Philae Temple nearly submerged in the huge lake made by the dam; then across the dam in a trolley pushed by Nubians, & back again on donkeys after lunch'. The route home would take him through Cairo and Venice.

Ten years later, this new trip to the Middle East had a particular flavour for the man who had done so much to pioneer aviation. He and his sister Elizabeth, known to him as Bay, walked across the airstrip at Gaza and climbed into one of the two passenger compartments in a large biplane. The *Hengist*, an HP 45, had two Bristol Jupiter engines fixed to the upper wing and one on each side of the lower wing.[10] The Imperial Airways flight roared them off to Baghdad and then on to Shaiba in the south of what was then Mesopotamia. A photograph shows the brother and sister being punted across the Shatt-al-Arab River in Basra, headed for Persia.

Haldane's work period involved visits to Abadan refinery, oilfields at Masjid-I-Sulaiman and Chashmeh-I-Ali, and a rig and test well at Pirgah, examining the effects of heat exhaustion.

He showed no apparent signs of heat exhaustion himself. A souvenir photo album of the visit sees him stooped, besuited and smiling all across Jerusalem, visiting Jericho, Tiberias, Kallia beside the Dead Sea, and the Virgin's Well in Nazareth; in Beirut; at both Larnaka and Nicosia in Cyprus, and in Rhodes. From Istanbul he moved on to the Acropolis in Athens, the old philosopher donning an overcoat and hat for his visit to Plato's Academy. Mining interests determined the next port of call, out to Lavrion near Cape Sounion, where silver, zinc, lead and iron have been mined since ancient times, and Mount Parnassus from where bauxite had been extracted. An old Roman village near Budapest and the castle of Nuremberg rounded off an extraordinarily arduous trip.

All should have been well. Back in Cherwell Haldane paid a visit to the sickbed of his wife, down with cystitis, and went to bed in his narrow room for a good night's sleep. He felt fine after his trip. However it was a high bed, and somehow he fell from it.

The fall provoked a bout of pneumonia. First Naomi, then Jack, and a troop of doctors and nurses rushed in to support the recovery operation. Haldane was intrigued by all their careful measures, discussing the elements with them, thrilled at the news that his temperature had reached a record low. An oxygen tent, the form of treatment he had pioneered, was raised around him. He sailed off on adventures in his dreams, fascinated to report these wanderings to those in the room, an idealist philosopher faced with a wondrous example of reality not existing outside of his own perceptions.

Naomi helped Kathleen out of her sickbed and across the corridor for just the one visit to her sick husband. He was delighted, greeting her with words of love. It was clear he was dying, though Jack would not have him told so. As a boy Haldane had drawn his son's blood for examination. Now Jack rolled up his sleeve for a series of blood transfers to his father.

Naomi and Jack's relationship was prone to its passionate outbursts. Down below the sickroom an argument developed in fierce whispers. Should Naomi have reported the illness to the press? Jack had strong Marxist ideological views on the matter. Naomi bit his arm. Jack twisted her wrist. The fire burned out of their anger, they returned upstairs to sit quietly beside their father's fever. In her own last years her father would come to Naomi in her dreams, dispelling the unease of nightmares. He came 'as the area of safety, occasionally as the exorciser or perhaps the explainer who makes it quite clear that as a matter of fact and once one grasps the pattern of what it is all about, everything is perfectly all right'.[11]

Treatment cleared his lungs, but Haldane's heart was too weak to support much more. He had been born at midday. He died on the stroke of midnight as the calendar moved to 15 March 1936. 'He had a look of intense interest on his face,' Naomi recalled, 'as though he were taking part in some crucial experiment in physiology which had to be carefully monitored. Jack and I watched him, one on each side. We could only go on the look, however much we longed to ask him. But it made me at least feel that here was an experience deeply worth having.'[12]

Haldane left his body to the Radcliffe Hospital. The staff there, his friends and colleagues, could not bear to dissect it. Instead it was carried to Golders Green cemetery in London for cremation. For J. Ivon Graham, the assistant director of the Mining Research Laboratory, the loss of Haldane brought a grief as profound as for the death of the closest family member. Haldane had steered him through his life, attended his wedding, and left provision in his will for the education of Graham's sons. Graham replied to those letters of sympathy streaming in to the family from Haldane's overseas colleagues, and took the lead in arranging the funeral ceremony. Alongside the family's chosen readings from Plato's *Phaedo*, he penned a passage from Haldane's own book *Materialism*. 'I am an old man,' Haldane wrote for his mourners now to hear, 'to whom death will soon come; but in proportion as I realise that God lives eternally, and that what is alone real in me is God's manifestation, I cease to fear the end of what is merely individual, and therefore, as such, unreal in my life, or to feel that their deaths have truly separated me from those I have loved, or whose memories I honour.'

The urn containing Haldane's ashes travelled up to Scotland on the luggage rack of a third-class compartment. Jack sat below it, trying to concentrate on writing a scientific paper, fuming that his sister and aunt had taken the capitalist route of a first-class sleeper. Calm would come beside the Gleneagles chapel on the Haldane estate, where John Scott Haldane's ashes were laid beside his brother Richard's, with 'the green turf and the mountains and the grey sky and the brilliant mass of flowers and the unaccompanied voices singing'.[13] The song was 'I to the Hills'.

'I am deeply grieved at the sad loss of Haldane,' C. S. Sherrington wrote from back in Oxford. 'He is a great man gone.'[14]

Haldane had pledged his body and his life to effect an astonishing range of improvements in public health, industrial safety and human possibilities. Men walked ocean beds, worked the deepest mines, dared scale Everest and envisage space flight, while doctors now had a bank of expertise and equipment to deploy in tending respiratory problems in their patients, all on the back of knowledge that he brought into the world. To an unusual degree, however, Haldane is worth celebrating not simply for his splendid array of achievements but for the sheer verve and impact of his life. His philosophy held that no organism could be seen in isolation from its environment. In life, the man exercised a very profound effect on all who came near him.

Out at Yale, Yandell Henderson read Haldane's obituary in the *New York Times*. 'Each year that I went to Europe my visit to Oxford, if only for a night, was my greatest pleasure,' he wrote to C. G. Douglas, his colleague from Pikes Peak. 'I feel now that I could not bear ever to set foot in England again.' As a physiologist Henderson had followed Haldane into the

trenches of the First World War, advising American troops on
gas protection. He had brought Haldane's methods into the
building of the Holland Tunnel. He knew as well as anyone
about soldiering on, but a man is allowed to be desolate now
and again.

'Well time goes on,' he concluded his letter, 'and I begin to
feel sad and old and tired. Yet to have known Haldane was
itself enough to have made it worth while to have lived.'[15]

ACKNOWLEDGEMENTS

My thanks to individuals who have provided support
and information along the way: Professors Dennis Mit-
chison, Murdoch Mitchison, Avrian Mitchison and Graeme
Mitchison; Lois Godfrey; Richard Haldane; Amanda
Mitchison; Peter Graham, David Graham, John Graham and
Robert Graham, the sons of J. Ivon Graham; Professor
Jonathan Meakins, Sally Jackson and Sandra Sackett, the
grandchildren of Colonel Jonathan Meakins; Howard
Thomas, of Tylorstown Post Office; Mick Brown; Professor
Philip James; Veena Rao; Krishna R. Dronamraju; Ian
Warden for research in Canberra; Sir Roger Elliott; Jeremy
Norman of historyofscience.com; P. R. Lewis; Steve Sturdy;
Simon Jones; Neil Wheelwright; Thomas Cunningham;
Nathan M. Greenfield; Liz Baird; Gail Joughin; Mrs Margaret
Torrance; John Morcombe; Mick Forsyth; the staff of the Big
Pit Museum in Blaenafon; Gareth Gill; the staff of the
Rhondda Heritage Park in Pontypridd and the Lewarde
Mining Museum; Lee Perry of the Charles Woodward
Memorial Library, UBC; Maggie Burns at the local studies
library, Birmingham, the Sir Benjamin Stone photographic

collection; Michael Young of Newcastle City Library; Moira Mackenzie; Dr Christopher Hilton; Professor Andrew Parker and Sally Harte of the Oxford Physiology Laboratory; the staff at the Tylorstown library; members of the Great War Forum. Ben Ball for acquiring the book; Andrew Gordon for adopting this book and editing it so handsomely; Ben Mason for encouraging, shaping and agenting it; James Thornton for continuous moral and editorial support; the Society of Authors for its Authors' Foundation Award.

PRINCIPAL ARCHIVAL SOURCES

The J. T. Wilson Papers, MS 035, Australian Academy of Science, Basser Library, Canberra (originals in the University of Sydney Archives)

The Haldane Papers in the National Library of Scotland

The Haldane Papers in the Charles Woodward Memorial Room, University of British Columbia, Vancouver

The National Archives at Kew

The Sound Archives at the Imperial War Museum

The British Library

The Burdon Sanderson and J. B. S. Haldane Papers in the University Library, London

The D'Arcy Wentworth Thompson Papers in the University of St Andrews library

The Haldane Papers in the Wolfson College Archives, Oxford

The Claude Gordon Douglas Papers in the Sherrington Library of the History of Neuroscience, Oxford Physiology Laboratory

Special Collections in the Penrose Library, Colorado Springs

NOTES

CHAPTER 1

1 From a blue-book on coal dust in mines by the mine inspector Henry Hall, reported in *The Times*, 12/9/1894, p. 14.

2 From a British Association report, quoted in *The Times*, 11/8/1894.

3 *South Wales Daily News*, 29/1/1896.

4 Ibid.

5 *The Times*, 28/1/1896.

6 J. T. Robson, *Report to the Secretary of State*, p. 11.

7 Henry Davies, *Silent Heroisms*, pp. 83–6.

8 *The Scotsman*, 28/1/1896, p. 5.

9 *Cardiff Times and South Wales Weekly News*, 1/2/1896.

10 Robert Woodfall, *Report to the Secretary of State*, p. 3.

11 *The Times*, 29/1/1896.

12 *The Scotsman*, 15/8/1894.

13 C. G. Douglas, pp. 115–39, 1936

14 *The Scotsman*, 28/1/1896, p. 5.

15 J. S. Haldane, *Report to the Secretary of State*, p. 36.

16 *South Wales Daily News*, 30/1/1896.

17 J. S. Haldane, 'Action of Carbonic Oxide', *Journal of Pathology*, vol. 18, London, 1895, p. 435.

18 Quoted from Piers C. Nye and John T. Reeves, 'A High Point in Human Breathing', *Attitudes on Altitude*, ed. John T. Reeves and Robert F. Grover.

19 UCL, BSP, 27/12/1895.

20 NLS #179, letter from J. Moran, Department of Mines, Canada, Ottawa.

21 Geoffrey York, 'A Canary in the Chinese Coal Mine', *Globe and Mail*, Toronto, 3/2/2007.

22 *China Daily*, 10/2/2007.
23 Ibid. 14/2/2007.
24 *Associated Press*, 18/2/2007.
25 *Associated Press*, reported in *The Guardian*, 2/4/2007.
26 *The Nation*, 12/6/2006.
27 *The Herald-Dispatch*, 16/2/2007.

CHAPTER 2

1 NLS, MS 20150, p. 85.
2 E. Haldane, *From One Century*, p. 94.
3 R. B. Haldane, *Autobiography*, pp. 8–9.
4 Reminiscences come from *Mary Haldane*.
5 J. B. S. Haldane, 'The Scientific Work of J. S. Haldane', p. 11.
6 Ruth Thompson's fine biography of her father included his reminiscences from an essay 'The Invention of the Blackboard'.
7 *The Edinburgh Academy Chronicle*, June 1936, from an obituary of JSH by D'Arcy Wentworth Thompson.
8 R. B. Haldane, *Autobiography*, p. 5.
9 NLS, MS 20150, 78, Mary Haldane's handwritten reminiscence.
10 Ibid.
11 R. B. Haldane, *Autobiography*, p. 11.
12 Ibid., p. 13.
13 Ghetal Burdon Sanderson, *John Burdon Sanderson*, p. 150.
14 R. B. Haldane, *Autobiography*, p. 25.
15 *The Times*, 24/1/1876.
16 R. B. Haldane, *Autobiography*, p. 27.
17 NLS, MS 6076.
18 J. S. Haldane, *The Sciences and Philosophy*, p. 76.

CHAPTER 3

1 Quotations from letters from Germany come from the 'Autobiographical Notes', mostly letters from J. S. Haldane to his mother, in the National Library of Scotland, MS 20231.
2 J. S. Haldane (as 'A Medical Student'), *A Letter to Edinburgh Professors*, pp. 19–20.

3 NLS, 41, 26/6/1879.

4 Seth later added the 'Pringle-Pattison' to his name, as a condition of a bequest he received.

5 NLS, 56–7.

6 J. S. Haldane, *A Letter to Edinburgh Professors*, p. 1.

7 J. B. S. Haldane, 'Darwin', *Keeping Cool*, p. 99.

8 J. S. Haldane, *A Letter to Edinburgh Professors*, p. 14, as with next paragraph.

9 Medical Act, 1858, Amendment (No. 3) Bill (Lords). Select Committee. Special report, proceedings, minutes of evidence and appendix, 1879. 1878–1879. Vol. XII, x, 524p. (Sessional no. 320), pp. 211–39.

10 NLS, letter of 19 August 1883.

11 J. S. Haldane, *A Letter to Edinburgh Professors*.

12 NLS, 113, letter to mother of 12 July 1883.

13 *The Scotsman*, 14/10/1933, p. 10.

14 E. Haldane, *From One Century*, p. 107.

15 J. S. Haldane and R. S. Haldane, 'The Relation of Philosophy to Science', from Andrew Seth & R. S. Haldane (eds.), *Essays in Philosophical Criticism*, p. 55.

16 NLS, Haldane Papers, IV, 10, handwritten draft.

17 *The Scotsman*, 29/9/1924, p. 7.

18 Quoted in Daniel Stashower, *The Teller of Tales*, p. 28.

19 L. K. Haldane, *Friends and Kindred*, p. 105.

20 Ibid., pp. 106–7.

21 NLS, f. 111, 4/7/1883.

22 NLS, MS 5902, f. 35, 13/7/1883.

23 NLS, f. 113, 12/7/1883.

24 NLS, MS 5902, f. 77.

25 NLS, to mother, 12.7.1883.

CHAPTER 4

1 This comes from a letter to his friend John Wilson, as do other quotations from the collection of letters among the Wilson Papers in the Museum of Canberra.

2 J. S. Haldane, 'Some Recent Advances in the Physiology of Respiration, Renal Secretion and Circulation', *British Medical*

Journal, 19/3/1921. Haldane's 8 litres of blood surpasses man's 5.6, the man's own physiology as extreme as his experiments.

3   J. S. Haldane, 'Some Recent Advances', *British Medical Journal*, 19/3/1921.

4   WCA, letter of recommendation for the Waynflete professorship, 15/2/1895.

5   J. B. S. Haldane, 'The Scientific Work of J. S. Haldane', pp. 13–14.

6   A letter in *The Times*, 13/8/1877, from a local resident, Mr A. C. Shelley, who complained of 'being nearly suffocated' by the sewer gas.

7   NLS, 139.

8   J. S. Haldane, *Transactions of the Sanitary Institute of Great Britain*, vol. 9, 1, 1887.

9   J. S. Haldane, 'Poisoning by Gas in Sewers', *The Lancet*, 25/1/1896.

10   *The Times*, 8/8/1895.

CHAPTER 5

1   E. Haldane, *From One Century*, p. 99.

2   UBC, XI 13.

3   E. Haldane, *From One Century*, p. 143.

4   WCA, letter supporting the Waynflete application, Berlin, 16/1/1895 – author's translation.

5   JSH was seeking permission for his sister Elizabeth to do this translation. After considering the matter for a couple of weeks, du Bois-Reymond declined the request.

6   NLS, 160.

7   NLS, 159.

8   Terrie M. Romano, *Making Medicine Scientific*, pp. 31–2.

9   Ibid., p. 26.

10   Ibid.

11   Handwritten account in NLS, with additions from a letter to Wilson of 1887, Canberra.

12   WP, Cloan, 25 Sept. 1887.

13   WP, Berlin, 4 Dec. 1886.

14   WCA, letter in support of the Waynflete professorship, signed by J. Lorrain Smith, W. Ramsden, M. S. Pembrey and A. M. Gossage.

15   WCA, Waynflete support letter, 1/2/1895.

16   NLS #164, 59 St Giles, letter to mother, 23/11/87.

17 NLS, MS 20659, to mother, 12/1/88.

18 NLS, 15/2/88.

19 NLS, letter of 4/5/88.

20 NLS, Karlsplatz 38, Freiburg, 17/6/88.

21 NLS, IV 1.2, 2/8/87.

22 J. S. Haldane, *A Letter to Edinburgh Professors*, pp. 39–40.

23 UBC, J. S. Haldane, 'Outlines of a Vitalistic Physiology', hand-written manuscript *c.*1890.

24 UBC, XI 13, Edinburgh lecture, 10/1/1896.

CHAPTER 6

1 UBC, letter of 17/8/1891.

2 L. K. Haldane, *Friends and Kindred*, p. 152.

3 Interview with the author at Murdoch Mitchison's home, 'Great Yew', on 26/4/2006.

4 R. B. Haldane, *Autobiography*, p. 8.

5 L. K. Haldane, *Friends and Kindred*, p. 150.

6 Reminiscence of Violet Markham, quoted in Mary Haldane, *Mary Elizabeth Haldane*, p. 157.

7 NLS, 192, 7/12/1891, from 11 Crick Road.

8 NLS, 53, 1889.

9 UCL, JBS Papers, 179/11, 30 Dec. 1891.

10 UBC, 11/8/1891.

11 UBC, 17/8/1891.

12 UBC, 26/11/1891.

13 NLS, 192, 7/12/1891.

14 L. K. Haldane, *Friends and Kindred*, p. 152.

15 UBC, 30/11/1891.

16 L. K. Haldane, *Friends and Kindred*, pp. 154–5.

17 Ibid., p. 150.

18 Ibid., p. 160.

19 NLS, JS to mother, 3/5/1893 and 3/6/1893.

20 R. Clark, *J.B.S.*, p. 17.

CHAPTER 7

1   NLS, 44, 15/10/1887.
2   NLS, 6/12/1887.
3   J. B. S. Haldane, 'The Scientific Work of J. S. Haldane', p. 13.
4   NLS, 202, 31/12/1893.
5   N. Mitchison in *The Listener*, 8/2/1973.
6   Robert L. Galloway, *A History of Coal Mining*, pp. 179–80.
7   This and subsequent sections from the same lecture come from UBC, XI 13, 'The Effects on Man of Vitiated Atmospheres', handwritten notes for a lecture at the Scottish Natural History Society, Edinburgh, 10/1/1896.
8   Ibid.
9   NLS, 206, JSH to MH, 18/10/1894, other details from J. S. Haldane, 'Notes of an Enquiry into the Nature and Physiological Action of Black-damp', *Proceedings of the Royal Society*, vol. 58, 24/1/1895.
10   UBC, XI 14 JSH.
11   C. le Neve Foster and J. S. Haldane (eds.), *The Investigation of Mine Air*. Haldane took over its editorial role on the 1904 death of Foster, who never fully recovered from the CO poisoning. Foster's diary entries are excerpted in an appendix to the book, and also in a report in *The Times*, 17/5/1897.

CHAPTER 8

1   NLS, 1/1/1898.
2   Fred T. Jane, 'Round the Underground on an Engine', *English Illustrated Magazine*, August 1893.
3   NLS, 30/4/1893.
4   UCL, 27/12/1895.
5   WCA, written by W. Hale White and J. W. Washbourn of Guy's Hospital, W. N. Atkinson, HM Inspector of Mines, and A. M. Anderson, Medical Officer of Health for Dundee, 30/1/1895.
6   L. K. Haldane, *Friends and Kindred*, p. 167.
7   Terrie M. Romano, *Making Medicine Scientific*, p. 131.
8   L. K. Haldane, *Friends and Kindred*, p. 167.
9   UCL, 27/12/1895.

10   WP, 29/4/95.

11   NLS, 5/12/1898.

12   NLS, 5/5/1898.

13   J. B. S. Haldane, 'The Scientific Work of J. S. Haldane', p. 19.

14   Letter to Mrs Roe, British Library 58570 – The Marie Stopes papers, f. 106, 5/4/1932.

15   UBC, talk to Wigan mining students, 18/10/1919.

16   Figures from *The Scotsman*, 13/6/1904, p. 6.

17   NLS, JSH letter to mother, Autumn 1888.

18   NLS, a Friday PS to a letter of 19/6/1901.

19   L. K. Haldane, *Friends and Kindred*, pp. 195–6.

20   DP, 26/12/1945, C. G. Douglas to L. G. Wicham-Legg.

21   DP, L. G. Wicham-Legg to C. G. Douglas, 17/12/1945.

22   NLS, 10/6/02.

23   N. Mitchison, *As It Was*, p. 84.

24   N. Mitchison, *The Listener*, 8/2/1973.

25   N. Mitchison, *As It Was*, p. 19.

26   N. Mitchison, *The Listener*, 8/2/1973.

CHAPTER 9

1   NLS, 83.

2   J. S. Haldane, *Report for the Secretary of State for the Home Department on Ankylostomiasis in Westphalian Collieries*, 1903.

3   NLS, #230, JSH to mother, from Duisberg station, 29/9/1903.

4   J. B. S. Haldane, 'The Scientific Work of J. S. Haldane', p. 22.

5   N. Mitchison, *As It Was*, p. 69.

6   *New York Times*, 15/8/1894.

7   UCL, letter to MEH, 10/11/1897.

8   L. K. Haldane, *Friends and Kindred*, p. 235.

9   UBC, J. S. Haldane, 'Some Recent Investigations on the Hygiene of Subterranean and Subaqueous Work', delivered at the General Meeting of the International Congress of Hygiene, Berlin, 26 September 1907. Handwritten notes.

10   J. S. Haldane, 'The Influence of High Air Temperatures', *Journal of Hygiene*, vol. 1, 1905, p. 494.

11   UBC, J. S. Haldane, 'The Relation between Pure Science and the Mining Profession', a response to students after a talk to the Mining

Students Association at Wigan, 18/10/1919.

12 Charles Blagden, 'Experiments and Observations in a Heated Room', *Philosophical Transactions (1683–1775)*, vol. 65, 1775, p. 111.

13 J. B. S. Haldane, *Keeping Cool*, p. 73.

14 WP, 8/11/1899.

15 JSH, intro. to unpublished textbook, 'Outlines of a Vitalistic Physiology', UBC, Box C.

16 Erling Asmussen, 'The Regulation of Respiration' *The Regulation of Human Respiration*, ed. D. J. C. Cunningham and B. B. Lloyd.

17 F.J.W. Roughton, 'The Chemistry of Respiration', Cunningham, *The Regulation of Human Respiration*.

18 J. B. S. Haldane, *Keeping Cool*, p. 96.

CHAPTER 10

1 NLS, letter to Elizabeth Haldane, 20/10/1903.

2 Frederick Maurice, *Haldane*, p. 136.

3 James Duggan, *Man Explores the Sea*, p. 52.

4 Ibid.

5 *The Scotsman*, 8/1/1908.

6 James Duggan, *Man Explores the Sea*, p. 93.

7 Jack Scoltock and Ray Cossum, *We Own Laurentic*, p. 36.

8 James Duggan, *Man Explores the Sea*, p. 95.

9 NLS, 20512, 17/8/1919.

CHAPTER 11

1 Violet Markham, *Friendship's Harvest*, pp. 49–50, including the J. M. Barrie story.

2 Ghetal Burdon Sanderson, *John Burdon Sanderson*, p. 148.

3 Interview with Lois Godfrey, Haldane's granddaughter.

4 WCA, Oxford house reminiscence.

5 NLS, 10/10/1901.

6 WCA, reminiscences of two Oxford houses by Naomi Mitchison.

7 Recollection of Kate Gielgud, the mother of Jack and Naomi's friends Lewis and John (the actor). She felt the rooms at Cherwell

'became as familiar and almost as dear to me as the rooms of my childhood'. Her husband was one of few casual visitors to be admitted to Haldane's sanctum, 'to chat late into the night while all the household slept'. Kate Gielgud, *Autobiography*, p. 208.

8   N. Mitchison, *All Change Here*, p. 70.

9   Sophie McBain, 'Smashing Job Chaps: An Exclusive Look inside the Bullingdon Club', *The Oxford Student*, 12/1/2005.

10 WCA, testimonial for lectureship at St Thomas's Hospital, 21/5/1895.

11 *The Times*, 15/5/1919.

12 Jimmy Wilde, *Fighting*, pp. 11–12. Jimmy Wilde's memory comes from the late 1890s. Born in 1892, he entered the Tylorstown colliery when he was twelve years old and went on to become flyweight boxing champion of the world, known as 'The Tylorstown Terror'.

13 L. K. Haldane, *Friends and Kindred*, p. 212; the other animal stories in this section all sourced from the same book.

14 DP, from a handwritten draft of a letter of condolence to Kathleen Haldane, 1936.

15 A letter to *The Times*, by someone styling himself 'A Biochemist', in response to the obituary of Haldane, 24/3/1936.

16 *Transactions of the Institution of Mining Engineers*, vol. 68, 1924–5.

17 DP C23, handwritten notes.

18 From three letters collected, WCA, this from 22 April 1905.

19 UCL, Burdon Sanderson papers, #131 Ms Add. 179/6, a letter from 17/10/1893.

20 Kenneth Franklin, *Joseph Barcroft*, p. 81.

21 *The Listener*, 8/2/1973.

22 The quotation, as with a great deal of the information on Mabel FitzGerald, comes from Robert Torrance's piece on her life and her contributions to the work on Pikes Peak, 'Major Breathing in Miners', from *Attitudes on Altitude*, ed. T Reeves and Robert Grover, published in a version he preferred in *Journal of Medical Biography*, vol. 7, August 1999.

CHAPTER 12

1   *The Colorado Springs Gazette*, 11/7/1911.

2   Ibid.

3   NLS, this and others from Haldane correspondence to his mother from the summit.

4   *New York Times*, 3/9/1911.

5   *Herald-Telegraph*, Colorado Springs, 18/7/1911.

6   *Colorado Springs Gazette*, 19/7/1911.

7   *Herald-Telegraph*, Colorado Springs, 11/7/1911.

8   'Physiological Observations Made on Pikes Peak', *Royal Society of London Physiological Transactions*, vol. 203, 1913, pp. 185–318.

9   *Colorado Springs Gazette*, 2/8/1911.

10   *Record Journal of Douglas County*, Castle Rock, Colorado, 14/7/1911.

11   *Colorado Springs Gazette*, 4/8/1911.

12   Official report, p. 270.

CHAPTER 13

1   'Just as the conceptions of mass and energy differentiated physics from mathematics, so the new biological conventions will differentiate biology from the physical sciences,' Haldane believed. 'When this time comes we shall have got out of the present rather barren controversies between vitalists and anti-vitalists. These controversies will die of inanition, just like the old controversies about the possibility of an absolute vacuum, which used to perplex the physicists and mathematicians. There will then be a distinctively biological way of looking at organisms *and their environment*, just as there is a distinctively physical and a distinctively mathematical way of looking at the world.' WP, letter to J. T. Wilson from 29/11/1896 – Haldane's own emphasis.

2   J. S. Milledge, 'The Great Oxygen Secretion Controversy', *The Lancet*, 21/8 December 1985.

3   A letter in *The Lancet*, 22/2/1986.

4   *The Times*, 10/7/1912 and 25/7/1912.

5   V. Markham, *Friendship's Harvest*, p. 10.

6   *The Times*, 18/11/1912, other information from Haldane's address to Wigan mining students, October 1919.

7   N. Mitchison, *All Change Here*, p. 26.

8   J. S. Haldane, *Mechanism*, pp. 63–4.

9 *The Times*, 20/10/1913.
10 Grover Smith (ed.), *The Letters of Aldous Huxley*, p. 55.
11 Quoted in Frederick Maurice, *Haldane*, p. 297.
12 Giles MacDonagh, *The Last Kaiser*, p. 332.
13 Stephen E. Koss, *Lord Haldane*, p. 87.
14 UPC, talk to Wigan mining students, 1919.
15 WCA, letter from W. Graham Greene of 14/10/1912.
16 E. Haldane, *From One Century*, p. 289.

CHAPTER 14

1 N. Mitchison, *All Change Here*, p. 101.
2 NLS 245, undated letter, 5/6/1911?
3 NLS, IV, 17, 18/1/1915.
4 WCA, letter of 2/11/1914.
5 J. B. S. Haldane, p. 17.
6 R. Clark, *J.B.S.*, p. 19.
7 All letters here from the National Library of Scotland's Haldane Archive.
8 Letter of 10 April 1915, in the author's collection.
9 Fritz Stern, *Einstein's German World*, p. 115.
10 NA, answers from General von Quirnheim, 22/3/22.
11 NA, letter of evidence from E. A. Beck, 1929.
12 Major Andrew MacNaughton, quoted in Tim Cook, *No Place to Run*, p. 21.
13 NA, answers from General von Quirnheim, 22/3/22.
14 NA, telegraphic dispatch 23/4/195.
15 IWMSA, #321, interview with Colonel Leslie John Barley, recalling in 1973 a conversation with Haldane in Flanders.
16 This and later information is taken from J. S. Haldane's typewritten memoir, quoted by Naomi Mitchison in 'The Haldanes: Personal Notes and Lessons'. She claimed to have the only typewritten copy, which has since disappeared.
17 NAWO, 142/281, the detail, as with others here, comes from H. B. Baker's diary.
18 J. S. Haldane, 'Lung-irritant Gas Poisoning and its Sequel', a lecture to the Royal Army Medical College on 8/10/1919, *RAMC Journal*, vol. 33, Dec. 1919.

19   NAWO, 142/153 CL/3/15, J. S. Haldane, 'Memorandum on Asphyxiating Gases and Vapours used by German Troops and on Means of Protection against Them', 3/5/1915.

20   NA, report on chlorine by J. S. Haldane, 4/8/1915.

21   Sir Hay Frederick Donaldson (1856–1916) was at the time Chief Superintendent of the Royal Ordnance Factories. He became Chief Technical Adviser to the Ministry of Munitions in September 1916, in which role he was accompanying Kitchener on his voyage to have talks in Russia with the Tsar. On 5 June 1916 HMS *Hampshire* struck a mine near the Orkneys and sank, killing Kitchener along with all of his staff including Donaldson.

22   NAWO, 142/281, H. B. Baker's diary.

23   NAWO, 142/184 ADG/18, J. S. Haldane and Professor Perkin, 'Report on Eye-Irritant Substances', 11/8/1915.

24   UBC, JSH, handwritten notes.

25   Daniel Charles, *Mastermind*, p. 166.

26   Ibid., p. 166.

27   NAWO, 95/744.

28   J. B. S. Haldane, *Callinicus*, pp. 68–9.

29   Huxley, *Letters*, p. 69.

30   NLS, 107, 9/7/1915.

31   V. Markham, *Friendship's Harvest*, p. 42.

32   Stephen Koss, *Lord Haldane*, p. 131.

33   J. B. S. Haldane, 'The Scientific Work of J. S. Haldane', p. 29.

34   WCA, proof of evidence submitted by JSH to counsel in the Home Office v. Clifton Colliery dispute.

35   N. Mitchison, 'The Haldanes: Personal Notes and Lessons', p. 13.

36   *The Times*, 16/9/1915.

37   NAWO, 142/90.

38   IWMSA, 10786.

39   NAWO, 142/91, DGS/23, letter to General Macready, 24/5/1915.

40   L. K. Haldane, *Friends and Kindred*, p. 176.

41   T. D. Spencer, 'Effects of Carbon Monoxide Poisoning on Man and on Canaries', *Transactions of the Institute of Mining Engineers*, vol. 118, part 8, 1958–9.

42   UBC, IV, 21, letter of 9/8/1917.

43   NLS, 10/10/1915.

44   Haldane family archive, Cloan.

45   NA, CAB 45/289.

CHAPTER 15

1   Address to Wigan mining students, 18/10/1919.
2   *RAMC Journal*, vol. 33, Dec. 1919, p. 507.
3   Ibid., p. 501.
4   This and subsequent passages come from Jonathan Meakins's hand-written memoir of his medical career, which he was writing at the time of his death in 1959. The material was kindly supplied by Meakins's granddaughter, Sandra Sackett.
5   Colonel Gorell, head of the unit, quoted in *The Toronto Star*, 11/2/1915.
6   Letter to Captain Means, historyofscience.com
7   'Therapeutic Administration of Oxygen', *British Medical Journal*, 10 Feb 1917.
8   From correspondence with Colonel Meakins's granddaughter, Sally Jackson.
9   Philip B. James (Professor of Hyperbaric Medicine, Wolfson Hyperbaric Medicine Unit, University of Dundee), 'Going Diving: Decompression Tables and the Genius of John Scott Haldane', paper read to the BSAC Diving Officers' Conference, 3/12/2005.
10 NLS, JSH to his brother, 27 March 1918.
11 Letter to Captain Means from JSH, 31/10/1918, historyofscience.com
12 *RAMC Journal* 33, Dec. 1919, p. 502.
13 Ibid.
14 Grover Smith (ed.), *Letters of Aldous Huxley*, p. 131, a letter of 3 August 1917.
15 IWMSA, #321, interview with Colonel Leslie John Barley.
16 UBC, Haldane XII, J. S. Haldane, 'Gas Poisoning in Warfare with Note on its Pathology and Treatment', hand-edited typescript of information for medical officers, p. 1.
17 Ibid., p. 37.
18 Ibid., p. 14.
19 NLS, letter to his brother.
20 UBC, Haldane XII, 'Gas Shell Bombardment of Ypres. 12/13 July 1917'. Marked SECRET, this was the investigative report of the first mustard gas attack written and filed by Haldane's colleague C. G. Douglas.
21 UBC, J. S. Haldane, 'Experiments on the Effects of Di-chlor-ethyl-sulphide', typewritten notes.

22 NA, G/59, J. S. Haldane, 'Poisoning by Nitrous Fumes and Sulphuretted Hydrogen'.

23 Ibid.

24 NA, AGD 18/21, J. S. Haldane, 'Physiological Action of Fumes from Arsenic Trifluoride AF_3'.

25 NLS, 276, letter to his mother, 14/8/1916.

26 NLS, June 20 1916, anticipating a visit to Cloan by John.

27 William Taft was the twenty-seventh president of the United States, 1909–1913. In 1916 he was Kent Professor of Constitutional Law at Yale, allowing for his attendance at Haldane's lectures. An advocate of peace, he went on to become Supreme Justice of the United States Supreme Court.

28 J. S. Haldane, 'Religion and the Growth of Knowledge', read at Guy's Hospital, 27/3/1924.

29 J. S. Haldane, *Organism and Environment*, p. 119.

30 NLS, MS 20512, pp. 27–8, 2/11/1916, as with the following quotations. The USA entered the war within six months of Haldane's visit to the USA, in April 1917.

31 J. S. Haldane, *The New Physiology*, p. 101.

32 NLS, 10/11/1916.

CHAPTER 16

1 This and the following excerpts come from a typescript entitled 'J. S. Haldane', NLS 10307, which begins: 'There is always the possibility that someone might write a book about my father J. S. Haldane and my brother J. B. S. Haldane. With that in mind I am now writing my own impressions of both my father and brother . . .'

2 This observation on First World War pilots comes from a discussion at the end of a symposium on carbon monoxide poisoning, recorded in *Transactions of the Institution of Mining Engineers*, vol. 118, 1958–9, p. 527.

3 Yandell Henderson, review of Joseph Barcroft's *The Respiratory Functions of Blood*, *Nature*, 1920.

4 D. Robertson, *George Mallory*, p. 151.

5 J. S. Haldane and J. G. Priestley, *Respiration*, pp. 203, 201.

6 ibid., p. 293.

7 D. Robertson, *George Mallory*, p. 155.

8 *The Times*, 3/2/1927, p. 10.

9 The two physiologists and sometime colleagues had their strong disagreements, but as Barcroft acknowledged in a closing statement as
   president of the Physiology section of the British Association in
   1920: 'Haldane's teaching transcends mere detail. He has always
   taught that the physiology of today is the medicine of tomorrow.
   The more gladly, therefore, do I take this opportunity of saying how
   much I owe, and how much I think medicine owes and will owe,
   to the inspiration of Haldane's teaching.'

10 Haldane did also take up Barcroft's challenge, describing the necessary oxygen apparatus for Everest in a lecture reported in *The
   Scotsman*, 27/12/1921, p. 3.

11 *Science News*, 22 October 1932.

12 Ridge's letter to Haldane states: 'Dr Jacob Schwartz, Mass. General
   Hospital, Boston, Mass., noted dermatologist to make study of
   animal to be taken aloft, animal shall be either monkey or pig; Prof.
   R. A. Millikan and Doctor A. H. Compton noted cosmic ray
   experts, are sending their cosmic ray machine aloft on ascension; Dr
   G. W. Pickard discoverer of the Heaviside layer in the stratosphere
   is to supervise radio short wave equipment; Dr K. O. Lange, Mass.
   Institution of Technology making meteorological study of condi-
   tion at highest point of ascension; Prof. J. Hardy of the same
   Institution interested in infra red ray photos to be made;
   Commodore E. G. Jay noted insulation engineer aiding in securing
   best method to protect the writer's body from terrific cold.'

13 NLS, MS 20513, Mark Ridge's letter to Haldane, from Dorchester,
   Massachusetts, 7 July 1933.

14 J. S. Haldane and J. G. Priestley, *Respiration*, p. 326.

15 The quotation, from a Boston dentist called Joseph Selif, was
   reported in *Time*, 19/3/1934.

16 Ibid., though I have taken out the misattribution to J. B. S. Haldane,
   one that is common throughout the public record of J. S. Haldane's
   life. He came to somewhat regret the closeness of his son's initials
   and name to his own.

17 J. S. Haldane and J. G. Priestley, *Respiration*, p. 326.

18 Details from Philip B. James, 'Going Diving: Decompression Tables
   and the Genius of John Scott Haldane', paper read to the BSAC
   Diving Officers' Conference, 3/12/2005.

19 NLS, 14/8/196, 276, with facts from 'Birmingham's Part in Mining
   Research', *Birmingham Post*, 18/2/1921.

20 UBC, 27/8/1916(?).

21 DP, from a 1936 letter of C. G. Douglas.

22 These details from J. Ivon Graham, 'John Scott Haldane'.

23 'An Account of Investigations Carried out or in Progress in the Mining Research Laboratory, Birmingham University, July 1933', p. 15, from the author's own copy of the original in the possession of the family of J. Ivon Graham, who took over as Director of the Laboratory on Haldane's death.

24 J. S. Haldane and J. G. Priestley, *Respiration*, p. 438.

25 Ibid., p. 442.

26 'An Account of Investigations', p. 15.

27 *The Times*, 15/5/1919.

28 *The Scotsman*, 10/12/1925.

29 J. S. Haldane, 'The Maximum Efficiency of Heat-Engines, and the Future of Coal and Steam as Motive Agents', *Transactions of the Institution of Mining Engineers*, vol. 68, 1924–5, pp. 383–411.

30 Comment by Mr Humphrey M. Morgans, who defended the orthodox view.

31 UStA, MS 16678, 22/5/1925. An interesting aspect of the joke is that the same letter speaks of the death of his mother two days previously.

32 UStA, MS 16695, letter to Thompson, 'damned' quaintly written 'd–d'.

33 NLS, MS 20512, f. 44, to Bay (his sister Elizabeth), 24/1/1924.

34 *The Scotsman*, 24/1/1929.

35 NLS, 8 May 1921, to Mary Haldane.

36 All details from J. S. Haldane and G. Scott Ram, 'Report on an Explosion in a House at Acton on February 19th, 1927', Electricity Commission, London, 1927. The house was 1 Beaconsfield Road.

37 Though the house has been demolished, leading thinkers and scientists are still attracted to its grounds. The site is now the home of Wolfson College, Oxford.

38 NLS, letter from Lord Haldane to Einstein, 26/6/1921.

39 The Gifford lecture audience, from J. S. Haldane, *The Sciences and Philosophy*, p. 243.

40 NLS, Haldane correspondence, letter from Mary Haldane to Einstein.

41 Ronald Clark, *Einstein*, p. 531.

CHAPTER 17

1   Some have questioned the attribution, since Tantamount dismembers a newt in the novel and Haldane has the reputation of experimenting on himself rather than on animals. However Huxley knew Haldane in the war years, when animal experiments were required of him. More conclusively, the dismembering of newts was a classic Haldane example drawn from biology to illustrate the self-regulation of an organism. In his first published work, the 1883 Edinburgh essay with his brother, he writes that 'the regeneration of the severed limb of a newt provides a similar example of teleological activity'. In his article 'Life and Mechanism', published in *Mind*, January 1884, p. 30, he extends the tale of the newt's regeneration, concluding: 'The purposive behaviour displayed in the attainment by organisms of such ends as the reproduction of a newt's limb cannot be due to the mere action of neuro-muscular or intracellular mechanisms.'

2   Aldous Huxley, *Point Counter Point*, pp. 62–3.

3   J. S. Haldane, *The Sciences and Philosophy*, p. 223.

4   *The Scotsman*, 11/9/1912, p. 8, reporting on a joint discussion between the zoological and botanical sections of the British Association.

5   J. S. Haldane, 'Presidential Address: The Values for which the Institution Stands', *Transactions of the Institution of Mining Engineers*, vol. 68, 1924–5.

6   NLS, quoted in Naomi's typescript about her father.

7   Julian Huxley, *Memories*, pp. 137–8.

8   *Newcastle Chronicle*, 28/3/1925, p. 12.

9   NLS, 29/3/1925.

10 UBC, letter of 30/4/1920.

11 UBC, 12/2/1917.

12 UBC, letter of 23/4/1923.

13 Mary Haldane, *Mary Elizabeth Haldane*, p. 143, letter of 15/9/1924.

14 From *The Times*, 21 May 1925, other detail from *Birmingham Mail*, 20/5/1925.

15 UStA, MS 16678, 931, letter to D'Arcy Wentworth Thompson, 22/5/1925.

16 Mary Haldane, *Mary Elizabeth Haldane*, pp. xi–xii. The son mentioned was most likely Richard.

17 Letter to Lord Rosebery, 3 July 1925, Rosebery Papers, quoted in Stephen Koss, *Lord Haldane*, p. 245.

18 These are official publications of the Royal Society.

19 UStA, MS 16673, 10/9/1920.

20 J. S. Haldane, *The Collected Scientific Papers of John James Waterston*, p. lxv.

21 J. S. Haldane, 'Biology and Religion', *The Modern Churchman*, September 1924.

22 UStA, MS 16693.

23 UStA, MS 16678.

24 The line is from Haldane's letter to Thompson, 25/6/1928, UStA MS 16693, and comes in the form of a quotation from Waterston's paper. The 1852 date also comes from that letter.

25 UStA, MS 16693.

26 NLS, MS 20513, from Ernest Waterston, 11/12/1930.

27 NLS, 2/7/1924.

28 *Transactions of the Institution of Mining Engineers*, vol. 68, 1924–5.

29 UStA, MS 27823, draft of a letter from D'Arcy Wentworth Thompson to his brother, 16/8/1928.

30 'A Biologist Seeks an Answer to the Riddle of Life', *New York Times*, 26/1/1930, p. 64.

31 J. S. Haldane, 'An Address on Biology and Medicine', *British Medical Journal*, 21/5/1927.

32 Peder Anker, *Imperial Ecology*, p. 119.

33 NLS, 305, 8/7/1929.

34 *The Scotsman*, 26/7/1929, p. 4.

35 NLS, 309, 30/7/1929, from the Rand Club, Johannesburg (wrongly ascribed in the archive to 1930).

36 NLS, 330, 16/9/1929, from Cherwell. Again wrongly ascribed to 1930.

CHAPTER 18

1 Delivered 13 October 1933 – the author's copy of the address kindly comes from the private papers of J. Ivon Graham.

2 DP, from a draft copy of an obituary notice by Yandell Henderson for *The Journal of Industrial Hygiene*, 'The Contributions of J. S. Haldane to Industrial Hygiene'.

3 All quotations taken from that Edinburgh address.
4 'Miss T' from Walter de la Mare's 1913 collection *Peacock Pie*.
5 Betty Ross, 'Famous Scientists Talk about Life's Secrets', *Sunday Graphic and Sunday News*, 5/2/1933, p. 13.
6 Karl Ludwig (1816–95) was the founder of the physicochemical school of physiology in Germany. An expert on the cardiovascular system, he was the first to keep organs alive outside of an animal's body, and was also regarded as an exceptional teacher of physiology.
7 DP, letter of 27/8/1935.
8 V. Markham, *Friendship's Harvest*, pp. 46–7.
9 NLS 328, letter from the SS *Arabia*, part of Cook's Nile Service, 22/2/1926.
10 The *Hengist* first flew on 8 December 1931. It was destroyed in a hangar fire in Karachi in 1937, a year after Haldane's flight.
11 N. Mitchison, *All Change Here*, p. 93.
12 N. Mitchison, *You May Well Ask*, p. 212.
13 DP, C13, letter from Naomi Mitchison.
14 DP, letter to C. G. Douglas, 16/3/1936.
15 DP, 28/3/1936.

BIBLIOGRAPHY

Altman, Lawrence K., *Who Goes First* (Berkeley: University of California Press, 1998)

Anker, Peder, *Imperial Ecology: Environmental Order in the British Empire, 1895–1945* (Cambridge, MA: Harvard University Press, 2001)

Asserud, Finn, *Redirecting Science* (Cambridge: Cambridge University Press, 2003)

Barrie, Alexander, *War Underground* (Staplehurst, Kent: Spellmount, 2000)

Barton, Peter, Peter Doyle and John Vandewalle, *Beneath Flanders Fields: The Tunnellers' War 1914–1918* (Staplehurst, Kent: Spellmount, 2004)

Benton, Jill, *Naomi Mitchison* (London: Pandora, 1990)

Burdon Sanderson, Ghetal, *John Burdon Sanderson: A Memoir* (London: Clarendon, 1911)

Charles, Daniel, *Mastermind* (New York: HarperCollins, 2005)

Clark, Ronald, *Einstein: The Life and Times* (London: Sceptre, 1996)

Clark, Ronald, *The Huxleys* (London: Heinemann, 1968)

Clark, Ronald, *J. B. S., The Life and Work of J. B. S. Haldane* (London: Hodder, 1968)

Cook, Tim, *No Place to Run* (Toronto: University of British Columbia, 1999)

Cornwell, John, *Hitler's Scientists* (London: Viking, 2003)

Cunningham, D. J. C. and B. B. Lloyd (eds.), *The Regulation of Human Respiration: The Proceedings of the J. S. Haldane Centenary Symposium* (Oxford: Blackwell, 1963)

Davies, Henry, *Silent Heroisms* (Newport, Montgomeryshire, 1901)

Douglas, C. G., 'John Scott Haldane', *Obituary Notices of the Royal Society of London*, Vol. 2, No. 5, December 1936

Duggan, James, *Man Explores the Sea* (London: Penguin, 1960)

Fiks, Arsen P. and Paul Buelow, *Self-Experimenters: Sources for Study* (Westport: Praeger, 2003)

Foster, C. le Neve and J. S. Haldane, *The Investigation of Mine Air* (London: Griffin, 1905)

Foster, R. F. *The Apprentice Mage (W. B. Yeats: A Life, Vol. 1)* (Oxford: Oxford University Press, 1997)

Franklin, Kenneth, *Joseph Barcroft* (Oxford: Blackwell, 1953)

Freese, Barbara, *Coal: A Human History* (New York: Perseus, 2003)

Galloway, Robert L., *A History of Coal Mining in Great Britain* (London: Macmillan, 1882)

Gielgud, Kate Terry, *An Autobiography* (London: Reinhardt, 1953)

Graham, J. Ivon, 'John Scott Haldane, 1860–1936', *The Mining Engineer*, no. 3, December 1960

Greenfield, Nathan M., *Baptism of Fire* (Canada: HarperCollins, 2007)

Haber, L. F., *The Poison Cloud* (Oxford: Clarendon Press, 1986)

Haldane, Elizabeth, *From One Century to Another* (London: Maclehose, 1937)

Haldane, Elizabeth, *The Scotland of our Fathers* (London: Maclehose, 1933)

Haldane, J. Aylmer L., *The Haldanes of Gleneagles* (Edinburgh: Blackwood, 1929)

Haldane, J. B. S., *A Banned Broadcast* (London: Chatto, 1946)

Haldane, J. B. S., *Callinicus* (London: Kegan Paul, 1925)

Haldane, J. B. S., *Daedalus* (London: Kegan Paul, 1924)

Haldane, J. B. S., *Keeping Cool* (London: Chatto, 1940)

Haldane, J. B. S., *Possible Worlds* (London: Chatto & Windus, 1932)

Haldane, J. B. S., *Science and Everyday Life* (London: Penguin, 1939)

Haldane, J. B. S., *Science in Peace and War* (London: Lawrence & Wishart, 1940)

Haldane, J. B. S., 'The Scientific Work of J. S. Haldane', *Penguin Science Survey 1961 Vol. 2* (London: Penguin, 1961)

Haldane, J. S., *The Collected Scientific Papers of John James Waterston* (London: Oliver & Boyd, 1928)

Haldane, J. S. (as 'A Medical Student'), *A Letter to Edinburgh Professors*, (London: David Stott, 1890)

Haldane, J. S., *Materialism* (London: Hodder, 1932)

Haldane, J. S., *Mechanism, Life and Personality* (Murray: London, 1921), 2nd edn

Haldane, J. S., *The New Physiology* (London: Griffin, 1919)

Haldane, J. S., *Organism and Environment* (New Haven: Yale University Press, 1917)

Haldane, J. S., *Philosophy of a Biologist* (London: Oxford University Press, 1935)

Haldane, J. S., *The Sciences and Philosophy* (London: Hodder, 1928)

Haldane, J. S. and J. G. Priestley, *Respiration* (Oxford: Clarendon Press,

1935), 2nd edn

Haldane, J. S., J. T. Robson, Robert Woodfall, *Report to the Secretary of State for the Home Department on the Explosion at Tylorstown Colliery on the 27th January 1896* (London: 1896)

Haldane, L. K., *Friends and Kindred* (London: Faber, 1961)

Haldane, Mary, *Mary Elizabeth Haldane* (London: Hodder, 1925)

Haldane, R. B., *An Autobiography* (London: Hodder and Stoughton, 1929)

Haldane, R. B., *Before the War* (London: Cassell, 1920)

Harris, Robert and Jeremy Paxman, *A Higher Form of Killing* (London: Random House, 2002)

Hayter, William, *Spooner* (London: W. H. Allen, 1977)

Holt, Tonie and Holt, Valmai, *Major & Mrs Holt's Battlefield Guide to the Ypres Salient* (London: Leo Cooper, 1997)

Huxley, Aldous, *Point Counter Point* (London: Panther, 1978)

Huxley, Julian, *Memories* (London: Allen & Unwin, 1970)

Jones, Christopher, *The Great Palace* (London: BBC, 1983)

Jones, Simon, 'The First BEF Gas Respirators, 1915', *Military Illustrated*, No. 32 (1991)

Jones, Simon, 'Gas Warfare the British Defensive Measures Part 1: The Second Battle of Ypres', *Stand To!*, No. 14 (1985)

Koss, Stephen E., *Lord Haldane: Scapegoat for Liberalism* (New York: Columbia University Press, 1969)

Lockhart, J. G., *Cosmo Gordon Lang* (London: Hodder, 1949)

Lorrain Smith, James, *Growth* (London: Oliver & Boyd, 1932)

MacDonagh, Giles, *The Last Kaiser* (London: Weidenfeld and Nicolson, 2001)

Macintyre, Lorn, *Charlotte Square* (Edinburgh: National Trust for Scotland, 1992)

Magnusson, Magnus, *The Clacken and the Slate: The Story of the Edinburgh Academy* (London: Collins, 1974)

Markham, Violet, *Friendship's Harvest* (London: Reinhardt, 1956)

Maurice, Frederick, *Haldane* (London: Faber & Faber, 1937)

Mitchison, Naomi, *All Change Here* (London: Bodley Head, 1975)

Mitchison, Naomi, *As It Was* (Glasgow: Richard Drew, 1988)

Mitchison, Naomi, 'The Haldanes: Personal Notes and Lessons', *Royal Institution of Great Britain: Proceedings*, Vol. 47, 1974

Murray, Nicholas, *Aldous Huxley* (London: Little, Brown, 2002)

Norton, Trevor, *Stars Beneath the Sea* (London: Century, 1999)

Nye, Piers C. and Frederick Maurice, *Haldane 1856–1915* (London: Faber and Faber, 1937)

Reeves, John T., 'A High Point in Human Breathing', *Attitudes on Altitude*, ed. John T. Reeves and Robert F. Grover (Boulder: University Press of Colorado, 2001)

Reeves, John T. and Robert F. Grover (eds.), *Attitudes on Altitude* (Boulder: University Press of Colorado, 2001)

Robertson, D., *George Mallory* (London: Faber, 1969)

Romano, Terrie M., *Making Medicine Scientific* (Baltimore: Johns Hopkins, 2002)

Scoltock, Jack and Ray Cossum, *We Own Laurentic* (Ballycastle, Northern Ireland: Impact, 2000)

Seth, Andrew and R. B. Haldane, *Essays in Philosophical Criticism* (London: Longman, 1883)

Smith, Grover (ed.), *The Letters of Aldous Huxley* (London: Chatto, 1969)

Sommer, Dudley, *Haldane of Cloan: His Life and Times 1856–1928* (London: Allen & Unwin, 1960)

Stashower, Daniel, *The Teller of Tales* (London: Penguin, 2000)

Stern, Fritz, *Einstein's German World* (Princeton, NJ: Princeton University Press, 1999)

Sturdy, Steven, *A Co-ordinated Whole: The Life and Work of John Scott Haldane,* Ph.D. thesis, Edinburgh University, 1987

Thompson, Ruth, *D'Arcy Wentworth Thompson* (London: Oxford University Press, 1958)

Wilde, Jimmy, *Fighting was my Business* (London: Robson, 1990)

ABBREVIATIONS:

DP – C. G. Douglas Papers, Oxford Physiology Laboratory, Oxford University

IWMSA – Imperial War Museum Sound Archives, London

NA – National Archives, Kew, London

NAWO – National Archives War Office Document

NLS – National Library of Scotland

UBC – University of British Columbia

UCL – University College, London

UStA – University of St Andrews

WCA – Wolfson College Archives

WP – J. T. Wilson Papers, Canberra

INDEX

Ch. 1, Tylorstown — *purif? H puzzled by carbon in [presence] of O_2 → oxidises to CO — but [so] supposedly takes mine canary to detect poison gas — really?
— was already working on CO prior to Tylorstown

— difficulty of reconstructing career
— disspirited, qp re science
— "phantasygia"?
— major physical findings only pp. 181–185 — + v. unclear

— luck of sense that this is about venture or form of scientific life that is not however taken up by others
— good on sheer energy, zest for the diversity of interest